urn /
w at:
ephon
D0358142
NML
QF

SOLITAIRE
SPIRIT

Acknowledgements

The author wishes to acknowledge the generosity of Dirk Kallis and Lymington Yacht Haven for providing *Solitaire* and him with a safe and contented home between voyages and a free berth for life. He also wishes to acknowledge Simon Horne, Royal Navy Chaplain, and his mother, Liz Hayes, for their encouragement and for typing the manuscript of this book onto computer.

Published by Adlard Coles Nautical
an imprint of Bloomsbury Publishing Plc
50 Bedford Square, London WC1B 3DP
www.adlardcoles.com

Copyright © Leslie Powles 2012

First published by Adlard Coles Nautical 2012

ISBN 978-1-4081-5415-1

All rights reserved. No part of this publication may be reproduced in any form or by any means – graphic, electronic or mechanical, including photocopying, recording, taping or information storage and retrieval systems – without the prior permission in writing of the publishers.

The right of the author to be identified as the author of this work has been asserted by him in accordance with the Copyright, Designs and Patents Act, 1988.

A CIP catalogue record for this book is available from the British Library.

This book is produced using paper that is made from wood grown in managed, sustainable forests. It is natural, renewable and recyclable. The logging and manufacturing processes conform to the environmental regulations of the country of origin.

Typeset in 10pt on 13pt Sabon
Printed and bound in India by Replika Press Pvt Ltd

Note: while all reasonable care has been taken in the publication of this book, the publisher takes no responsibility for the use of the methods or products described in the book.

Parts of this book were previously published under the title *Hands Open*.

SOLITAIRE
SPIRIT

Three times around the world
single-handed

LES POWLES

ADLARD COLES NAUTICAL
LONDON

For my younger brother, Royston.
A loving and devoted son.

CONTENTS

FOREWORD

by Paul Gelder

Editor of *Yachting Monthly*, 2002–2012

This book should probably carry a government health warning. It could change your life. For many people, sailing beyond the horizon is the ultimate adventure, whether alone, or with a partner or crew. The inspiration to cast off comes in many forms. For some it might be a book, like this one, or a hero they have met, or some more intangible, divine intervention. Intrepid solo sailor Mike Richey once said it was 'the splendid company at either end of a solitary voyage' that gave him part of the reason. The ocean in between gave him 'a kind of harmony with the universe'.

Les Powles' Eureka moment happened as he walked along a yacht club's pontoon. He realised a sailing boat symbolised escape: freedom from mortgage, the bank manager and a career, plus a means to transport himself and a set of golf clubs around the globe.

He spent £7,000 and two years building a bullet-proof 34ft yacht named *Solitaire*, after the card game. But the cards were stacked against Les from the start. After logging just eight hours' sailing time, only two of them solo, he impetuously – some might say recklessly – set off across the Atlantic in 1975, bound for the Caribbean.

He described how he sailed to the wrong hemisphere in his first published article, 'Barbados or bust', which appeared in *Yachting Monthly* magazine. The sub-title was 'Les Powles has trouble at the 19th hole'. His landfall turned out to be in Brazil, some 1,000 miles south of Barbados! The magazine's editor, Des Sleightholme, was careful to add a footnote: 'A highly amusing account that could have been far from funny. Mr Powles was lucky to get through with his life and his boat and learned from his experience. We would not condone anyone attempting anything similar to this voyage.'

Never underestimate British pluck and the spirit of adventure. We breed intrepid lone voyagers – from Francis Chichester and Robin Knox-Johnston to Chay Blyth, Mike Golding, Ellen MacArthur and Dee Caffari. A psychologist has profiled this unique band of brothers and sisters as 'impulsive, certainly eccentric, though not entirely barking mad'. Though it's surely no coincidence that the title of one best-selling sailing book is *A Voyage for Madmen*.

After surviving his first circumnavigation (1975–8), Les set off two years later on a second (this time non-stop) and returned in 1981 to be awarded the Yachtsman of the Year accolade by the Yachting Journalists' Association. He joked: 'Like the chap released from a mental home, I now had a certificate to say I was not completely bonkers!'

In June 1988, aged 67, he set off on his third solo circum-navigation, returning eight years later in July 1996, to be awarded the Ocean Cruising Club's Award of Merit. By now dubbed 'the Ancient Mariner', this third epic voyage was, as usual, packed with incident. He was knocked unconscious, ran out of food and lost 5st, having rationed himself to a quarter of a tin of corned beef and two teaspoonfuls of rice a day. He was given up for dead before he eventually sailed into Lymington, four months overdue, to a media frenzy. Newspaper headlines proclaimed 'Alive! (thanks to a teacup in a storm)' and 'Reports of my death are greatly exaggerated'. The *Daily Mail* reporter said: 'He is so thin you could play a sea shanty on his ribs.' As weather-beaten as his 34ft sloop, Les, 70, finally declared: 'I'm not going round the world again. Three times is enough. You start to get giddy.'

It was fear, as well as a crazy kind of courage, that inspired Les to sail around the globe three times. He had no desire to be one of 'tomorrow's people' – whom he characterised as 'We're off tomorrow... when we've bought a new mainsail. We're off tomorrow... when we've painted the topsides. We're off tomorrow... when we've bought a bigger boat.'

He foresaw the final excuse: 'We're off in a hearse.'

Now aged 86, Les still lives on his boat, in Lymington Yacht Haven, on the Solent, where he has a free berth for life. He has recently been seen re-painting the decks of *Solitaire*. He still calls himself an 'amateur sailor' and he still has that knowing twinkle in his eye. Above all else, he still remains an inspiration.

PART ONE

first time round

CHAPTER ONE
On a Whim or a Wind's Whisper

Lymington
1975

From a deep sleep to panic: Christ, she's aground on the reef again! Struggling from my bunk on legs that will not respond, I hear a baby's cry and a man's soothing voice, speaking in a language I cannot understand. Trying to pierce the gloom through sweat-filled eyes, I realise I am no longer aboard my sinking boat, but bed-bound in a small white room. Moonlight through a window touches wall-mounted posters about pregnancy before outlining rafters that disappear into blackness. Then memory floods back.

The population of Tutóia, a small fishing village on the Brazilian coast, had increased that day with the birth of a child howling its first protest at the same moment that a wreck of a man lay near to gasping his last. I had been half carried, half dragged from my boat and into their hospital, blister-faced, with feet infected and groin swollen. Sailing, I had once read, was a peaceful pastime punctuated by moments of extreme excitement but after my experience on the reef a week earlier 'extreme excitement' seemed the ultimate in understatement. As to those pregnancy posters on my wall the only thing I'd given birth to was a yacht called *Solitaire* or, as she was registered, *Solitaire of Hamble*.

She was conceived in South Africa towards the end of 1968: before this I had spent two years working as a radio engineer in

South Yemen where I had taken to golf. But knocking little white balls over the desert held no future and I had flown to South Africa to practise my newly-acquired skills on grass, which led first to employment by an electronics company and then, indirectly, to sailing. One morning I wandered along Point Yacht Club's jetty in Durban where cruising yachts from all over the world had come to rest, colour splashing from their fluttering flags, and was struck by their freedom. They were not shackled to land by chains whose links were forged by careers, mortgages and fashion: their mooring lines were but spiders' webs so fragile that they could be broken on a whim or a wind's whisper. Suddenly I wanted to throw my arms wide and scream at the heavens, 'YaaaaaaaaHoooooooo!'

But an Englishman of course doesn't do that sort of thing, not at ten o'clock on a Sunday morning, not in Durban.

I gave thought neither to sailing nor to the vessel itself, simply appreciating that a boat could be both home and transport for self, suitcase and a set of golf clubs from A to B at minimal cost. Early 1969 found me back in England with only £2,000 to my name, a sum that was hopelessly inadequate for the sort of boat I coveted. So I took a contract in Saudi Arabia as an aircraft radio engineer and pushed my savings up to £4,500, only to return home to yet more inflation. At this stage I met a young English couple just back from two years' sailing in the Mediterranean, who were now off around the world in a beautiful 45ft sloop. Believing them to be experienced I considered myself lucky when asked to act as crew, but we motored most of the way to Gibraltar and I can recollect no single incident or experience that proved useful on subsequent voyages, unless it was a strong desire to sail alone. I would make blunders but they would be mine rather than someone else's: they were certainly not the yacht's and never the sea's, whose roar can burst an eardrum, but, when it comes to excuses, is profoundly deaf. No, I would sail single-handed. Alone.

After another stint in Saudi Arabia the beginning of 1973 found me possessed of the respectable sum of £8,500, by which time the price of the type of boat I wanted had jumped to more than £12,000. Then I chanced on an advertisement in a yachting magazine: 'Come to Liverpool and build your own Nor-West 34, hull and deck, £1,300'.

I promptly made an appointment, and one cold morning in January drove through Liverpool's leaning dock gates, easing the throttle to prevent tyre slip on the oily cobblestones. The dock's stagnant waters housed a waste of pans, cans and blackened bottles and on the adjacent rusty railway lines weeds flourished. A mouldering brick building, about 900 x 90ft, with a high sloping roof showing gaping holes, was the boat builders' headquarters. Two modern cars, parked by high sliding doors, hinted of better things to come inside.

I edged mine alongside, wondering whether to brave the drizzle that was turning to rain. Making a dash for the doors, I grabbed the padlock and heaved. Nothing happened. Minutes later I was still attempting to get in, only now I was being tried out for Arsenal and taking running kicks at the door. All I wanted was to force my way inside and tell them what they could do with their stupid boat.

A polite cough as an immaculately-dressed man emerged from a side door. 'Mr Powles? We've been expecting you. My name is Keith Johnson, managing director. This way, please.'

And he escorted me into this derelict slum as if it was a Hilton Hotel. Inside were two enormous plastic tents. 'This is where we lay off the hulls: the plastic prevents dust falling onto the resin.'

All was spoken in a serious voice, despite the heavy rain still soaking us. We moved further into the building in search of a drier spot where, in Nelson's time, the floor might have been of stone and was now, after centuries of dust, but a puddled dirt surface.

The managing director still rattled on: 'We have two plugs for building the hulls, one used by the company, the other for do-it-yourself people. The company can build a hull and deck for £2,500. Have a look: as it happens a couple of our self-building customers are just about to remove the plug from their hull.' With that he pointed to the far end of the shed where a crane hovered over the vague outline of a boat.

It was love at first sight. Instinctively I knew this I had to have.

'What's the specification, Keith?'

'She's a Bermudan sloop in foam sandwich and glassfibre designed by an Australian, Bruce Roberts. She's 33ft 6in long, 24ft 6in on her waterline, with a beam of 10ft 6in and a draft of 5ft 6in. Classed as a cruiser racer she can sleep up to seven people.'

She would have more room than the Contessa 32 that I had seen at the London Boat Show but could not afford, but had the same clean lines as the Contessa with a fine entry, keel and skeg. Though I could not see my wanting ever to sleep seven people aboard her.

'What will she cost complete?'

'Around £4,000 to £5,000, but that's up to the individual. We charge a basic £1,300, which includes the use of the plug for a month, a female mould for the deck and all building materials, a set of plans and fitting-out instructions and free rent for a month. After that there's a small charge if you remain longer.'

I would need a place to live. 'If I bought a small caravan, could I keep it alongside the hull?' I asked. A quick nod to that. 'If I gave you a cheque for a deposit today, when could I start?'

There was a pause. 'It's short notice but you could start in a month's time.'

I wrote a cheque for £400.

The womb that was to develop *Solitaire*'s embryo would not be safe and warm, but she could still be a beautiful baby and with my £8,500 I would give her the best start I could in life. On the 80-mile drive back to my home town of Birmingham I considered two priorities: first I had to buy a caravan, second I would need help for a few days.

Having bought a second-hand caravan for £200, I arranged for a school-leaver to spend a week with me, contracting to feed him, to take him to the cinema once, and to pay him £10 in wages. A couple of home-town mates agreed to spend a long weekend helping me to fibreglass in return for a slap-up meal and all the beer they could drink. Ken Mudd and Tony Marshall were both quality control engineers, Ken with British Leyland, Tony with Lucas Electronics. Ken I had met when I worked on guided missiles after returning from Canada in 1956 following the breakup of my first marriage. Tony came on to my scene in 1970 together with his wife, Irene, and their two lovely blonde daughters: their home was to become a workshop and a haven where I was always welcome.

The plug, or former, looked like an inverted hull built of wooden laths with half-inch gaps. While upside down, sheets of polyurethane foam (up to 3 x 4ft and half an inch thick) are sewn onto it, using a forked 'bogger'. String is forced through the foam and between the laths, forming a loop into which nails are placed. When tension is applied the nails prevent the string pulling out, forcing the foam hard against the plug, much like a bobbin in a sewing machine.

The building of *Solitaire*, as I had already named her, went to schedule. After nine days, thanks to the help from one boy and two friends, the hull was covered with rough fibreglass, which left three weeks of my month for the miserable part – screening and sanding. Talcum powder and resin are mixed to form a paste, then a catalyst (hardener) is added with which to plaster the rough hull.

For smoothing I hired heavy industrial sanders with vacuum attachments but white dust flew everywhere. I had to dress in overalls, taping the cuffs and trouser bottoms, and wear a face mask and hat. Ghost-like figures would move as if they had fallen into flour vats, self-raising puffs for their feet or shimmering haloes round their heads, careful never to leave the building in their disguise by night lest the local people be diminished by cardiac arrest.

As the weeks passed the weather warmed and more people started building. The shed became a village community with its own characters: some, like driftwood, bumped alongside briefly, leaving but a faint impression before disappearing. Others would weave themselves into the fabric of my life with acts of kindness and consideration. I would make my own voyages and have my own moments of glory but without such friends it is difficult in retrospect to see how.

Stan turned up one morning in a 20-ton tipper to build his hull. Until then there had been no facility for removing the mountain of rubbish in the middle of the floor. The rats that infested it grew tame, no longer scurrying away at the approach of a human but stopping to clean their whiskers, lift a paw to their forelocks and give an apologetic half smile, as if to say, 'Morning, gov'nor.' This always started my day well, for I would nod and even consider raising a hand in the weak-wristed wave favoured by royalty.

The yacht builders arranged for a tractor to load our mountain onto Stan's truck, to be carted away when he left. From then on we threw our waste directly into his lorry. At the end of ten days, Stan's hull looked great. He and his father had worked hard and had benefited from the experiences of previous builders, even using steel rollers to smooth out the raw fibreglass. Glittering, it stood there, still wet, waiting for the catalyst to dry and harden it. Next morning it was still golden, gleaming and wet, but streams of yellow syrup were falling from its edges into gooey pools. After a week of trying everything including heat and nearly pure hardener, it was finally agreed that the resin was faulty. Since Stan had already lost three weeks' work with his truck, he asked for a replacement hull already brought to the same stage as his own. The company offered to supply a man and materials, whereupon Stan rebelled. Next day his tipper had gone, having upended our mountain on the floor, bigger than ever. Only the rats were smiling.

Bing, a scientist, was helped by two teenage daughters. His keel had been formed along with the hull and was a box section some 8ft long, 3ft deep and 9in in the middle, tapering to rounded ends. This box took two tons of ballast which would prevent the yacht, with sails raised, from flopping onto its side. In theory you could stand the boat on its nose, roll it upside down, or simply drop it from an aircraft and it would still bob right side up. There was a disadvantage: if you ever put a large hole in the bottom of your craft, your life savings would go down like a brick.

At this time we could use two materials for the keel: iron or lead. The first to build a hull (Berny and Vic) had made a plaster mould of the inside of the keel from which a local foundry would make a 2-ton iron casting for £90. Lead, which took up less room and gave a lower centre of gravity (thus making for a stiffer boat), would have been preferable, but the price was more than double – £250.

Bing called a meeting and described how we might use the non-active atomic waste, heavier than lead, which the British government was dumping in the North Atlantic. Bing thought we might get a load cheap. We were all keen on the idea until someone asked, 'Since we will be walking over the stuff, what would happen if it became active?'

Without hesitation Bing replied, 'It would have the same effect on your sex life as the loss of your testicles.'

As I hurried away I said to a newcomer, Rome Ryott, 'I don't mind risking one but not both.'

'I'm risking neither!' said he.

Rome had arrived in my life with dash and style, driving directly into the building in a sporty red Capri, complete with beautiful blonde passenger. He was tall, broad-shouldered, narrow-hipped and as he walked in with quick, bouncing steps, full of purpose, I fully expected to hear James Bond theme music. His first words were not 'Anyone for tennis?' as I had anticipated, but enquiries about the boat he was due to start building the following week. His soft, educated voice had a Wodehouse stutter assumed to give him time to choose his words. He became my closest friend.

The yacht's deck was made from a female mould, a process that took only a few days. The principle was much the same as housewives have used for years to turn out fancy jellies. First you coat the mould with wax (release agent) which in turn is given a heavy coat of paint (gel coat). The laying up, as for the hull, starts with very fine lengths of fibreglass, looking much like tissue paper, and is built up to heavier grades, with a layer of woven rovings. Water is then forced between the deck and mould to break it loose, and there is your completed deck, already smoothed and painted.

One Sunday night at the end of his month, Rome, packed and ready to set off, called at my caravan. 'I have to be at work tomorrow morning,' he said. 'Since I've just had one leave I'll only manage to get here for long weekends to build the deck. I... I... was wondering if I gave you a hand to build your deck, would you help me to get mine finished?'

'Sure, Rome,' I replied. 'By the way, what *do* you do for a living?'

'I'm a pilot in the RAF,' he answered.

From that moment I knew Rome would not figure as one of my pieces of driftwood: it was perhaps because I had always wanted to be a pilot but more, I suspect, because with his quiet unassuming manner Rome accepted me for what I was, ignoring my background, lack of education, working-class accent and financial standing. Rome was someone I could always look up to, yet he never once looked down on me. His father had been a silent movie actor (hence the son's exotic name) who had died leaving a widow, Grace, with two young children, Rome and his sister Terry, to bring up. After a short period in the Merchant Navy, Rome joined the RAF, where he learned to fly first helicopters, then jets. Interested in sailing since an early age, he had already owned several boats, which he changed regularly along with sporty cars and even sportier girlfriends.

I was born in Birmingham which, for an Englishman, is about as far from the sea as you can get, on October 24th, 1925, and was brought up there, living in a small terraced house with parents and young brother, Royston. We were a normal working-class family, never well off, my father employed as a foreman at the Rover car factory. During the Depression the rent man would bang on the door while we cringed inside: they were terrible years for my father, a proud man who stood on his own two feet and never failed to pay his debts.

The Second World War broke out when I was 13, and the following year I went to work in an aircraft factory as a machinist on Pegasus aero engines. But my ambition was to be a pilot. As a boy I had spent hours at the local airfield watching Tiger Moths, Hawker Hinds and Gloucester Gladiators drop over the boundary fence. Aged 17 I joined the RAF, not as a pilot but as a wireless operator/air gunner.

Having completed the training I became a sergeant but the war was over before I could join an operational squadron. My service career ended running a station laundry in Italy, with 12 lovely young women to look after – an occupation in which I upheld the finest traditions of the British Empire but for which, unfortunately, no medals were awarded. Since then I had had many different jobs, in many countries. In my time I belonged to four skilled unions, only because I had to in order to work. I had had my own businesses including a garage, a haulage firm and shops. I was always a loner, never feeling I belonged.

My introductions to the opposite sex started with Nancy in Crewe, courtesy of two American Eighth Air Force bomber wings. As I had just been promoted to sergeant Nancy came in the form of a celebration and I shall always remember her with gratitude for her understanding, kindness and tuition. 'Navigator to pilot, left, left a bit. Hang in there old buddy... bombs awaaaaaaaay!'

I married two charming ladies and was divorced from two charming ladies. No children came from these associations, only cocker spaniels whose custody was fought over with more bitterness than the D-Day beaches of Normandy – the battles were always lost when it was pointed out that I was a wandering soul, unable even to provide a proper home for them.

Brian Gibbons reached Liverpool to build his boat – by Jaguar. He owned a factory in the Midlands (not far from my home town). He was a boss who wasn't frightened to get his hands dirty and, without doubt, the finest all-round engineer I have ever met. Married, in his mid-thirties, his friendly, rugged face was topped by a mop of unruly hair. His clothes, like his hands, were likely to show oil or grease stains and he spoke with assurance and authority in a Midlands accent.

Brian had bought a finished hull and deck and would turn up with lumps prefabricated in his garage or works which slotted precisely. He overtook us all: I was for ever seeking his advice which he seemed to encourage, mulling over problems with the same sort of concentration some people show for *The Times* crossword. It was never long before he would return, a stub of pencil and scrap of paper in his hand. 'This is what you do, our kid.' And you had your answer.

Once the plug was removed, the hull was placed in its cradle. Then 3in channels were chiselled out of the foam to form stringers and bulkhead recesses. The plans called for three layers of 2oz fibreglass to be laid up inside the hull but I went way above this specification, trying to build more strength into the boat. As bulkheads were fitted and glassed into position we started to use new terminology: we would be working in the forward compartment, the heads, or main cabin.

After completion the decks would be lowered into position with a 2in lip running around the outer edge until it came flush with the top of the hull. It was then through-bolted, and later capped with wood to make the toe rail. The inside corner would be glassed-in to give more strength and make it watertight.

Brian asked for layers of fibreglass to be left out as he wanted a lighter, faster yacht, but he put strength back by running two Iroka beams along each side of the boat, under the deck, which were then glassed in position. He also put a third beam across the rear cabin bulkhead. Through-deck U-bolts took the standing rigging.

I followed Brian's example despite the fact that I had been adding weight instead of reducing it. By this time people were saying I was over-building *Solitaire*, using backup systems to back up systems but I knew she would have to look after both of us until I could learn the ways of the sea and sailing.

If you asked the driftwood what they remembered about me, they would probably reply, 'Leslie? Oh yes, he was the one who cut a blooming great hole in the bottom of his boat.' In fact it was 9in wide and 4ft long. I had never liked the skeg, which was hollow, and, when banged with a fist, would vibrate. I spent a weekend in Tony Marshall's garage building a replacement of Iroka, a modification which one day was to save *Solitaire* – and me. The size was increased to allow 10in to extend into the hull for bracing with a hole drilled ready to take the stern tube and propeller shaft.

For a few days the boat sat with a gaping hole in her bottom. To lifted eyebrows and inquiring looks, I would merely say, 'Mice.'

In June my mother was taken to hospital which meant that I had to return home. I managed to find a good position with Ken Mudd as a quality assurance engineer for British Leyland. *Solitaire* was moved 80 miles overland into a field where I fitted her out, buying unplaned planks of Iroka for her interior. Most of the work was carried out with the help of an old friend, Tony Marshall, who had started out as a carpenter. Len Westwood, a foreman motor mechanic at British Leyland, helped to fit a new 18hp Saab diesel engine.

When the time came to install *Solitaire*'s ballast, I bought 2 tons of scrap lead but could not decide how to pour the casting. I considered using an old bath as a melting pot, but the snag was manoeuvring this lump into the boat now that her deck had been fitted. When in doubt I did what I always did – phoned Brian Gibbons. He had got over this problem by building an adjustable die with which you could make ingots to suit the shape of the keel. Having borrowed it I spent two days in Tony Marshall's back garden where we cut a 32lb gas bottle in half for use as a cauldron. For heat we used coke with a couple of car air blowers. The resultant 80 castings fitted to perfection and with a few gallons of encapsulating resin the job was completed.

Solitaire began to show her beauty and was ready to be christened in seawater. A government agent had visited and presented her with a British birth certificate. She was painted and antifouled; mast, boom and rigging ready for fitting.

Although Rome had been stationed up north we kept in contact with weekly letters and the odd visit. He already had a berth in Lymington, his home town on the south coast. In March 1975 he took his yacht there, so I went along to lend a hand and to learn the ropes. There I was introduced to his mother, Grace, a fitting name for such a lady with her easy smile and quick laugh. Born in South Africa, she still had tinges of the accent. I met her lovely daughter Terry and Terry's husband, Martin Maudling, son of the former Chancellor of the Exchequer, which started another lasting friendship.

By now I had reached the stage where people began to say, 'It must be great to own your own yacht and sail around the world. I'd love to do the same but...'

'But' is always the crunch. Invariably it would be followed by 'I'm still paying the mortgage' or 'the wife's not keen' or 'the cats have had kittens'. If people were honest with themselves, they would admit they led a contented life and had no reason to change it.

As for me, I was 49 years old, had a well-paid, secure job, with no possible chance of finding another if I gave it up, but I had no buts. The dream I had had in South Africa six years earlier was stronger than ever so I surrendered my safe future and moved *Solitaire* to Lymington where she was immersed in seawater and baptised.

The launch went without a hitch, *Solitaire* bouncing like a beautiful baby, just above her waterline. The father, however, was to find himself in embarrassing situations over the next few months in trying to understand his child.

John, the dockside foreman, and his lads had gently lowered her into the water and stepped the mast. Only one end of the rigging wires had connectors, which had to be secured to the tangs on the mast. Everything was held in position by the halyards. Later I would cut the stainless rigging wires to length and fit Norseman connectors... I had been telling John how I had built *Solitaire*, impressing everyone with my plans to sail around the world single-handed. Then I asked where I could park my boat. John pointed to a berth less than 50 yards away.

'Would you please take us over?' I asked.

He was busy, he replied, and since there was no wind or current I would have no problem. 'Slack water' was what he actually said. I then explained that I had to check the engine, look for leaks and change my socks. When I finally ran out of excuses, I admitted I had never berthed a boat or tied one up in my life. We chugged over at a third of a knot to catcalls, cheers, and cries of 'Bon voyage' and 'Send us a card from Cape Horn'.

Two days later I was in trouble again. I had completed the work on the rigging and had fitted the boom when a stranger asked, 'When are you fitting your kicking strap?' What on earth was he talking about? Suspecting that he was pulling my leg, I gave a vague wave of my hand and said, 'Maybe tomorrow'. The solution seemed easy: go to the chandlery and buy one. Next morning I was waiting for them to open.

'Good morning. I'd like to buy a kicking strap, please.'

'We don't have any made up.'

'When will you have some made up?'

'Well, we never make them up, we sell the parts.'

'Fine, I'll buy the parts.'

'What size, sir?'

'What do you mean? I'll take average.'

'How much rope do you need, sir?'

'Oh, a few feet.'

'Don't you think you should measure the length you require... sir?'

'Right, I'll be back.' As I left the shop I had a brainstorm. Back in the marina I found the first yacht with someone aboard who looked intelligent.

'Hello, that's a fine craft you have there. And a nice kicking strap.'

A puzzled look. 'What are you on about? Mine's in the locker.'

Rome arrived to help me buy the necessary pulleys and ropes to put tension on the boom – the kicking strap. After that he took *Solitaire* into the Solent to supervise my first faltering steps. She handled better than his own yacht, he said, with less weather helm, which might be due to my using lead ballast instead of iron. My sailing, however, was less impressive. I took over after Rome had shown me how to set the sails for different points of sailing. An hour went by with Rome becoming very quiet. Fine, I thought, he's taught me all I need to know. Now I can pop off round the world.

'Nice day, Rome.'

'Not bad, we could do with a bit more wind.' (We were becalmed at the time.)

'Er, that's it then, my old mate. I'm all set to go, eh?'

'Well, Les, I'd give it a bit longer.'

'How much longer, Rome? A couple of days?'

'Maybe a year.'

Later, when he had jumped in the dinghy to take pictures of my sailing by, I said, 'Rome, just one quick question before you paddle off. How do I stop the bloody thing?'

'Les.'

'Yes, Rome?'

'Make it two years.'

The following week I took *Solitaire* out alone, a single-hander for the first time. I had given much thought to this, deciding that the cautious approach would be best with the engine on slow tick-over so that if I bumped into other boats only small pieces would be removed. I realised my mistake soon after leaving the pontoon when wind and current revealed how quickly *Solitaire* could move sideways. Craft that minutes before had seemed deserted became festooned with happy, smiling yachties joyously waving fenders, old truck tyres... and boat hooks. Out in the less restricted Solent, things went better until I hoisted the mainsail and genoa. There was a tangle on the genoa winch due to my failure to feed its sheet through the deck block, and the mainsail was not filling properly as I had forgotten to slacken the topping lift. Thereafter I had no other problems. She would sail close to the wind unattended, even allowing me to make a cup of tea!

The mechanics of sailing were never to trouble me, but I deeply regretted not having had the opportunity to start in dinghies as a boy, to learn to do things correctly from the start. Bad habits take years to break, whether swinging a golf club, driving a car or sailing a yacht. I had some help in that I had been born a coward.

I disliked arguing and would always walk around people when possible. As a boy I had stood in my school playground with blood streaming from my nose and soaking a torn shirt, hands open by my side. The bully had continued to slap my face, egged on by the jeers of the other children. It wasn't that I was afraid, just that there seemed no point in fighting. Only when I realised I was trapped did my hands become fists.

I approached the sea in the same way, hands open. I had no wish to fight the sea, to claim false achievements, to feel anger. At the first sign of the sea's disapproval I would lower my colours and drop sail: only when *Solitaire*'s life was threatened would I fight back. The sea was far stronger than any ship so I had to always try to live with it, hands open.

I stayed out a couple of hours, anxious then to return to the marina to try out a new theory. My approach to berthing had been quite wrong; far too slow, it allowed outside elements to take over. The marina berths consisted of long pontoons, both sides of which had fingers to form an H, each U-portion taking two yachts. Should you fail to stop when entering your berth, the bow of your boat slowly rises up the pontoon before sliding gently back into the water.

I went down the long line of boats at approximately 5 knots in a graceful curve, sweeping round at the last moment to line up on our berth. A boat's length away, I pulled back on the pitch control lever, which provides forward, stationary and reverse drives – and it jammed. In the next few seconds I broke several world speed records, none recorded. When I opened my eyes it was to find *Solitaire* lying alongside her berth docilely, indignant at the delay in having her lines made fast.

Later a twit arrived. 'I say, old boy, everyone was concerned by your departure, but jolly impressed by your return.' I would spend much time wondering whether he was serious or sarcastic.

The main hold-up to our departure now was the lack of self-steering gear. This had been a long drawn-out affair starting in Birmingham a year before. Three leading manufacturers had quoted roughly £250. After Rome's remarks about *Solitaire*'s lack of weather helm, I felt she could be steered by any of these gears, and settled for one that was compact and neat with a direct drive onto a balanced rudder. This was the beginning of a long association with Hydrovane, one I have never regretted. Indeed, the independent rudder would one day save *Solitaire*.

Group Captain Rex Wardman turned up at crack of dawn one morning soon after my arrival in Lymington and banged loudly on *Solitaire*'s side.

'Come on, Rome, you lazy devil, time to get up.'

I stuck my head out of the hatch. 'It's not Rome, it's Les, and you've got the wrong bloody yacht.'

Rex was a little shorter than me, and a little older, having joined the RAF in the 1930s to fly many of the aircraft I had watched and admired as a boy. A jolly man, he lived life to the full, brushing problems aside with logic and a flick of the hand. As an experienced sailor Rex had been one of the first to take a berth at Lymington. Over the coming years it would be hard to count the number of times he and his wife, Edith, were around when I most needed them.

On this occasion, after inspecting *Solitaire*, Rex muttered, 'It seems hardly fair to keep buying yachts when some people go into a field with a bucket of resin, a roll of fibreglass and build their own.' The final insult, on seeing the piece of old wood I was using as a tiller, was 'I don't think much of that.'

He enforced the point by taking a kick at it and left me thinking that that was the last I would see of him. Minutes later he staggered down the jetty with two beautifully laminated tillers on his shoulders.

'I've changed my yacht to wheel steering. Give one of these to Rome and keep the other for *Solitaire*.'

Without even waiting for thanks, he was off again.

Rex took me racing in the Solent a couple of times, not that I really enjoyed it. I found the sport a bit hair-raising, especially the starts, watching all that money being thrown about with seeming abandonment. On one occasion Rex had a beautiful crew member whom I assisted in the galley, and by the end of the day felt I had made a fair impression. Helping her ashore she belched in my face. 'Leslie, how could you?' she said and stalked off with another crew member, which just about summed up yacht racing for me – expensive, attractive and often with nothing but a belch at the end.

By August 1975 time was running out and so were funds: with berthing fees of £10 a week, only £300 remained in the kitty. *Solitaire* was still uninsured and the risk of damaging another yacht due to my lack of experience was worrying. Soon it would be autumn with a bleak English winter not far behind, making sailing difficult. Although I had a reasonable amount of food on board, I had no accurate timepiece, liferaft, flares or transmitter. Charts, too, were in short supply, along with navigational books.

Rome was still insisting I wait another year, while Rex Wardman was threatening to break both my legs if I started on a world cruise so ill-prepared. But despite shortages I wanted off, to have *Solitaire* to myself away from prying eyes and to learn our lessons together in solitude, listening to sounds we had not heard before, riding on waves, skirting their edges, gliding over peaks, surfing down valleys, seeing over horizons, controlling our own destinies.

I had no desire to be one of tomorrow's people: 'We're off tomorrow when we've bought our new sail', 'We're off tomorrow when we've painted the topsides', 'We're off tomorrow when we've bought a bigger boat'. I foresaw the final excuse: 'We're off in a hearse. We ran out of tomorrows.'

I had wanted to start six years before, not tomorrow but yesterday. Whenever asked about my first port of call, I would say, 'Barbados'. To avoid technical or navigational questions I would become flippant. 'I'll potter down the middle of the English Channel and when 300 miles into the Atlantic, I'll turn sharp left and sail between the Azores and Portugal. Then I'll fork right onto Barbados' latitude of 13°20′ and I'll stay on it until the island appears over the horizon.'

At that time I believed celestial navigation to be beyond my limited education, a belief which goes back to the early days of sailing when captains hugged the secrets of navigation to themselves, fearing that mutinous crews might take over their ships. The fact that the young couple with whom I sailed to Gibraltar took no sights, despite having a first class sextant on board, did nothing to rid me of my apprehension. Rome showed me how to correct for sextant error but then I made the mistake of asking him to explain the formula. There is no need to know this, any more than there is to grasp the working of a car's gearbox: simply accept that it works and try to understand the rules. To learn to use a sextant takes less than an hour, a noon sight for latitude no more than a day. Yet I was foolish enough to sail without this basic background.

I had neither timepiece nor navigation tables, so there was no possibility of my carrying out sights for longitude. I possessed a small portable receiver but this had only long and medium waves with limited range and was unable to pick up BBC overseas broadcasts for time checks. My navigational equipment consisted of charts, compass, Walker trailing log (to register distance covered), Seafarer depth sounder, and a Seafix radio direction finder (one of my main hopes for safe navigation since I remembered my morse code from RAF days). A major mistake was not to carry the *Admiralty Book of Radio Signals*, which gives the stations around the world: instead I had *Reeds Almanac*, which only printed European call signs. However, *Reeds*, with a £10 plastic sextant, would give the information for sights for latitude. With my limited sailing experience it would have been more sensible to have studied two or three English ports, using daylight, tides and weather to coastal hop.

Ken Mudd and his family came down to spend the last week with me. Ken, a born do-it-yourselfer, fitted gas bottles, radar reflector, hatches, battery and goodness knows what else. At the end it seemed only fair to take him and his family for a sail, as in any case I wanted to try out the newly-fitted self-steering gear. However, Ken gave me no chance of doing this, seizing the tiller as soon as we were under way and refusing to give it back, glaring down at me from his 6ft 2in at any intrusion on his new-found pleasure. He managed to chalk up one first with *Solitaire* when he ran us aground.

We had dropped sail and were motoring back to our berth. 'Stay just this side of the black markers,' I had instructed. 'Watch out for the ferry'. I was fiddling with the self-steering gear again, leaning over the stern, when...

'Les, we seem to have stopped.'

'You stupid clot, Mudd. You've put us *on* the mud. Where's the marker?'

He pointed to a blackbird sitting on a post. Too late I remembered the day I had first met him. We were standing a few feet from a works clock as big as a barn when he asked me the time. Ah well, no one's perfect. With a bit of jumping about we soon got off. Ken and his family returned to Birmingham that night, not out of embarrassment but simply because it was the end of a holiday. It would be nearly three years before I saw him again.

I was passing the point of no return: my old banger was sold, there were last-minute calls to my parents, to Tony Marshall, Irene and their children, Tracy and Sally, with a few belated words of thanks for all their kindness.

By the night of August 17th, *Solitaire* was just about ready to sail. Covers were off, and the number one genoa and working jib hanked onto the twin forestays, the Avon dinghy half-inflated on deck ready to act as a liferaft. Grace Ryott came down to wish me well with a box of chocolate bars. Anne and her daughter, Susan, invited me aboard their boat for a late supper, as they had done so often before. This time there was too much to do, but I was grateful for their help in turning *Solitaire* so that she was pointing in the right direction (I didn't want her kissing the other yachts goodbye!).

Monday, August 18th, I showered and mailed a dozen postcards. A kiss on the cheek from Anne and Susan, a final wave. *Solitaire* and I were off around the world, unfortunately not to fame and fortune but ultimately to laughter, pointing fingers and cries of 'You're the one who finished up in a maternity hospital.'

CHAPTER TWO
Which Way Barbados?

Lymington – Tutóia, Brazil
August – November 1975

As the boat moved slowly downriver that Monday and into the Solent, I hoisted the sails at nine o'clock to start a voyage that would take us 34,000 miles around the world and last more than two-and-a-half years. It was a beautiful morning with south-westerly winds in a blue sky patched with a few scattered clouds. I had some anxious moments when the self-steering failed, until I discovered I had repeated an early mistake and had set a reciprocal course. I streamed the Walker trailing log to start registering *Solitaire*'s journey.

Half an hour later we were sweeping past the Needles in company with another boat, both close on the wind, neck and neck, red ensign saluting red ensign. Then I showed off, leaving the cockpit to sit on the pulpit forward as if to say, 'Look, no hands.' *Solitaire* surged ahead while I yearned to climb the mast to look down on the arrowhead her bow was making, to watch her long white wake, longing to run alongside to see her hull in graceful flight. God, it was marvellous. I turned on the radio full blast and made entries in the log. 'Yipppeee', I concluded, 'Yipppeee!'

I decided to come about and follow the coast. *Solitaire* hesitated for a second, wondering why we were separating from her new playmate. Then she saw the distant headland and was off again, heeling for more speed, like a puppy seeking a new interest. The wind blew free with no bills to pay at the end of the month for that! Oceans lay ahead like orchards of succulent fruit: we could gorge ourselves and feast. All free, free, free.

The rent man called that evening, first with a light tapping on the door, followed by a more insistent banging and whistling. Initially I paid no attention. Then, growing nervous and weary, became too exhausted to care. By six that evening we had problems. The wind was increasing, the sea becoming choppy as I reduced the headsail to working jib. With darkness, the lighthouse on Portland Bill started flashing but *Solitaire* was much too close inshore to clear the headland and its race, so I came about and headed south. France was 60 miles away, with plenty of sea room in that direction. Then a fog descended, thick, grey banks obliterating the lighthouse which prompted me to start the engine in order to maintain a compass course. The outlines of large ships waltzed by, partnering *Solitaire* in a dance of disaster, faint shapes towering above us, their unfamiliar lights confusing me. Sometimes I turned away, sometimes circled back, sails a-flap. Terror!

During one of these panics I managed to tangle the trailing log line around the skeg so that now I would have no idea how far *Solitaire* travelled on her manic course. Tuesday morning saw us still beating into angry seas, completely lost. I tried to keep heading west, confused and legless. My radio direction finder would certainly have supplied the answers had I not managed to leave it switched on with the result that the batteries were now flat.

Turning *Solitaire* off the wind I headed north-west to bring us back to the English coast. Late that night shore lights showed faintly through the murk so I dropped sail and stayed on watch until morning when the fog lifted. Land! We were sitting in the western end of a vast bay, in the far distance, a harbour. From the chart Falmouth was shown to the west of a large bay.

Full of confidence, *Solitaire* motored over to a young lady in a rubber dinghy and, in what I thought to be a swashbuckling manner, I shouted, 'Ahoy there, missy, could you please tell me where you anchor in Falmouth Harbour?' A look of horror crossed her face. Ye gods, I thought, my flies are open. The poor creature's legs seemed to give way and she collapsed in the bottom of her craft whence weird sounds emerged, followed by a tear-stained face.

'Miss, I only want to know where you anchor in Falmouth Harbour.'

'About 100 miles westwards,' came a shrieked reply.

Brixham is a delightful place. For a while *Solitaire* circled its harbour like a cat looking for a comfortable place to settle, this my first attempt at anchoring. Exhausted, I used my remaining strength to tie a length of rope onto a 25lb CQR anchor and throw it over the side. With that I sat on deck, head in hand, until a man in a dinghy appeared alongside.

'Are you alright?' he asked. I nodded, whereupon he suggested that it would be advisable to put a length of chain on the anchor before the rope. I fetched up about 20ft and after helping me to re-anchor he invited me to dinner with him and his wife. Next morning they were gone. I forgot their names, even their faces, but I will always remember their kindness.

I stayed only a few days in Brixham, using the yacht club's showers but not daring to enter the bar as I could still hear the girl's laughter ringing in my ears. Perhaps the word had gone around: we have a fool in the harbour.

The sail to Falmouth, starting at dawn one morning, arriving early the next, proved easy. Close on the wind all the way we made a fair course without overmuch tacking, sailing with main and number two genoa in a reasonable Force 3 to 4. I managed to pick up all the headlands by day and identify the lighthouses by night, and having replaced the RDF batteries I could now confirm my position with radio fixes. *Solitaire* and I enjoyed this part of the voyage, arriving fresh and slightly more confident. As Falmouth seemed crowded, we moved to the other side of the river and the picturesque village of St Mawes. *Solitaire* has no fitted tanks, she carries her water in six 5-gallon containers. When these were filled,

I bought a roasted chicken, some vegetables, and prepared for our first long voyage together across the Atlantic.

On August 28th, 1975, I hauled up the anchor at the start of a lovely English summer's day with the dew still wet on *Solitaire*'s deck, motored out of the sleeping harbour and raised sail. A faint breeze from the north-west seemed reluctant to speed us from our homeland so *Solitaire* drifted south, her self-steering debating whether to hold her on course or give up and go back to bed. By afternoon we were only 12 miles south of Falmouth. A large ketch headed towards us, passing down our side under full sail. I could hear shouting, see its crew waving their arms as though in distress. Quickly dropping the headsail I started the engine, turned into wind and made after them. It turned out their motor had broken down and they were lost.

'Which way Falmouth?' they called. 'And how far?'

That I could give them this information amused me and for the rest of the day I kept chuckling to myself. Had they but known!

Good humour came to an abrupt end that night when I managed to rip the mainsail. Soon after the ketch had left us, the wind started to pick up so I hoisted a smaller genoa, then, just before dark, with heavy clouds forming and the wind increasing, I reduced to working jib. That stormy night, still on a broad reach, I tried to drop the main without turning into the wind but the sail caught on the crosstrees and ripped. When it was finally down and lashed, I was violently sick. I was to be sick at sea only twice, due to my idiocy rather than an upset stomach. On this occasion I was concerned about the sail repair, having previously sewn together nothing more complicated than an old pair of socks. What bothered me most was removing the sail from the mast, as Rome had fitted it for me when I had been elsewhere. Did you take it from the mast first or from the boom? It was only a passing fear. I tied the sailbag onto the mast and fed the sail directly into it – successfully.

When next I went below I had my first experience of the different worlds of sailing. On deck it was cold with a screeching wind, breaking waves and glowing phosphorus. Below it was peaceful and warm. *Solitaire* broad-reached comfortably, delighted to be off the wind and the pounding sea. The rip proved to be only a few inches long and easily repaired, so *Solitaire* and I learned another lesson. There's an old saying of the sea, 'When you think of reefing (shortening sail), that's the time to reef.' I have always taken this to extremes.

The number two genoa and working jib were permanently fixed to twin forestays and I invariably changed down to the smaller working jib at the slightest excuse such as increasing wind, heavy swell, unusual clouds... and, after many months at sea, on instinct that all was not right. I liked to clear shipping lanes as soon as possible. Once in open sea, I would switch off lights to preserve the batteries and sleep through the night, relying on intuition to wake me for weather changes, deviation from course or ships in the vicinity. That way of thinking would have been different if there had been other people on board when I would have been responsible to them for keeping a good watch at all times. Besides, there is no way you can develop this intuition when other people are around.

After leaving the English Channel I stopped using the number one genoa. It provided insufficient extra speed for its size and, hard on the wind, with the foot running along the deck inside the stanchions, it restricted my forward vision. I was to become lazy at sea. If I could make 100 miles a day I would be content and, should I fail to achieve this distance, who cared? When I found *Solitaire* slamming into heavy seas, I would drop all sail, batten myself below and read or sleep. If the winds turned into storms and they were aft of the mast I would simply run with them on a broad reach under working jib. I was never frightened and indeed found comfort in gales by thinking either of Chay Blyth, who had rowed the Atlantic, or Bombard, who had crossed it in a rubber dinghy.

My boat was strong so why should I worry? I enjoyed the solitude and there were plenty of books to read. I had never to be in a certain place at a given time, the crazy world could wait until

I chose to join it again. Meanwhile I had friendly dolphins who entertained me nightly with their ballet dancing. Like a king before his court I sat back applauding, enjoying a last cup of coffee at the end of another halcyon day. Navigation was proving easier than expected. I had stayed as far out of the Bay of Biscay as possible and still received limited RDF signals from England, Spain and Portugal. Two or three such bearings gave me a reasonable fix, which was confirmed by dead reckoning using a £20 bosun's compass and the trailing log for distance travelled.

When I had been at sea for ten days I read the instructions in *Reeds Almanac* and used my Ebco plastic sextant to take my first sight for latitude. It took longer than is normal as I had no accurate timepiece aboard. My old car clock lost 40 seconds or so a day which meant I had to guess when the sun would reach its maximum height, following it on its upwards curve to the top of its arc, and only too relieved when my calculations tied in with the pencilled RDF positions. For a few days I continued this cross-checking until we were 300 miles into the Atlantic, when the signals faded. Now we would have to depend on dead reckoning and the sextant.

Dropping below the Azores, *Solitaire* picked up the beautiful trade winds, constant at Force 3 to 4 over our stern. There were times when I thought she had stopped: surprised by the silence, I would put down my book and go on deck only to find the log spinning merrily away at a steady 5 knots.

In these conditions, I started to learn the importance of a varied food supply. Cooking would have given another interest, another pleasure, were it not that nearly all the food on board was tinned: the fresh food I had bought in Falmouth had been eaten in the first week. One meal I relished was rice and curried chicken, and I regretted having no more. In time I would learn to carry the things that would last and were cheap to buy: rice, flour, onions, cabbage, eggs.

The main event of our Atlantic crossing took place on September 23rd, at precisely 1400 hours GMT. It would be many weeks before I learned the importance of this day and the changes it would make to my life. All that is recorded in the ship's log for that day is 'Distance travelled 2,442 miles. Latitude 23°41′North.' From then on things would happen that made no sense. I would go over incidents again and again, sometimes believing I was losing my sense of reason as I tried to understand why, after things had gone so well, suddenly I seemed unable to do anything right.

I kept pushing *Solitaire* south but the reduction in latitude was too slow and simply would not agree with the compass course or dead reckoning. I checked the compass against that on the RDF set but both gave similar readings. I went over my latitude figures repeatedly, always getting the same answer. It could not be my method of working out sights whose correctness I had confirmed long since. I tried to remember where the fast-flowing Gulf Stream started its journey north: I knew its current sometimes reached 5 knots but I had no charts to guide me and the sea tells no secrets. Could it be I was under the influence of the Bermuda Triangle, where ships and aircraft had vanished, perhaps, it was suggested, as the result of large compass variations? Day after day we pushed further south into dangers that would subsequently make me shudder at my stupidity.

As the trade winds began to drop we had periods of calm punctuated by vicious squalls, the first of which started at night. Previously there had been light rain squalls but these were something quite different. I would wake up in the night to an eerie silence. Suddenly, screaming winds would start whistling in *Solitaire*'s rigging, whereupon she would come off her broad reach and luff up. I would dash on deck naked, stopping only to throw on a life harness, to find sheets of warm water pounding the sea flat. I would drop the mainsail and within a few seconds all would be normal, with *Solitaire* back on course under a clear, starry sky, as if nothing had happened.

Two days later I saw these squalls for what they were – seemingly atom bomb mushrooms, starting at sea level and spreading upwards to blank out the sun. Normally I would drop the mainsail as quickly as possible and free the genoa sheets if it seemed the squall would blow for any length of time. Later I was to question many seamen how they reacted. One said he merely allowed the yacht to luff up, arguing that you were through a squall quicker than trying to run with it. Most of those I spoke to seemed to drop or slacken sail. During this confusion and despondency, I learned a lot about the sea, *Solitaire* and myself.

One day we were beating into a breaking sea with a long swell, *Solitaire*'s bow being thrown high in the air every now and then, only for her to fall back, burying her nose, waves streaming up her decks towards the cockpit. I needed to take off the large genoa that was driving her into these seas to slow her down, but as I have never been a strong swimmer (a cross between a breast-stroker and a dog-paddler) I did not fancy going forward for a ducking. In the middle of a sail change *Solitaire* started to lift and, just as I thought she was about to take off in flight, we started down again. Seas broke over the bows, whirling first around my feet and then my chest. I grabbed the forestay in panic, drawing in each breath as though it were my last, before sinking into a green world, which sucked me away from *Solitaire*. Water filled my nose and I choked. After what seemed like a lifetime I was lifted clear, terrified, trying to draw breath into burning lungs, spitting out mouthfuls of neat sea.

At that moment, strangely, I stopped being afraid. My fear was replaced by anger and I screamed obscenities, using every backstreet gutter word I could remember, even managing to invent a few. Within minutes using hand-like steel claws, I had changed sails and was back in the cockpit, sucking the salt from my lips which I spat over the side.

'You bloody bitch,' I said. It was not until I had towelled myself down, and was sitting with a cup of tea, that my hands stopped shaking. Then I began to think about the strange chap I had met on the foredeck, this Jekyll and Hyde character. If I could control him and harness his anger to give me the strength to survive, I would have learned another valuable lesson which must serve me well.

At ten o'clock that night, October 13th, after being at sea for 57 days and having logged 4,340 miles, a lighthouse flashed which should not have been there. By dead reckoning, we were still 200 miles from Barbados. Our noon sight that day had put us 14°40′N, more than 80 miles above the island. My sole chart, which covered the whole Caribbean, reduced Barbados from 20 miles to one inch, and showed two lighthouses but no flashing codes. I decided to sail down the island to pick up the other light but soon thought better of it and headed out to sea to await morning.

Dawn found *Solitaire* sailing on a southerly course parallel to an island with sandy beaches, palm trees and hills in the distance. A few dhow-type vessels about 40ft long with large triangular sails made of odd pieces of material were in sight, each with two or three dark-skinned men on board whose curiosity made them come alarmingly close. By noon, sea and sky had taken on the same shade of blue, the horizon hazy.

Despite problems in getting a decent sight it appeared to confirm the previous day's latitude. Using my RDF set I was surprised to pick up a loud SLI Morse signal, which indicated I had sailed above the Barbados Islands and was cruising down the coast of Martinique with St Lucia to the south. Although I had no radio codes for the area, that would surely account for the SLI call sign. Barbados then was 90 miles to the south-east. Although it meant retracing my steps, I decided to sail there because a young girl had once said it was 100 miles to Falmouth and her laughter still rang in my ears.

Since we were sailing into open seas I slept well that night. In fact I even had a lie-in, made a leisurely cup of tea and came out of the cabin yawning. A glance at the compass revealed we were still on course with the trailing log behaving satisfactorily and the self-steering working well. To starboard I was surprised to see land about 3 miles away but, over the bow, *Solitaire* was facing huge breaking seas. The cup scalded my legs as I dropped it scrambling over the hatchboards. I was halfway to the tiller when the air filled with flying spray. As there was no time to tack I fled below, slamming the sliding hatch: for a moment silence endorsed a short-lived sense of relief, then the earth spun out of orbit as *Solitaire* was lifted sideways. Believing this a new game, she went willingly, flying in her eagerness to please until struck viciously by a gigantic hammer, which stopped her dead, knocking her legs from under her. And I heard a baby howl...

In the cabin movement was too fast for the eye to register. As the boat fell on her side, I found myself on the floor: lockers burst open and I was bombarded by books, tins, bottles. Whatever could fall fell and sea water gushed in.

The seas had her, like a tiger bringing down a fawn, swinging her in a complete circle. She shrieked. I tried to escape through the hatch but solid water flung me back to the floor, the cabin darkened by green shades that covered its windows. Now she was dragged sideways, leaving skin and blood on jagged rocks, and crying in her agony, but there was nothing I could do for her. Trying to restore sanity to this madness, I picked up a book from the shambles to blank out her screams.

Then her cries changed to defiance, although the sea still pushed her sideways. Now she was riding with the blows, staggering to her feet after each knockdown. She would take stumbling steps, sit down, then quickly push herself upright, complaining the while at such treatment. Again and again she was slammed down but with each knockdown her stubbornness increased until, after being turned again in a complete circle, she finished up standing when the noise subsided. She stood there swaying, quietly sobbing, but on her feet and proud.

I slid back the hatch cover and emerged shamefaced, embarrassed by the dangers I had left her to face alone and bitterly repentant of my hope that some small part of her would be found so that my family would not spend years wondering if I were alive or dead. From the cockpit her decks appeared to have been swept clean: dinghy, fuel containers, spray dodgers... all had disappeared. Later I found them hanging over the side secured by old bits of lashing. The mast still stood, heavy spray running off the untorn sails like rivers of tears. The battens in the main had broken and the headsail sheets flew free but were intact.

A glance into the cabin showed the wreck that had been my home. Rubbish floated in deep water, not as bad as I had thought, locked below, when I would have sworn she was half-full. That had been with *Solitaire* on her side. Now that she was upright water ran to her bilges, reducing the level. The boat was held in soft sand. The reef she had survived lay to one side, the distant shore to the other, the sea brown and shallow. After hauling everything back on board and securing, I started pumping, but as it took an age to clear the water in the cabin, I feared her hull might be cracked. The tiller was jammed to one side, but by pushing with both feet I managed to centralise it and the plywood weather vane on my self-steering gear had broken but I could soon fit a spare.

Solitaire started to come alive again, and with a little encouragement she might even be away. I thought of using the motor, but after that pounding doubted it would ever start until I turned the key. The engine gave a half-turn and roared into life. *Solitaire* shuddered with pleasure and as I pulled in her sails she leaned, sighed and moved. I felt her sweating forehead on my cheek as she whispered in our secret language, forgiving me my faults and weaknesses. Life was full again – the music of Bach, the birth of Christ. It was Christmas, Christmas Day in October. We were off to Barbados.

Solitaire edged her way nervously back along the reef where the echo sounder gave no reading. The distant water seemed even shallower, so we stayed close in, eyeing the sea warily lest it brought on fresh assaults. Salt water and spray still showered us but as we rounded the end of the reef the air cleared and I could see again.

The first thing I spotted was a green and white sail. 'Americans,' I thought, setting off in hot pursuit. I wanted to inspect for damage and clean up the mess below so, as she was holding a good course, I switched off the motor and let the self-steering take over. Water oozed through the cabin floor and worriedly I started pumping again. We were still in sandy seas that stretched to the horizon, the echo sounder occasionally registering a few feet. Old Green Sails was even closer inshore. Still trying to catch him, we rounded a headland with a lighthouse perched on it but the other craft pulled away and disappeared. Where had this land come from? I tried the RDF again and the SLI signal came through loud and clear as ever. I checked the chart. Martinique had coral banks halfway down its east coast: a lighthouse was shown a few miles north of these. Maybe we had hit these banks and rounded the light so I decided to follow the coast.

At noon the horizon was even hazier with no chance of a sight. Then a second island appeared which, if we were sailing down the west coast of Martinique, had to be St Lucia. I decided to pass between the two and then head for Barbados. A few hours later I realised that these islands were merging and that we were entering the mouth of a river! At that point I realised I badly needed help for there was nothing in the Caribbean that looked like this.

Solitaire was sailing in shallow waters where the charts showed 50 fathoms or more. The riverbanks continued to close in on us, now 3–4 miles apart. Small open fishing boats and canoes appeared with the same patched triangular sails I had noted on the earlier vessels. I closed them, pointing downriver, and shouting 'Harbour', which brought only smiles and shrugs. Then I tried shouting 'Porto' at which they waved me on.

Moving through the same dirty brown water the echo sounder read 7–8ft. Now and again *Solitaire* would hesitate as we touched soft sand but in no way put out she would shake herself and continue on her way. A Spanish-style village began to appear above a bay to starboard, first a church, then white buildings with red-tiled roofs, and finally a jetty with a flat-bottomed canopied boat tied to it. A walled road ran up a hill, with people lining it. I attempted to anchor but such was the current it would not hold and *Solitaire* was swept towards the shore which made me decide to carry on upriver and find another haven.

Just before dark the river ended in forest. I dropped anchor and was contemplating inflating the dinghy and rowing ashore when a canoe appeared manned by a man with a dirty cloth at his waist tucked between hairy legs. He passed with thrusting strokes, bulging muscles and furtive looks. A forked spear lay in the bottom of the canoe, most likely for fishing. Holy cow, I thought, I wouldn't like to meet him on a dark night, so decided to stay where I was.

It had been a long day but there was still much to do. For the first time since the knockdown I dried out *Solitaire*, including her bilges. Water had been coming in pretty fast and I had been pumping her every 2 or 3 hours without tracing its point of entry.

By now it was dark and the sky full of stinging insects. Thinking of food I went below into an oven where I managed a cup of tea but spent so much time defending myself with flailing arms that food was not worth the effort. Perhaps those tropical marauders fancied some real English roast beef. I closed the hatch and slept so deeply that dragon bites would not have wakened me. When I came to at dawn, my face was puffed and swollen. Having feasted heartily off me through the night, the dragons had limped off home – gorged. Now all I wanted was to get back to sea. The trip upriver had taken six hours. Two days later, after forcing a way back through thick, brown chocolate, I was to remember those few hours as pleasurable!

At first the return was not too bad. In the cool of early morning I hoisted the sails and started the engine. At the end of each tack I would simply turn the self-steering onto its new course and stand with a genoa sheet in each hand, letting go on one, taking up on the other as we came through the wind. The slow-running engine kept her moving as she came about, easing her through any soft sand. Hard-in sails helped her to heel, which lifted the keel slightly. Every now and again I would pump the bilges but progress was slow.

The mid-day sun reflected off a burning deck. Standing in the cockpit was uncomfortable even in a minimal shirt and shorts as I sought relief from the hot breeze, quite unconscious of the sun's damage to my skin and eyes. The previous night's bites were now sore and itching and when darkness fell we still had not reached the village. I tried to continue sailing but islands of hard-packed sand constantly delayed *Solitaire*. When we ran hard into one particularly shallow patch, I called it a day, anchored and made tea, for again I could not face food. All I wanted was the night's cool comfort. Bliss... then the dragons arrived for another feast.

I sailed next morning as soon as I could make out the shoreline. The river began to widen and by noon *Solitaire* was a mile or two beyond the village, still running into islands of hard packed sand just below the surface that were impossible to see. Normally they did not cause too much concern: we invariably hit them on their downriver side and the wind soon floated us off again. Then, after running into one soft patch, *Solitaire*'s motor stopped. The engine uses seawater as a coolant but the muck we were sailing in did not agree with its digestion, so it overheated and gave up the fight. Lacking its thrust we drifted astern and finished on the wrong side of a hard-packed island. For the first time since leaving England I inflated the dinghy and stepped off *Solitaire*, dropping our anchor with 200ft of rope in deep water.

A few fishing boats closed to see what was going on. One came alongside with a crew of three who I invited aboard *Solitaire* and gave them cigarettes, the first people I had spoken to since the lost souls on the ketch off Falmouth. Not that I could understand these men's language. I felt they had originally come from Spain or Brazil, and spoke Portuguese or heavily-accented Spanish. Peasants in rolled-up trousers, secured by string, they wore tattered shirts and, above all, battered straw hats – which I envied. One or two of the words they used I recognised, 'please', 'yes', 'no', with which I tried to obtain my whereabouts.

One pointed to me and asked, 'Saint Lucia?'

Getting somewhere at last, I thought. I shook my head and said, 'Barbados.' Waving in the general direction of the DF signal, I asked 'Saint Lucia?'

To this they all nodded their heads enthusiastically. I fetched my chart of the Caribbean, and pointed to my position. It was as if it had a curse, they would not even look. I kept pushing it under their noses, pleading, 'Please, señor.'

Then I noticed *Solitaire* was leaning further over, a foot of sand showing around her. It could not be happening. The Caribbean has no such tide. My guests sat back smoking and smiled confidently, waiting for *Solitaire* to float. I watched the miracle of the waters rising until she pulled on her anchor line and swung into deep chocolate whereupon I farewelled the fishermen, hauled up the sails, and again started reaching for blue waters.

Within an hour it was dark but the river grew wider as we tacked by the stars. I nipped below and made tea, putting marmalade on a cheese biscuit. Next moment I was spread-eagled over the forward bulkhead. *Solitaire* had hit an island and was on her side. Before I had time to panic, a wave had picked her up and gently deposited her in deep water where she continued serenely as though nothing had happened. That would teach me to go below without permission.

As I picked up the lighthouse and made towards it, I started to hear a strange but familiar sound I could not place. Dropping sails, I put down the anchor and, head on tiller, fell asleep having sailed and pumped for nearly 40 fasting hours. Dawn found us close inshore, a shore covered by bushes. Then I remembered and recognised the sound I had heard: crickets! Once clear of the land, I studied my chart, trying to identify the coast with the compass. Nothing made sense. There was no river that size on Martinique, nothing like it in all the Caribbean, the brown water too shallow, the tides quite wrong, the land too flat.

I could not just sit there; we had to sail in some direction. I would sail north, back the way we had come, so I brought *Solitaire* onto that heading. But that could not be right, we must sail south and home in on the RDF to St Lucia. I turned *Solitaire* south. In the end I was changing course every few minutes and circling, circling. I gave up, apologised to *Solitaire*, made tea and ate my marmalade biscuits. Since first hitting the reef three days ago I had accomplished nothing. The trip downriver had ended with me burned by the sun and savagely bitten.

The locals had said St Lucia again and again. My last latitude had been 14°30'N so, river or no river, I must be on the west coast of Martinique. Nothing else was possible. Finally I headed north. On Sunday, October 19th, *Solitaire* was back on course for Barbados which I believed to be south-east and I followed the coast until clear of land when I found that sailing in clear water had increased the leaks. I was now pumping out *Solitaire* every two hours.

Next morning I hallucinated, believing that my brother Royston was sleeping in my bunk. Should I disturb him and ask him to have a go at pumping? Later I made two cups of tea, and took him one in the cockpit. Just before dark, standing in the hatchway, I felt a chest pain. Looking down I saw I was pushing hard against the hatch cover to make room for family and friends standing behind! Of course I saw no one. There was no fear, nothing worse than having too much to drink and making a fool of myself. Too much worry, too much sun.

Thoughts of sailing direct to Barbados were given up on Tuesday, October 21st. Then one of the twin forestay bottle screws, which allow the standing rigging to be adjusted, broke. Later I learned that it failed because there was no universal coupling at its base. With loose rigging I turned *Solitaire* and ran westwards. My condition was deteriorating, my skin so burned that even a light shirt proved painful, yet I had to spend hours in the cockpit pumping and sailing *Solitaire*, the sun ever blazing, the spray stinging. I could no longer see the horizon. There was no mirror aboard, but I knew my eyes were nearly closed and my head was blistering.

Wednesday, October 22nd. A week had passed since hitting the reef. Sailing back into the brown shallows, I saw a large bay with the same fishing boats and canoes, the same peasant crews. My spirits rose when I saw a large marker buoy, the type used to mark shipping channels. I circled it, but the echo sounder showed only a few bitterly disappointing feet. Ashore were palm trees and several thatched huts. Motoring down I found flat water with no current, so anchored in 7ft or so, backing away to allow the chain to run out. I went below, glad to be out of the flying spray and burning sun, and lay on my bunk for the first time in many long days. I moved my eyelids a fraction to close them. Beautiful, deep soothing sleep. Then a bump on *Solitaire*'s side.

I staggered on deck to find a dug-out canoe alongside with a man and woman, both with broken teeth and flat faces, and a coloured, handsome man with Spanish features. He made signs indicating the sea would soon leave the lagoon, precisely what I needed to allow me to sleep in safety and, later, inspect *Solitaire*'s hull. To please them, I thought I'd move *Solitaire* a few feet. I started her motor, removing its cover to make sure it was not overheating and, stumbling, pushed my leg against the revolving flywheel. A quick burning pain... I watched the blood run without the slightest interest, switched off the motor, gave my visitors cigarettes and pumped the bilges. Finally, lovely sleep.

I awoke spluttering, my face immersed in sea water. *Solitaire* was lying on her side and water had collected – into which I had submerged my face when turning in my sleep. On deck I could see we were about 200 yards up the beach, the sun about to make its appearance. Clambering over *Solitaire*'s side, I felt cooling sands on my grilled feet. Ecstasy! A bent old man was examining the beach pools and extracting stranded fish, which he belted over the head before dropping them into his sack. I joined in the game for a while, laughing and dancing like a clown until, tiring of the sport, I went to lay out anchors as close as possible to the sea.

By now *Solitaire*'s starboard side was completely exposed and I could examine the wounds she had endured on the reef. A large piece missing from the bottom of the skeg accounted for the jammed rudder. Halfway along her hull on the waterline was one area that had been pushed in the depth of a dinner plate, another (larger) area simply flattened. Other parts were scratched and gouged, although none an inch deep, the thickness of her skin. In the hot sun, *Solitaire* soon dried out. Still searching for the cause of the leak, I saw dampness where the after end of the keel joined the hull which I had reinforced with fibreglass at least an inch-and-a-half thick. When I cleaned it with a file, water trickled out.

Fortunately I carried resin and fibreglass on board in sealed containers; unfortunately I had no brushes or gloves to protect my hands. Despite making a brush from a rope's end, I still managed to cover my hands with resin, which I tried to clean off with rag and seawater. Then I had the brilliant idea of using sand and finished up looking as if I were wearing brown gloves, which at least stopped me scratching my face. It is inadvisable to glass over a damp surface but, by adding extra hardener, I made a half-decent job.

By the time I had finished, a crowd of locals had gathered. The last job was to inspect my stock of 18 bottles of spirits and some 600 English cigarettes which, as I was a non-smoker, were mostly for trade. I came across about 40 sodden yachting magazines and took them on deck, intending to dump them. A girl reached up, so I gave her one. Next minute I was besieged by fighting, screaming women and out of the newspaper business. I decided the men should also have a treat and dished out half a dozen bottles of whisky and gin and, to add to the party spirit, started handing out cigarettes. While this was going on I tried to hold some kind of a conversation without much luck. Suddenly I heard the name 'Pele'.

'Football!' I shouted, and pretended to dribble a ball. Pointing to myself I said, 'Golf.' The best I could get from my fans was 'Goof'. I still had a set of golf clubs on board so fetched them, made a round hole in the sand, marched back 150 yards, selected my trusty five iron and asked the admiring public to stand back. With my 'sandpaper' gloves I had a good grip on the club. Making my first back swing as wide and slow as possible, I came down and through what I saw as two blurred balls, holding my stance at the end of the applause. A slight titter. Looking down I could still see two balls.

On my fourth attempt I managed to move them 10ft. I tried to explain that my first three swings had been practice, not that I minded their laughter even if they were drinking my grog. I looked for revenge. My old fishing partner, rolling about much the worse for wear, seemed a likely victim. Prising a gin bottle from his shaking hand I gave him the club, pointed to the ball, the general direction of the hole, and stood well back. The poor old man could hardly stand and I started to feel sorry for what I was doing. Encouraged by his mates he finally swung and made solid contact. The ball flew off in a majestic trajectory to land a few feet from the hole. He was carried around on the shoulders of a cheering crowd as though he had just won the British Open. I handed out all the balls, three dozen or so, and the rest of my golf clubs, not particularly caring if I got them back.

With that I went to join the only friend I had in the world. From *Solitaire*'s deck the beach took on a festive atmosphere: golf balls were flying like white meteors over sands covered by drying magazine pages while staggering drunks held cigarettes like prize Havana cigars. I had brought havoc to this sleepy village but felt content for the first time since hitting the reef.

Around noon a Land Rover came down the beach with two uniformed men and a civilian who was the first to speak.

'No problem,' he said.

Thank the Lord, I thought, for someone who could speak English. Quickly I told him of my adventures since leaving England, finishing up with a question, 'Where am I?'

'No problem,' he replied.

We went in this circle three times before I realised 'no problem' was the extent of his English. Passport and ship's papers were handed over and for the first time I heard the name Tutóia. It was decided that Maurice, one of the uniformed men, would stay with me to help refloat *Solitaire* and then navigate us to this Tutóia, a fishing village 2 miles or so away at the other end of the bay. The tide came in just before dark and *Solitaire* stood on her feet again. Some 40 yards offshore, Maurice took the tiller while I watched the echo sounder. Then it grew dark, which confused Maurice, and we hit the mud. In the near vicinity were several canoes using lights. When Maurice called, one came over and without a word he stepped in and was swallowed by the dark.

I spent a worried night trying to sleep on deck, wrapped in a sail. *Solitaire*'s keel was held as though set in concrete and there was no way of getting ashore unless I grew wings.

When Maurice returned at dawn *Solitaire* was again afloat. I started the engine and Maurice navigated us through a winding path of water cut in the forest until I had my first sight of Tutóia, a dirty beach with a single wooden jetty against a background of a few red-roofed modern bungalows among scattered palm trees.

I was given to understand a naval officer wanted to see me and tried to make myself presentable, covering my blisters with light-weight trousers and a long-sleeved shirt. As I could not get shoes on my feet, I cut off the bottoms of some old pumps and bandaged them on. A local named Tony came out in his canoe and Maurice indicated that in future this man would look after me, so there would be no need of my rubber dinghy. I was taken to the largest of the bungalows, which turned out to be Navy Headquarters and after a short wait was shown into an office sparsely decorated with pictures of ships. Behind a large desk sat a handsome officer wearing American-type light khaki Navy uniform, silver bars agleam.

This was the commanding officer, Lieutenant Orland Sapana. Later I was to hear villagers refer to him as a saint and within a few days I was agreeing with them. The only other piece of furniture in the room was the biggest, softest, most luxurious easy chair whose arms reached out to me like those of a beautiful woman. My aching body longed to be engulfed by her and when I became aware Orland was inviting me to sit, I slowly lowered myself with closed eyes, only to receive another full-throated belch. The seat had no springs and I was sitting on the floor. Lieutenant Orland had disappeared: all I could see was the underside of his desk. I pulled myself up until my nose rested on its surface from where I tried to carry on an intelligent conversation. Although Orland could speak no English, he used words that were nearly international.

'Military... sporta?'

I gathered he wished to know if I was in the services.

'Sport,' I replied.

'English?' he asked.

'Si, yes, English,' I repeated and then pointed at him.

He said he was Brazilian which confused me as I had always thought St Lucia was British.

'Saint Lucia? Brazilian?' I queried, shaking my head.

'Si, si.' He stretched his arms wide and said, 'Brazil.' Putting his hands close together: 'England'.

I was not having that, so I bent both arms intending to say 'England stronger' but having let go of the desk I was again swallowed by the armchair. When I re-emerged Orland was rocking back and forth, pretending to hold a baby and smiling. At first I thought he wanted to know if I had any children. He then picked up my papers and pointed first to the date in the calendar, then to my birth date, October 24th. Today was my birthday!

His face took on a look of concern and, pointing to my own, spoke the one word I'd been fearing, 'Hospital.' I tried to make my way out of the office repeating, '*Solitaire, Solitaire*', too frightened to leave her, however much I needed medical attention. It was like being on the moon with someone suggesting you leave your space craft, your only means of returning to earth, plus the normal concerns of entering any hospital, wondering when they would release you. Orland understood this because he kept repeating, 'No problem, no problem.'

Maurice then returned and I was told to accompany him to a hotel for a meal. Most of the houses around had been standing for years, their whitewashed walls, 2ft thick, broken by heavily shuttered windows as if under siege from the scorching sun. Poorly-dressed peasants offered fish and over-ripe bananas for sale but the village smelt of decay, flies seeming to cover its filth. Whenever Maurice and I came into view all movement would stop. I walked through statues that moved only to watch my stumbling progress. Now and again I would stop to tie the bandages on my feet when, seeing me kneeling on the cobbles, they would move forward to help, only to retreat with shy smiles, wishing me 'Good morning' as I looked up.

The hotel was another terraced house, larger than its neighbours and with a small courtyard in front. Behind its shutters it was cool. The main room had long scrubbed tables, kitchen chairs and sturdy sideboards: the walls were covered with browning family photographs such as I had last seen as a boy in my grandfather's house. Would I like to shower? I was shown across a dirty yard to what I first thought was a lavatory but inside which was a 40-gallon oil drum filled with water and a pannikin for throwing it over oneself. There was no soap or towel, but it proved the finest shower of my life. I patted myself dry with my shirt and tried to finger-comb my hair. As this hurt I simply pushed it back from my forehead and replaced the four-knotted handkerchief I had been using as headgear.

I was given two boiled eggs, some bread, and the worst cup of coffee I had ever tasted. There was another person in the room, a young Castro, with thick black hair and beard. About 30 years of age, he could speak a little English and introduced himself as Professor Maguil, a visiting teacher. He asked if I would visit the local girls' school that evening and give a talk, explaining that although the children would be unable to understand what I was saying, nevertheless they were trying to learn English and would welcome an opportunity to meet their first Anglo-Saxon.

A second man entered, Maguil's age, slightly built and beardless, a Dr Benedito Carvino. They talked together awhile, and from their glances clearly they were discussing me. I heard Lieutenant Orland's name mentioned.

Maguil turned. 'Leslie, hospital,' he said seriously.

Already I felt I had been separated from *Solitaire* too long, so I shook my head and returned to her. Tony took me back to my boat in his canoe and spent the afternoon aboard. Married, with six children, he lived in a small concrete box containing several beds built from odd pieces of wood, covered with bits of blankets, with a cooking fire in the middle of the dirt floor. Whenever I wanted to go ashore, I would blow a whistle: either he, his wife or children would row me.

The youngsters added a touch of drama to this task. With a paddle as big as they were and a fast-flowing current, they had to drag the canoe well upstream before starting across, timing their meeting with *Solitaire* before being swept past. I showed Tony how to use my gas stove and where the tea and coffee was kept. Considering their poverty Tony and his family were the most honest people it has been my privilege to meet and nothing was ever taken without my say-so.

Just before dark a single-engine aircraft, a Cessna 126 I reckoned, landed close to the village. That night I returned to the hotel for dinner, ready for my solo performance at the girls' school. Seated at the table with eight or ten other men eating prawns and rice, the man opposite me spoke in English. He was Ivan, the pilot of the aircraft I had seen land, and someone with whom I thought I could hold a conversation at last. Alas, he knew only a few phrases and words. In fact I was having difficulty myself with sentences, remembering only a few words at a time: if anyone spoke for too long I would forget the earlier part. In fact I found it easier to understand Orland, who spoke no English, than Ivan who in normal circumstances I would have been able to hold in conversation.

What happened that evening frightened me. At the school I was introduced to the teachers and then taken into a classroom with around a hundred females, aged between 14 and 60, all wearing grey skirts and white blouses, a government perk for attending school was the impression I got. There was a good deal of laughing and shouting and the odd word of English. Since I knew they would not understand if I just talked, I drew a chart on the blackboard showing my voyage from England to Martinique, then out to sea and back to St Lucia, at which point the shouting and laughing suddenly stopped and a chill ran up my back. When I turned around my audience stared at me as though I were mad. I had experienced this type of thing before when talking to the fishermen and Orland. I was trying to be friends with these people and I could not understand why they kept trying to frighten me. An attractive girl, aged about 20, was about to leave, her provocative wiggle marking her out as the village flirt. She stopped in front of me, eyeing me up and down with a smouldering look as she said something to Maguil. The silence was broken by roars of laughter. Maguil indicated she wanted to kiss me goodnight. My answer was to point to my blistered mouth and say, 'Problem!' I started to enjoy life again.

Next morning Tony arrived early with a gift from Orland of a plate of toast which we spread with marmalade and shared for breakfast, helped down by coffee. Later Ivan joined us and we sat talking in the cabin for a while. When he said he had flown to many islands and, indeed, Miami, I produced my Caribbean chart and pointed to Miami. He nodded, then, smiling, pointed to Havana. I tried Barbados and got another 'Yes'. Warming to the game I pointed to St Lucia and was amazed when he shook his head. I did not appreciate his sense of humour. I had seen him land, he was with me now. Why was he trying to worry me? My head started to ache again and Tony led Ivan away shortly afterwards.

While they were ashore I found a stainless-steel mirror which I cleaned and polished. The reflection surely was not me, not this ugly mass of blisters and yellow, weeping sores? The ginger beard was encrusted with filth, the eyes barely visible, just red swollen lids with slits which started to run as I became sorry... not for myself, but for the poor fool in the mirror.

That afternoon Orland, Maguil and Dr Carvino came on board. Again I was told I must go to hospital, and again I refused. There would be no charge they said, apart from for medicines and food. Finally I gave $10 to Tony to fetch the antibiotics and disinfectants the doctor prescribed. Professor Maguil was leaving to visit another school and promised to ask the teachers to look after me while he was away. The doctor cleaned my face, gave me some tablets and then they all left.

On October 26th I cut my feet, swollen like glowing balloons, with a razor blade to release the fluid. Later Orland arrived with the doctor and for the first time they saw me in shorts. The condition of my legs seemed to make them angry but lying on my bunk I had the feeling that it had little to do with me. Now and again I tried to explain that there was something wrong inside my head, that I could no longer understand anything. I kept making circular movements by the side of my head saying, 'Loco.'

I was asked again if I would go to the hospital, and again refused. The doctor cleaned me as best he could and angrily pointed to the swarms of flies. 'Englishman loco,' he agreed. They left, none of us happy.

I spent a restless night, my only relief to keep the blood from my feet by holding them above my head. In the morning I asked Tony to fetch the doctor, who inspected my legs.

'Hospital,' he said again, shrugged his shoulders and closed his bag. 'Fini,' he said, which I took to mean the poor man had had enough of me.

It was my turn to say 'Hospital' and I even managed, 'Please, doctor.'

Satisfied, he gave me some tablets that seemed to ease the pain. Later he returned with Orland and a stranger. John, who had been in the Merchant Navy and had spent a good deal of time in British ports, spoke excellent English. The fault was mine that it took so long to explain things.

Tony, who had been pumping *Solitaire* dry every day, would now live aboard and look after her. I was asked to write a brief statement to the Captain of Ports, along with a sketch of *Solitaire*'s damage and a rough chart of my voyage, which I duly did and included a thank-you note for all the kindness and hospitality of the people of St Lucia.

It was arranged I should enter hospital next morning. I spent those last few hours on *Solitaire* with my feet above my head before being carted off to hospital on October 28th, Tony canoeing me to the jetty to save the long walk. Our trail up the cobbled streets was marked by flapping bandages I could no longer be bothered to tie, and the bottom of my pumps dropping off as I staggered into the village square. I went forward bare-footed, vaguely aware of a green building on my right, a church in the left-hand corner with two buildings alongside.

Tony pointed to the far one and said, 'Hospital', towards which I stumbled drunkenly.

As I entered I looked up, my embarrassment at finding myself in Brixham about to be surpassed. Over the door for all the world to see were the words *Hospital Maternidade*. I considered trying to return to *Solitaire* but a light nudge from Tony pushed me into Tutóia's Maternity Hospital!

Maria da paz Rodrigues – a long name for someone so gentle and pretty, so I shortened it to Maria that first day. She started working on my suppurations as soon as I arrived. The bed had clean white sheets and since I could not wear pyjamas because of my weeping sores, I lay on top of them clad only in boxer shorts. Maria had her back to me when I suddenly drew in my breath as though hurt. She looked round, her large brown eyes full of concern, until I started laughing, at which point she joined in. When she had cleaned my face, I made signs I wanted to shave off my beard, which she did for me. Already I was feeling much better.

The first week passed quickly. Tony turned up each morning to report on *Solitaire*. Orland would visit and the teachers and girls from the school stayed with me until lights out. After their departure the main entertainment was provided by bats performing acrobatics in the open rafters to the screams and groans of pregnant women – so much better than any late night horror film, with the added spice of finding yourself a blood donor if the bats included you in their act.

During the second week things improved and my head pains eased. I learned a few Portuguese words – and the names of the girls who were visiting me. The doctor's wife would sit with me at night and we would read together from an old English textbook of hers, trying to increase her tiny vocabulary. Little old ladies would stay for hours without speaking, just holding my hands. Lovely young ladies would lean over, their black hair cascading down the sides of my cheeks, and would slowly moisten luscious red lips and expect me to repeat some Brazilian words after them as they tried to teach me their language.

The night before my release a fisherman, a new patient, came to my room to complain about the noise. Although I thought it a bit of a liberty, I asked the young ladies to take away their tape recorder. I would learn the Bossa Nova another night, I explained.

'What's your next port of call?' the fisherman asked.

'Barbados,' I answered.

'How long will it take?' he queried. When I said two days, he told me it was impossible. We argued awhile and he left, saying he would give me some charts. Next morning he handed me two of Brazil which I promptly gave back, saying I had no intention of going there. He looked at me as though I'd just landed from another planet and pointed to a chart showing Tutóia.

'No,' I said. 'We're on Saint Lucia.'

He pointed to a town 80 miles away called Sao Luis. For a moment I stared at the charts, expecting my head to explode.

I was in Brazil.

I was 1,000 miles south of the Caribbean St Lucia and had sailed over the Equator to hit a reef 100 miles south of the Amazon. How could I have made such an incredible blunder?

On my return to *Solitaire*, I re-read the instructions for taking a noon sight for latitude. 'Declination, North and South. These two elements are additive or subtractive according to the following simple rule. Same names add. Different names (one N and one S) subtract.' On September 23rd, when halfway across the Atlantic, the declination had changed from North to South (the sun moving south of the Equator) and I had added instead of subtracted it.

The day I hit the reef the declination was 8°S, so from 16°S should have been subtracted the assumed latitude 14°40'N for that day. I had hit the Brazilian coast about 1°20' south of the Equator! Eighty miles further south is Sao Luis, the capital and port in that area of Brazil, its call sign SLI. Had I carried the *Admiralty List of Radio Signals* I would have found that St Lucia's call sign in the Windward Islands was, in fact, SLU! But the elementary error that had brought me to this pass I now found difficult to live with. In a sense that second week in hospital saw the start of my wish to make a second, non-stop voyage around the world.

Before *Solitaire* could continue I had to do something about her broken bottle-screw and loose rigging. As I had no spares I removed one from the twin backstays, replacing it with four links of anchor chain, and used it on the forestay. Once more *Solitaire* had tight rigging.

Feeling pleased with myself, I heard a disturbance on the shore. A man in brightly coloured shorts ran up and down waving his arms and jumping in the air. We watched him awhile until I concluded that it might be a new dance craze and sent Tony over to see if he would like a partner. He was captured and brought out to *Solitaire* where his crew-cut and accent proclaimed him an American. He revealed that he was the aircraft pilot for the Captain of Ports in Sao Luis. When the Port Captain received my letter acknowledging the kindness of the St Lucian people, he could not read it so passed it on to the American to translate.

'Jesus Chriiiist, this guy doesn't even know which hemisphere he's in,' he had exclaimed and came to inform me.

I thanked him for his trouble, claiming that I had now recovered my marbles. After a couple of shots of my whisky and his camera, he was gone.

I had just got my breath back when Tony returned with another visitor who looked like Rock Hudson, except that he had thick grey hair and a deeply tanned face and his baritone voice hinted of a French extraction. Lord knows what effect he had on women, but they were out of luck for he was a French-Canadian priest, Father Le Brun, who had heard of my troubles on his aircraft radio and had flown down to see me. I now had visions of the village airport starting to look like Heathrow.

He asked two questions, why did I wish to sail around the world alone? And would I go to church that night? I told him about solitude and contentment: of sailing into setting suns, of shoals of flying fish lifting from the bows, of colours beyond the skills of camera or painter which only God could have created. I had been having trouble finding words so, to make him understand, I had been using my hands to show fish in flight and dolphins dancing. Yes, I believed in God, but I considered the world to be His church, it was what was in your heart and mind that made you a Christian. There was no necessity to go into a stone building to pray. If Father Le Brun did not understand my reasons for avoiding church, he nevertheless seemed content.

Later that afternoon I faced another mystery: jazz music blasting from the sky, over as quickly as a squall. That night I was invited to dine with the doctor and his wife and a few friends whose house adjoined the church. We had been enjoying both food and conversation when the musical earthquake struck and windows started to shake. I looked at the walls expecting to see cracks appear before the house disintegrated, calming down only when I noticed that the other guests ignored this interruption. Conversation continued, but now we were lip reading. Then I solved the mystery of the heavenly music. To call the faithful in a 100-mile area, the church was using four loudspeakers instead of bells, one speaker directed into the doctor's window and my left ear.

His wife was trying to persuade me to take her to church that night, pretending she was unable to appreciate my reasons for not going. In the end she employed the normal feminine method of getting her way. Earlier I had refused more food although still hungry. She overcame my objections by saying I did not like her cooking so, not wanting to give offence, I had allowed my plate to be filled again. Now she claimed I was ashamed to be seen with her so I had to agree to accompany her to church.

The village square was crowded and I thankfully turned to go back but mysteriously a path opened up in front of us, people stepping aside as we moved towards the church. Inside it was packed, but again the people let us through. For a moment I panicked, thinking they were going to marry me off to one of the nurses but finally I found myself in front of the pulpit, looking up at Father Le Brun, who was smiling at me. He preached in Portuguese but I recognised my own name and *Solitaire*'s, after which the congregation repeated them the way you might say 'Amen', echoing through the speakers to the crowd in the square. Then he used his hands like flying fish and dipped them like dancing dolphins, having clearly understood what I had told him that morning. The scheme to get me to church had been a well-contrived plan involving Mrs Doctor!

After the service he explained how the villagers wished to bless my voyage but had not anticipated the problem of getting me into church. Had he explained the reason I would have been delighted, I replied, adding that he had pinched all my best material for his sermon for which I would forgive him if he would pay another visit to *Solitaire* before he flew off.

This perfect day was still not over. Back on the beach I found six of the school ma'ams waiting for me. Aboard *Solitaire* they produced a guitar and tape recorder and started recording the songs of Brazil, in the intervals one of them reading from some pencilled notes in Portuguese. The performance ran for half-an-hour or so, whereafter all gave our Christian names just before the tape ran out. I have no idea how long it took them to perfect their timing but it must have been hours. It was a tape I would keep all my life and play a thousand times. I cherish it still.

Next morning Father Le Brun and I discussed my ports of call en route to the Panama Canal. Cayenne in French Guiana – 650 miles to the north – seemed a good prospect, and English was its second language. There I could pick up stores at reasonable prices. Shortly after he left, a light aircraft flew over *Solitaire*, dipping its wings. A kindly man was off to see if any more of his flock had strayed.

Food in Tutóia was hideously expensive and in short supply, but I still had £200 left so I indulged in a couple of tins of spam and sardines and 10lb of potatoes and bananas to add to my store of three jars of marmalade, six tins of mixed vegetables and a bottle of salad cream and another of mustard. Orland presented me with a sack of oranges and 5 gallons of diesel while Tony was asked to fill my water containers. Later in the day I watched a football match and, on the way back, was shown a ditch filled with water in which children and dogs were playing. A woman filled a jug from it and Tony made a drinking movement with his hand. It seemed I would be carrying 30 gallons of well-used bath water!

I was delayed for a few days awaiting my papers from Sao Luis, which did nothing to help my nerves. Like being thrown from a horse, the quicker you're back in the saddle the better, although I wasn't keen on coming within a mile of the horse or the sea in case I received another kick in the teeth from sun, sea and reefs.

At first light on Tuesday, November 18th, I switched on the engine, but the diesel grumbled and showed her displeasure at being ignored for so long by emitting clouds of blue smoke before screaming at full pitch to shatter the quiet of the morning. Crickets in the mangroves on the far bank stopped their insistent chattering and the birds took flight, screeching at the noisy intruder. Pushing the throttle forward, the sound reduced to a slow, sexual throb. Tutóia slept on, palm trees lying limp with bowed heads. Over the dew-covered roofs I could see the steeple of the church in which I had received my service of blessing, and nearby the maternity hospital in which I'd spent two weeks flat on my back. Would Tony arrive to help lift the anchor or could I play safe for another day?

No such luck! Already he was making his way down the beach, followed by his wife and children. Orland, in full uniform for the occasion, was there too, with his wife and young son, scuttling any chance I had of not sailing. Tony came aboard and quickly pulled up the anchor and, on his return to the cockpit, I gave him the parcel I had made up for his family.

'Adios, Leslie.'

'Adios, Tony,' I said, and then he was gone.

As I rounded the bend in the river, I looked back to wave farewell to my friends, a final glance at the kindly village of Tutóia, the home of Samaritans.

CHAPTER THREE
The Hallelujah Chorus

Tutóia – Fatu Hiva, Marquesas Islands
November 1975 – May 1976

Slowly we motored through the watery forest into a nightmare of shallow brown waters, waves breaking over the sandy islands that threatened our passage. I raised sail, trying to lift the keel by heeling but without success. Ahead I could see the black marker buoy that had greeted our arrival, towards which *Solitaire* made her way, picking her steps as though walking through a minefield, with nothing showing on the echo sounder. She lifted and dropped heavily on hard ground, her mast shuddering, and I was promptly and violently sick over the stern. Slowly, so very slowly, we struggled to the buoy.

The sea was still brown but Orland had shown me on the chart in his office that if I sailed north I would soon find deep water. Moreover, I now had the two charts the fisherman had given me and a list of RDF call signs all the way to Panama. Although I had no harbour charts, the ports I was considering would be well-buoyed, with Cayenne, 650 miles away in French Guiana, the first.

The first 24 hours were nerve-wracking, what with gusting winds, choppy seas and the bilge pump packing up, thanks to a ripped diaphragm. *Solitaire* needed pumping dry twice a day so I made do with a bucket and sponge until I contrived a new diaphragm from some plastic 'rubber' left over from the seat covers.

My noon sight on November 19th, put us 22 miles below the Equator and as we made our first intentional crossing that night, the wind came light from the east enabling *Solitaire* to broad-reach contentedly for Cayenne, dozing along under main and working jib. I should have put up a larger headsail but relaxed with 80 miles a day, plus another 20 miles or so from the favourable current. My nerves steadied, the cool sea breeze refreshing my scarred skin. To celebrate crossing the Equator I dined on spam and chips.

As the days slid by the winds continued to decrease but I refused to fly more sail for I was enjoying this voyage too much. I found some flour in a plastic bag inside a box of sponge mix, and made my first-ever pancakes, spreading them with my favourite marmalade as the radio started to pick up delightful French music.

One morning I saw what I first thought was a low flying aircraft coming over the horizon, followed by another and another. As they neared, I could see they were modern fishing trawlers with their arms extended. All day, stretching from horizon to horizon, they streamed by *Solitaire*. With darkness they became a blaze of lights, making me think I was sitting on a main street. Then, like a body of soldiers, they turned together, headed out to sea and disappeared. A last arrival came scurrying by, late for parade. 'Get a move on, you hooooooorible little man...' I cried in my best sergeant-major voice. When he had gone we had the night to ourselves, and a French woman sang me to sleep with love songs.

On Tuesday, November 25th, *Solitaire* lay a couple of miles off Cayenne. I could see trawlers heading inshore but could pick up no RDF signal, although Paramaribo in Dutch Suriname was coming in loud and clear from 160 miles away and, since it had a lightship to help with the landfall, I decided to sail there instead.

We arrived late on Thursday and lay off, keeping the lightship in sight until morning. Although I had tried to hold our position, *Solitaire* had drifted to the north with the current and had to be forced back. Again the waters were chocolate-coloured but a clearly-buoyed shipping lane made navigation easy. A strong outflowing current slowed progress and as ocean-going ships were using the main channel, I pulled to one side, dropped sail and anchored for the night. Food was getting short so dinner consisted of a tin of mixed vegetables, salad cream and an orange, as did breakfast the next morning.

We arrived in Paramaribo fairly quickly and rode the broad river on a favourable tide. The port seemed prosperous enough, with clusters of docks housing fleets of shrimp trawlers, the town a mixture of old Dutch buildings and modern stores, a bustling fruit, fish and vegetable market on the dockside. Flags and bunting were everywhere as a week earlier Suriname had gained its independence from the Dutch. The harbour itself was spoilt by a massive cargo ship parked in the middle, upside down, scuttled by the Germans during the last war. I felt *Solitaire* shudder when she caught sight of it but I hastened to disclaim any responsibility.

However, I soon managed to get us in trouble again. I dropped the hook about 20ft from a structure of girders but was suspicious of *Solitaire*'s position in the fast current. If I attempted to lift the anchor again or she started dragging, we could find ourselves trying to climb over the top of the sunken German ship. On the girders, wearing green overalls and plastic helmet, stood a black man, looking for all the world as if he had been working on a New York skyscraper when it had sunk.

After my experiences in Brazil I knew you could work wonders with the odd packet of English cigarettes, so I waved a pack in his direction, making a diving and swimming action with arms, shouted 'Amigo' and waved him over. His eyebrow merely lifted, whereupon I increased my offers to two packs, still without joy. Perhaps he could not swim? The solution was easy: I would throw him a rope which he could tie onto a girder. I would then pull *Solitaire* over and he could lift the anchor while I steered. My throw was perfect, landing plumb at his feet at which he raised the other eyebrow. We both watched with interest as the current slowly snaked the rope back again. After three more perfect throws I grew despondent.

'For Pete's sake, will you please tie the rope to the girder,' I cried.

To my surprise he picked it up and secured it. Roy turned out to be the dockyard foreman and spoke excellent English, Paramaribo's second language, probably because the Americans run most things there. Roy took me to the Dutch manager who could not do enough. The structure Roy had been standing on was part of a dry dock for lifting prawn trawlers. *Solitaire* could be hauled out at the same time at no expense to me but I turned down the kindly offer, wanting to push on to Panama.

The only other cruising yacht in port at the same time belonged to a Frenchman, Stephen, who with his wife and young daughter was preparing to leave on the out-going tide when I arrived. I was invited on board to share their last meal before they sailed: steak, salad and bread washed down by fresh milk! They put me ashore with the last of the steak in a crusty roll. As I let go their lines, Stephen asked what my next port of call would be.

'British Guiana,' I replied.

Stephen's mournful plea came back: 'Oooooh, Leslie, don't go there. Very bad people. You will be robbed.'

So I said, 'Right, I'll go to Trinidad.'

'Oooooh, Leslie, don't go there. You'll be robbed.'

So I asked where they were going.

'Grenada in the Caribbean,' they said.

'Right,' I shouted, waving goodbye with my steak sandwich. 'I'll see you there.'

My stay in Paramaribo, thanks to my first real taste of American hospitality, was longer than expected. They were either visiting *Solitaire* or taking me to a barbecue party, the movies or whatever. I bought what tinned food I could afford, always looking for the cheapest buy which did not always pay off as I had to throw away a dozen tins of canned mackerel. The Dutch manager presented me with oranges and a sack of grapefruit. My last day in Paramaribo was spent chiselling through *Solitaire*'s cabin floor and reinforcing the cracked hull with fibreglass.

The 500 miles voyage to Grenada took eight weary days. The currents between the islands are strong and as Grenada had no

RDF station and those available on other islands were weak, dead reckoning became paramount. The last two days brought heavy rain with bad visibility which cleared up at midnight on December 16th when a large black cloud appeared on the horizon with a star in the middle – Grenada with a house light high up in the hills.

At dawn I motored to St George's main anchorage where I performed my usual party piece of putting *Solitaire* on a reef. To be fair I don't think we should count this one as another yacht was coming out, leaving insufficient room for two boats to pass. *Solitaire*, the perfect lady, stepped to one side and we had virtually stopped when there was a crunching sound and *Solitaire* rolled from side to side, shaking her mast as if to say, 'I don't believe it.'

Instantly a flotilla of small craft, power boats, yachts, gin palaces, even rowing boats, tore out as if they had been awaiting our arrival, the air filled with flying ropes and people clambered over our decks attaching them to every conceivable place. Within minutes, *Solitaire* was swinging to her anchor, dazed by so much attention. Where, I wanted to know, had they been when I needed them in Brazil?

We had just got shipshape when I heard 'Ooooh, Leslie' from a dinghy racing towards me. 'Ooooh, Leslie, I've been robbed,' said Stephen, which had me in stitches.

The following night I was laughing on the other side of my face. Men would silently raft around the anchored yachts by night intent on robbery, so it was unwise to leave craft unattended. New arrivals were quickly made aware of the danger and, in turn, I had already warned another crew that day.

I had met David, an American, through his English crew member, and had been invited to his yacht *Rolling Stone* for dinner that night. David had built his boat in England before sailing across the Atlantic to pick up his parents and a girlfriend for a holiday. I thought *Solitaire*, anchored no more than 40 yards away, was safe enough since I could still keep an eye on her and, for added protection, fitted strings to the deck light switch and attached them to the sliding hatches. There was a good crowd on *Rolling Stone* and for a while I sat drinking in the cockpit, watching my boat. Finally we disappeared below for a curry meal although every few minutes I would pop my head outside to make sure everything was all right. Then *Solitaire*'s lights came on.

David and another large American, Tom, rowed me over. I thought the thieves might still be aboard but the hatch cover had been ripped off and every locker, drawer and door opened, including the oven's. I would not have thought it possible to wreak so much malicious damage in so short a time. The engine's instrument panel had been uprooted and the spare money I kept there stolen. My portable radio, clothes, tools and two torches had vanished. The ship's papers, my passport and £80 in travellers' cheques should have been at the back of my chart table, but they had gone, too. It was a kick in the crutch. I could sell my outboard motor, WC, even the stove, and still continue around the world but without a passport or ship's papers, I was stuck.

I told David and Tom the reason for my looking so sick, whereupon they started pulling out the charts... and found my wallet with the papers and cheques which meant that I could leave for Panama in the morning after all! My visitors had kindly left my RDF sextant and compass and had also missed a camera. The police were called but showed perfunctory interest and I was still upset next morning, as if *Solitaire* had been violated. David suggested I hang on for a couple of days and tie alongside *Rolling Stone* for protection, and again Americans came to my assistance. Tom and his girlfriend, Karen, presented me with a large bag of food, claiming that it had been stored in the bilges too long and was going bad. On inspection I found a recent label from the local supermarket!

Christmas was but a few days away. David and his family were sailing to Prickly Bay, 6 miles along the coast, where it would be quieter, with less chance of being broken into, and *Solitaire* accompanied them, feeling that one violation in a girl's life was one too many. I did not set off for Panama until a fortnight later but in the interim became friendly with more Americans, including Bill and his girlfriend, Dean, who had started on a world voyage but had been forced to give up the idea. Since they couldn't go, they decided to help me on condition I wrote to them detailing my progress with pre-addressed envelopes they supplied!

One other thing the Americans in Grenada offered was advice: stay at least 20 miles off the Colombian coast and ignore distress rockets. Pirates were using them to attract unsuspecting yachts, then murdering the crews and using the craft for drug trafficking. Finally, take care walking the streets of Colon, even in daylight, as muggers formed queues to rob tourists.

Solitaire set off on January 10th, logged 1,124 miles and arrived on January 23rd, 1976. Sailing to Panama is like entering the neck of a bottle: trade winds that have swept thousands of miles across the Atlantic can become quite strong and compressed; steep-breaking seas build up but fortunately for us they were from the east and hence over our stern. I left Grenada with a comfortable Force 4 from the south-east but by the third day winds had increased and we were down to working jib only, breaking seas speeding behind us. At times *Solitaire* would find herself surfing on them: at others, unable to move fast enough, she would receive a firm pat on her stern, and would turn indignantly as if to say, 'How dare you, sir.'

On one such occasion a wave shot a bucketful of water through the open hatch, soaking the cabin carpet again. Thereafter I kept the hatch boards in, closing myself below and emerging only to take noon sights for latitude, obtain fixes, or check sails, rigging and self-steering. Most of the time I spent reading the books Bill and Dean had given me and eating strange American foods including stuffed tomatoes, which I had never heard of!

The night of my Panama Canal landfall I panicked. As I had been warned to keep 20 miles off the coast, I played safe and doubled it, then when it was time to turn towards land, I had the Cayenne problem over again: I could not pick up the Canal's RDF signal. However, call sign TBG came in loud and clear, indicating the island of Taboga lying at the Pacific end of the Panama Canal, and since it was in the right direction, I set course for it.

At about the time I had estimated, I saw the loom of a light in the night sky and made for the glow, which swung up and became two blooming great headlights. Pirates! Turning off my lights I started the motor to shoot off back the way I had come, only to find another set of headlights blocking *Solitaire*'s escape. At that moment I saw the Canal lighthouse flashing and made for it. Astern were two looms of lights in the sky; I'm sure now they were fishing boats using their lights to work by. Maybe I scared them more than they scared me. Maybe.

I waited for daylight before easing through the breakwater where, after anchoring on mud flats, an American Customs launch came over and gave me the good news that I would have enough money to pass through the Canal. It would cost only £30, half of which was a deposit and would be returned later. That was not my only piece of luck: I also received my first letter from Rome who, as an ex-merchant seaman, knew I had to pass through the Canal. I had reported all my blunders and how *Solitaire* kept getting me out of trouble, to which Rome replied that, despite so many mistakes, at least I was making them only once. I wrote back immediately... omitting to mention the reef in Grenada!

To arrange our transit I moved *Solitaire* into the Colon Yacht Club, one which does not encourage you to linger as they double their prices every three days to make room for new arrivals. You can stay on the mud flats free of charge, but from there it is difficult to arrange for a pilot and crew.

The Colon Muggers must be the world's best and if you haven't been mugged by one of them, you haven't been mugged. Colon is in one of the few countries that runs schools for these gentlemen, with courses in drug trafficking, kidnapping, and plain everyday murder. After successfully completing their training, many graduates are exported to less well-endowed regions, such is the demand for their talents. I made their acquaintance soon after my arrival. Communication between them and the chaps in Grenada must have broken down or they would have been informed that I had already been nobbled and there was little left.

My partner in this drama, Terrell Adkisson, was not exactly my idea of a Texan, as I had been brought up watching John Wayne and Gary Cooper knock ten kinds of rice pudding out of the Indians. Needing fuel for my trip through the Canal, I was hitting the trail along the Old Pontoon when I heard a slow, drawn-out, 'Hooooowdy.' I spun round, dropping my hand to my hip, then quickly removed it in case I conveyed the wrong impression. I was confronted by a scruffy individual wearing checked shirt, glasses and a pair of ex-army trousers four sizes too big. At first the stubble on his face and grey crew-cut hair suggested he was older than I. In fact he was younger, proving again that ageing is a deception practised on people after a long sea voyage and nights without sleep.

Terrell owned *Altair*, a new 28ft glassfibre Bermudan sloop, and had recently given up teaching mathematics in Texas to sail around the world with his 22-year-old nephew, Leo, a blond young man who had previously spent his spare time playing guitar in a pop group. Terrell needed petrol, or gas as he put it, so we started out on the first of our many adventures together to a garage only a mile away in the Colon district. I had enough money to buy 5 gallons of diesel; Terrell had his wallet in his back pocket. The garage attendant warned us to be careful, his darting, frightened eyes telling their own story.

Groups of men were watching us but it was ten o'clock in the morning, broad daylight, so why worry? Halfway back to the yacht club I turned to speak to Terrell and spotted three of the biggest men I've ever seen coming up behind us, with knives. I had dreamed of moments like this. I would push the women and children to one side, take a flying leap, legs drawn to manly chest to shoot out like two murderous pistons, taking the two nearest villains in the throat, killing them instantly. The third would be despatched with a karate chop to the head.

What I actually did was to shout a warning to Terrell and run in front of a line of oncoming traffic. A screeching of brakes... I bounced off a car, the fuel can turning into a tiger that wanted to go walkies. It bolted across the intersection, dragging me with it, to get clobbered by a truck coming the other way. When I staggered to my feet, Terrell had a man on each arm, with knives at his chest, while a third tore at Terrell's wallet.

I shouted as loudly as I could to let the men know I really meant it, 'Hang on, I'm coming.'

There was a sound of ripping and Terrell stood in the main street minus trousers – and wallet. He started running after them, with me trying to stop him. If he caught up with them, they would surely kill him but, outdistanced, he abandoned the chase.

Terrell had lost a few travellers' cheques, no cash. Soon his sense of humour returned. 'Just my luck to be arrested for indecent exposure,' he said, looking down at his fancy underpants. He was attacked a second time in Panama City, but this time Leo came up behind with a tin of peaches and started hammering the would-be mugger, who ran off. In Colon that could be described as a bad day at the office. It is inadvisable to linger long in Panama.

The 40-mile canal trip is straightforward enough, through pleasant lakes and waterways, with three locks at each end. You require a ship's pilot (normally an ex-Merchant Navy captain), four line handlers and four 100ft lengths of rope. The handlers adjust your lines to keep your craft in the centre of the dock as you rise and fall, for which you supply the food and grog for the day and their rail fare back. In 1976 that was just $1. Line handlers are not hard to come by. They reckon it's a nice day out.

I arrived at the Balboa Yacht Club on the Pacific side with precisely $3 so I sold my outboard for $200 to put me back in funds. Again I bought the cheapest food available: unmarked tins of corned beef that turned out to be mostly jelly, tins of tuna that looked and tasted like grey sand, a sack of rice alive with weevils, flour, baking powder and a large tin of treacle as a treat.

For my Pacific crossing (8,000 miles or so) I bought two charts. My first landfall would be Hiva Oa in the Marquesas Islands, a voyage of 3,500 miles or so. Navigation to date had been by dead reckoning with noon sights for latitude and radio direction finding; now I would be sailing into areas of reefs, few lighthouses and fewer navigation aids. Accurate navigation would be essential so I would have to learn how to take sights for longitude. I managed to buy a 1976 Admiralty Almanac and a second-hand set of reduction tables, and for accurate timekeeping (one minute in error can put you 15 miles out of position) I helped antifoul another boat whose owner gave me a small portable receiver in payment. This one had short wave, enabling me to pick up the American station WWV which broadcasts time checks 24 hours a day. There was one small problem: the mirrors on my sextant had lost their silvering. A lady presented me with the mirror from her handbag. Cut to size, it made my sextant serviceable again. I made one major mistake when, trying to save money, I bought a gallon of cheap antifouling. As things worked out it would have been less expensive to have paid more for a better quality.

My custom ashore was to sit on the edge of a group of cruising people, listening to their tales of the sea, trying to pick up tips. *Solitaire*, the only craft I knew anything about, had now carried me 7,000 miles or more, but I still had not picked up much sailing terminology: talk of schooners, ketches or heavy weather sailing and I was lost. I tried to fade into the background with the odd 'Hear, hear' and 'Dashed good show', trying to pretend I was one of them.

On one such occasion I was with a crowd at the Balboa Yacht Club discussing the particularly bad weather at that time of year in the Caribbean. One American had lost his trimaran. He and his crew, over-tired on the trip from Grenada, had tried to come through the breakwater at night, missed the lights and hit it, but managed to get off before it sank. A Canadian family had tried for ten days to sail in the other direction but after a fierce battle had given up and retraced their steps through the Canal. Another five boats were hoping for an easterly passage, meanwhile waiting for the seas to die down. A Frenchman had ripped the floor out of his yacht to cover the cockpit and give protection from breaking waves. I thoroughly enjoyed their talk: you could virtually taste the salt on your lips.

'Leslie, you've come through the Caribbean from Grenada single-handed,' someone commented.

'Er, yes.' A mass of weather-beaten faces turn towards me.

'How bad was it in your opinion?'

'Pretty bad,' I replied.

'Yes, but how bad?' the voice insisted.

I didn't want to tell them I spent my time below, reading, while *Solitaire* and the self-steering did the work. I couldn't talk about wind speed as I had no wind indicator and I would not know a 20ft breaking wave from a 10ft, yet I desperately wanted to be accepted by these adventurers. I came out with the incident that made me put in my hatchboards. 'Well, my carpets got wet.'

There was a deathly silence.

I escaped next morning to the island of Taboga, 6 miles away in the Pacific. Terrell and I had heard of a wartime landing barge on the beach there, against which it was possible to tie alongside, wait for the tide to ebb and then antifoul the hull. *Altair* was done on one day, and *Solitaire* the next. Not too keen on the idea, my boat started acting like a spoilt child on bath night until I tied her up, when she settled. I made a better job of the wound in her side and then applied my cheap antifouling which went on like weak whitewash. *Solitaire* deserved better, but with only $60 left in the kitty I had little choice. At least we would be sharing discomforts, I thought, remembering my jellied corned beef and gritty tuna!

Terrell and Leo sailed a week ahead of us, as there were a few jobs still to do on *Solitaire*. I was sorry to see them go, but we would catch up later. I felt like I was living in Germany, when a knock on the door could mean a call from your local friendly Gestapo, inviting you to sample the delights of a lovely prison camp. Only now, in Taboga, it would be the army or police searching your yacht for drugs.

They paid a visit the day before I left, bringing a dinghy I was supposed to have left on the beach, one I knew belonged to a nearby yacht whose mast had been broken coming through the Panama. A young man with a large Dalmatian dog was looking after the parent boat while its owner was away. As I towed the dinghy over to tie it on the yacht's stern, I could see the dog running on the beach. Later I heard the full story. The young man had taken it ashore for a walk, the army had tried to shoot it and the boy had put his arms round it for protection. He was now in hospital, half his hand blown away.

I sailed for Hiva Oa on Thursday, February 26th, 1976, and for two days *Solitaire* made good time in light winds, gliding along effortlessly on her clean bottom. Conscious of my earlier mistakes I spent hours in *Solitaire*'s cockpit, listening to WWV for time checks while I took sights for longitude which, in the early days of the voyage, I could easily confirm. As the days passed I began to feel more at home at sea than on land. *Solitaire*'s constant movement and my spartan diet kept me slim and fit. As I am blessed with ginger hair and freckles, the sun enjoyed itself colouring my skin anything from brilliant red to deep purple. It was a surprise to find it browning me as well.

No webbed feet or gills yet, but I was metamorphosing into marine life. For instance, storms and calms are treated differently by sea animals. To land life, a storm is a personal attack, knocking down a man's chimneys, flattening his crops, whereas calms go unnoticed. Sea life, however, accepts storms that may sink ships but are not malicious, and realises that the patient ocean recognises no flags, is not vindictive and, far from finding pleasure in rolling you over, does not even notice you. But a calm is a personal attack and in early days could mean back-breaking weeks in a longboat, towing a square-rigger while searching for life-giving winds, half the crew dying of thirst or hunger.

Solitaire hit her first long calm east of the Galapagos Islands. After the early days at sea progress had slowed with runs of only 30 or 40 miles a day, periods without wind, the self-steering on a knife edge. Now she was about to spend four days in an ocean of thick blue oil below a sky whose solitary, unmoving cloud would retain its shape and position hour after hour, leering down on our discomfort. We carried no burgee at the mast top to indicate wind direction but on our backstays bore long, red tell-tales which became skirts covering the most beautiful legs in the world, legs that made Betty Grable's look like matchsticks. They would lift slightly, showing trim ankles and then, seeing they had my interest, drop teasingly.

Just over the horizon was a Giant bathing in this lake of oil, his movements causing a long swell that swayed *Solitaire* monotonously from side to side. I grew to hate him and the Leering Cloud and the Teasing Skirt. The slapping sails, the rattle of the rigging, the strange sounds that would take hours to find... a shifting mug, a loose can. One sound had lasted longer than all the rest, a bruuuph, bruuuph, over and over again. Whenever I moved from my bunk I would alter *Solitaire*'s balance and the noise, hearing me, would stop. Even if I slid along the floor on my belly, holding my breath, I could not catch it. Then the Giant scrubbed his back, and I had it. Bruuuph, bruuuph. A new drill was rolling back and forth in a drawer. I watched it with pleasure for a few minutes, like a cat with a mouse, then I pounced. Clutching it in my fist I took it to *Solitaire*'s stern, and threw a brand new drill worth a bag of rice 50 yards into the sea. You really should not do that sort of thing. Later I learned the secret of destroying calms. You simply ignore them.

Once the sea was flat I would drop the headsail, and put a reef in the main to reduce chafe, which drives the chappie taking the bath bananas. Invariably I would spend my first day on deck busy with odd jobs, always remembering to smile and whistle from time to time for Leering Clouds hate happy whistling. To attract the Teasing Skirt I would bring out my secret weapon, a couple of good books, and while reading would watch her advances from beneath lowered lids. Red skirts hate being treated in this way and soon show all they have. There are compensations to long calms for at the end you will hear the Hallelujah chorus played by the London Symphony Orchestra. It's like sitting in the Royal Albert Hall, eyes closed, waiting, waiting, waiting. Then a faint cough; a ripple touches *Solitaire*'s side. A flute softly tunes up and the sails stop flapping. The string section plays a few bars and her rigging hums. The conductor taps his baton, a slight pause and *Solitaire* is sailing and the most marvellous music in the world is heard. The chorus sings Hallelujah, Hallelujah, higher and higher, Haaaaaleeeelujah...

Solitaire sailed 200 miles to the east of the Galapagos Islands, passing through areas showing six per cent calms on the charts. She had to overcome a north-flowing current of 15 to 20 miles a day as she struggled over the Equator for her third crossing to the free-flowing trade winds that started 300 miles to the south. She was sick as she told me but again, because of my inexperience, I took no notice. She lost her will to live, dragging through the sea on legs too tired to move. I assumed the slow progress to be due to the adverse current and light winds, and fought back with every sail arrangement I could possibly manage to contrive.

The first light breezes from the east indicated the start of the trades. *Solitaire* carried no whisker poles for holding out twin headsails simply because I could not afford them. Instead I had made do with two 13ft aluminium poles to which I had fitted eyes at both ends. I tried using these with both the number one and two genoas hanked on, plus the full main. Still she would not budge. Seas flowed past her and the self-steering lost control, even the tiller having little effect upon her erratic course. She would broach continually, swinging 180° and backing her sails.

When finally we came into the true trades, constant Force 3 to 4 (7 to 16mph), I sailed on a broad reach, with a quartering wind, the number two genoa poled out, a reef in the main. Yachtsmen would have considered me crazy to have so little sail, and in such conditions I would have loved to have set a spinnaker, had I possessed one. Half of the course settings were by sail adjustment as the self-steering was of little practical use.

Unknown to me a cancerous growth was spreading its tentacles around her. *Solitaire*'s cries for help quietened as it entered her mouth, silencing her. Now she was wallowing, hardly noticing the winds that entreated her to frolic.

Wednesday, March 24th, found us at latitude 6°05′S. We had left the Equator 365 miles astern and were 300 miles below the Galapagos Islands. A favourable current gave us an extra 10 to 15 miles a day in south-east winds around Force 4. In these ideal conditions *Solitaire* should have been romping along, covering at least 120 to 140 miles a day. All she produced was a limping 50 miles. Our trailing log clocked only 1,115 miles in 27 days, not a third of the way to Hiva Oa, with half our food and water already consumed.

On the self-steering rudder and under the stern I found pink stalks up to an inch-and-a-half in length with a white and grey bud on each top which I cleaned off with a paint scraper. Could these growths be the reason for *Solitaire*'s illness? I rejected the idea when I remembered antifouling her hull only five weeks earlier. Surely that could not be the cause.

During one of those cleaning sessions I found myself in one of those stupid situations that happen only to single-handers. I had pushed myself through the bars of the pushpit as far as I could, leaning well out and holding on with one hand while scraping with the other. I felt a pull on my hair and threw the scraper into the cockpit, grabbing at my head. My hair had become tangled in the trailing log line! It took me a good half hour to free myself. After that I had a dread of getting stuck up the mast, only to be discovered a year later as a swaying skeleton.

Afloat it is difficult to see all of *Solitaire*'s hull as it rounds sharply just below the waterline and falls away to the keel, so I decided to lean out as far as possible, using a lifeline and an extra rope for support. I had expected to find someone's old sail or a bunch of rope tangled on the keel. Instead I found a swaying pink and white garden completely covering the hull, keel and skeg. No wonder *Solitaire* had wept. Again I felt as I had when the bruuuph, bruuuph drill had come to light. I prepared to pounce then, deflated, realised it had us in thrall, that I had a plague of goose barnacles.

There were three reasons why getting rid of them would cause problems: I'm a poor swimmer, there were sharks in the area, and I'm a confirmed coward. I spent the morning making every conceivable excuse I could think of for not going over the side. *Solitaire* listened in silence except for a muttered slop slop, slurp slurp. I suppose she could have nagged that I had been the one to give her a cheap coat of antifouling and was thus responsible for her sickness but she didn't, which made the need to be forgiven the more dramatic. I badly needed to hear her whisper and laugh with me again.

In the afternoon I dropped her headsail and under the main brought her onto a reach, allowing her to roll in 3–4ft waves. The rubber dinghy was inflated and secured to leeward. With two lifelines and armed with a scraper, I dropped into it and then, holding onto the toe rail, reached down the hull as far as I could on each roll. I spent an hour or so on one side, clearing only a foot and a half of the barnacles, their rubbery feet still clinging below the waterline.

Hanging onto *Solitaire*, trying to keep a grip with my toes as the dinghy dropped away, made me want to give up and throw up. Oh well, tomorrow it would only be worse so I climbed back on board, turned *Solitaire* around and worked on her other side. Then we were back on course, broad-reaching, with our number two genoa filling with only a slight improvement in her performance. All the thanks I got for my trouble was slop slop, slurp slurp.

For the next few days I lost interest in everything but trying to ease the pain in my arms and stomach. We became a couple of tetchy invalids reluctantly settling for a desperately slow passage. To save water I stopped shaving and started my first intentional beard as we slurped across the Pacific in perfect slurping conditions. I would spend hours in the cockpit marvelling at this sailing paradise with cool trade winds and clear, blue skies broken only by a few wispy clouds. The transparent waters provided a private aquarium of beautiful tropical fish that would look up, saucer-eyed, to admire our exotic garden of pink stems and nodding white heads which grew larger with each slurping mile.

At night I had an I-hate-barnacles hour. No longer content

with merely scraping them off I wanted to inflict pain and hear their screams, to collect every last one and lay them on *Solitaire*'s decks so that we could both witness their death throes. The day of reckoning was drawing near.

On Friday, April 23rd, after eight weeks or so at sea covering 3,020 miles and with 600 miles still to go to Hiva Oa, we sighted our first ship. To be honest, it was not a ship but a yacht and they sighted us, not I them. I had felt like a spot of work that morning and spent half an hour picking the weevils out of my daily cup of rice. Despite this strenuous exercise I still felt pretty active, but could think of nothing that demanded attention until I remembered my golf clubs, which were as dirty as old boots. So I spent the morning below cleaning them.

Towards noon I heard the sound of a trumpet. If that's Gabriel, I thought, I'm not going, and banged my head to clear it. Then it sounded again. On deck, clutching my five iron, I saw a 40ft boat off our bow manned by an elderly couple and two in their mid-twenties. Canadians by the home port on their stern. Their twin-poled headsails had been eased and they were holding position a few yards off. I walked up to *Solitaire*'s pulpit.

'Ahoy,' they shouted. 'We've had you in sight all morning. Seeing no one on deck we became worried.'

'I'm fine,' I said, waving my iron. 'I was cleaning my golf clubs.'

There was a thoughtful silence. 'Do you know if there's a bank in Hiva Oa?' they asked. 'We need to cash a cheque.'

'I'm sorry,' I replied. 'I'm a stranger here myself, don't often play this course.'

Another long silence. 'You sure you're all right?'

'Perfectly,' I assured them.

With that, they pulled in their sails and drew away. I couldn't believe it. After eight weeks with no one to talk to, they were leaving without even an invitation to coffee. I wanted to say something really mean but the best parting shot I could think of was, 'You haven't seen my bloody golf ball, have you?' The I-hate-barnacles hour that night was extended by 30 minutes.

On Monday, May 3rd, the noon sight put us 47 miles from Hiva Oa. Looking back over my life I seemed to have done few things right so now I wanted desperately to recompense by making a good landfall. I had nothing to confirm my longitude calculations, apart from some days when I had taken two sights, morning and afternoon, which gave position lines crossing at about our latitude.

Slow progress, a flat sea and clear skies helped my navigation. Today I checked and re-checked a dozen times, for failure to sight land next morning would mean I had let down *Solitaire* yet again. In the afternoon I decided to test the engine, which normally I ran every two or three weeks, just to circulate the oil and top up the battery. I turned the key but nothing happened so I went over all the connections. Those on the solenoid seemed loose and dirty. Cleaned and tightened, we had a motor again!

The Marquesas Islands stretch for about 200 miles, half a dozen of them 3,000ft high or more, and on a clear day they should be visible for 30 or 40 miles. Hiva Oa, at 3,520ft, should not be difficult to spot, despite having no lighthouse or radio direction beacon. But, with one error of more than a thousand miles to look back on, anything was possible!

As night fell the sky filled with stars, although a sea mist obscured the horizon. *Solitaire* should have been within a few miles of the island but I could see nothing, no lights, no black shape. The sea was empty. I dropped all sails and waited for dawn. As the sky grew lighter, there was still no land. The sun had not appeared but it was daylight. Now I would settle for anything, a smudge in the distance, even land birds. All one could see was sea. I could not face another Brixham, another Brazil, another broken marriage. I went below, recorded another failure, and made myself a cup of tea. All I could do now was to take fresh sights and try to discover my mistake. Defeated, I climbed back into the cockpit.

I heard the Hallelujah chorus so loud it almost took my head off and tears of joy ran down my face. She had been there all the time, hiding beneath the early morning mist, the most beautiful island in the world. Her purple and blue mountains reached up for the sky, green palms swaying in the breeze, surf breaking on golden sands. After 68 days at sea, *Solitaire* and I had made it and had got something right. I savoured every precious second.

Terrell had lent me one of his charts, from which I had sketched the island. The anchorage was at the far end of a bay and we spent the morning motoring there, *Solitaire* still rolling drunkenly with her cargo of barnacles. That morning I hated nothing, not even the blasted barnacles.

The bay we wanted turned back on itself. There was a moment of doubt when I could not see it, then I spotted a beach, palm trees, a few homes up in the hills and two boats at anchor. *Solitaire* turned to meet new friends, a blue ketch flying a French flag, an American flag on a trimaran with people on its spacious decks.

I dropped anchor and started to put *Solitaire* in order, making a final entry in the ship's log: '23.15 hours GMT. Anchored Hiva Oa, distance by trailing log 3,655 miles after 68 days at sea. On board one gallon of water, two pounds of rice, two tins of corned beef, six Oxo cubes.'

A dinghy left the ketch and started across. The men and women aboard could speak good English with a heavy French accent. Did I need anything?

Where could I buy bread? There was a store in the village, an hour's walk away. They left but the man was soon back with half a loaf, a jar of marmalade and a can of beer.

Later another dinghy came over from the trimaran with an Englishman in his early thirties and a beautiful doll-like creature whose golden skin and almond eyes showed traces of the Orient. Jeff and Judy were the couple I would spend most time with in the Marquesas. There are few men I have grown to admire more than Jeff. Born in Britain, he became a veterinary surgeon and moved to the west coast of America where he built his trimaran, *Dinks Song*, to escape the more mercenary practices of his profession. Each day shared with him brought fresh surprises. It started with his playing the guitar, singing in a voice that would have earned him a living anywhere in the world. He went through numerous instruments which finished one spell-binding night when he stood on his foredeck at anchor in the bay at Fatu Hiva, playing the hauntingly lonely music of Scotland on his bagpipes – unforgettable!

I learned more and more about this man, mostly from Judy. He held an aircraft pilot's licence. With his high-powered rubber dinghy he water-skied and taught the Polynesian locals to emulate him. But what I remember Jeff for most was the 3-mile walk to the village, his face covered with dust, sweat and pain, never complaining. Jeff had only one leg. He had lost the other as a small boy in a coach crash in Scotland. People like Jeff make you humble – even after your first true landfall.

Now that *Solitaire* was about to be cured of her barnacle sickness, I found that I had contracted a terrible disease, the worse because you inflicted it on your friends. It is a disease of brain and mouth and is particularly prevalent among single-handers. It normally lasts for a few days after any long voyage and is called verbal diarrhoea. The brain keeps sending messages, 'For God's sake shut up, you are boring the pants off everyone', which the mouth refuses to receive and continues to spew out garbage. On that first night in Hiva Oa Jeff and Judy made the mistake of inviting me back to *Dinks Song* for dinner. Judy, a first class cook, had spent most of that day baking. I completely demolished her work and was finally got rid of in the early hours, being bundled into their dinghy with a mouthful of cake, still trying to talk.

I awoke next morning from a deep sleep to a glorious day. A warm breeze rippled the still lagoon, palm trees barely a-sway while *Solitaire* slept on. I tried not to disturb her as I moved forward to check the anchor but managed to shake her slightly, whereupon she yawned and stretched. Her chain lay limply on its sandy resting place 3 fathoms below, looking as if it could be touched from the boat. I walked softly back. 'Sleep on, love, you've earned a holiday.' With a contented sigh she snuggled back into her clean, warm bed.

There was no movement from the other boats; perhaps Jeff was watching from behind portholes, frightened lest I return for more cake and conversation. Then I heard a faint chugging and round the headland came the bow of a boat, standing on which was an attractive woman, complete with movie camera. Her long, blonde hair streamed down her back, caught by the breeze but held partly in place by a fawn-coloured topee of Indian vintage. The bow belonged to a lifeboat with an ultra-short mast. At the tiller, like an old-time film producer complete with thick black glasses and also hiding under a fawn topee, was a man. Ye gods, I thought, it's Bogie and the *African Queen*. They circled around the lagoon a couple of times, still filming. I dashed to comb my hair and emerged in time to see them anchor, whereupon I rowed across.

Juli and Dontcho were Bulgarians permitted by their government to carry out an experiment in the *Kon-Tiki* vein. They had left the coast of South America intending to sail to Fiji, proving that you could survive long periods at sea by dragging a fine mesh net behind and collecting plankton, the small organisms that are found in the oceans. Soon after leaving they had lost their mast and were making do with a jury-rig. Dontcho was a scientist with black hair to complement horn-rimmed glasses. Shorter than myself, he was a bit overweight so the plankton must be doing their stuff, I thought. He could speak little English and relied on his lovely wife, Juli, a concert pianist, to translate. Slim and tall, she could well have been in films, her skin darkened by the sun to contrast strikingly with her blonde hair.

Their lifeboat was madness. The Bulgarian government had insisted that they carry a powerful transmitter and had supplied a 24 volt set, knowing the boat had only a 12 volt supply so that it could never be used. Heavy gauge stainless steel bottle screws and shackles that made my mouth water were used to put tension on thin ropes. The fibreglass water tank had been built with the wrong resin, souring their water. Their method of navigation included timing sunset to obtain longitude. They had been trying to correct their watches with BBC time checks, ignorant of the constant time signals from the American station WWV. Although they had three portable receivers on board only one worked, and that poorly.

After all my own blunders, and remembering the help I had so freely received, it was satisfying to contribute in return. We soon had all three sets blasting out WWV signals, and the water tank cleaned. Doncho and Juli made a great deal of any kindness shown them, a truly brave and lovely couple of whom I became very fond.

Solitaire and I will always look back on the Marquesas as a Shangri-la, an earthly paradise. On the morning after our arrival I walked to the nearby ramshackle village situated on a hillside. Looking down on the lagoon I could see *Solitaire* still slumbering in clear waters. I cleared the French Customs and then tried the village store. Some of the things on display, eggs and tomatoes for instance, I was not allowed to buy. Items in short supply were kept for the villagers but there was no shortage of mouth-watering delicacies.

Stalks of bananas, coconuts and bread fruit, which makes the world's best chips, were plentiful as was that goddess of fruits, pamplemousse, a grapefruit as large as a football, sweet and streaming with juice. Eaten for breakfast with a cup of coffee, you were set for the day. I bought some of the cheaper food including flour, rice and baking powder.

Everyone was going back that night to dine and watch some native dancing. Tickets were $3 each so I decided to give it a miss. I had less than $60 left and there seemed little chance of my finding work until reaching New Zealand or Australia, more than 5,000 miles away.

On the way back to *Solitaire* I spotted the Canadian boat we had met in the Pacific and went over, minus golf clubs, to inquire if they had managed to cash their cheque. They apologised for not stopping with me longer and made up for it by inviting me to dinner the next day.

At six that evening I sat on *Solitaire*'s deck drinking a coffee and watching the other yachts and their crews preparing for the native dancing. As the dinghies moved ashore, Jeff and Judy came over to *Solitaire*. The crowd had realised, by the food I had bought, that I was short of money and had clubbed together to buy me a ticket, deciding not to collect me until the last minute so that I could not refuse. I tried always to repay this sort of kindness, but it seemed that I always ended up at the wrong end of the stick.

An American yacht with five young men on board came into the lagoon with alternator-charging problems. A broken holding bracket was the only trouble so I fitted one of my spares for them. During our conversation it was mentioned they had a taste for English gin and as I still had two bottles on board left over from my Brazilian beach party I wanted to make a present of them, but this they refused, insisting on paying the full local price. The battle went on for a week, with me holding the ace and the only two bottles on the island. I would go over with my gin and describe the pleasure of rolling this nectar around the mouth, of feeling it trickle down a parched throat, watching them grow more desperate. It seemed like stalemate. On the morning they left, I waited until they had their anchor up, rowed over and placed the bottles on their deck as they slipped by with cries of 'Up the British!'

An hour later they were back again with engine trouble so I went over to lend a hand. The battle of the gin bottles was not mentioned. Good, I thought, they've accepted their defeat with grace. At dawn the next day I was rudely awakened as they sailed past *Solitaire* to raucous Yankee battle cries. I waved them good luck, then breakfasted on pamplemousse and the $20 bill they had stuck in my coffee jar. One of them must have swum over while we were messing with the motor. There was a note: 'No Englishman's going to get the better of a Yank.'

One of the people never to visit *Solitaire* was the filthiest old man I have ever met. The store had run out of bread one day and I was directed to an overgrown path on the village edge down which, they told me, was a bakery. I pushed through the creaking door of a ramshackle shed into a black interior, adjusting from the tropical colours to dusty gloom within. I felt rather than saw the diminutive Chinese man, who shuffled forward smiling, saying the only words I ever heard him speak, 'Me British.' He reached in a pocket and brought out a tattered British passport. Reluctantly I bought one of his hot rolls and, halfway down the path, hungrily broke off a piece. My taste buds turned my feet in their tracks to buy another.

Each day thenceforward I bought two of his rolls and each day he would show me his passport and say, 'Me British.' I wished I had an old medal to give him – if not for his bread, then for being a true patriot.

Solitaire and I loved our easy life. A freshwater stream ran into the lagoon, diluting its sea-salt concentration. The goose barnacles nodded their heads worriedly, turned black and died. I had relished much contentment, particularly during my second marriage, but if you had asked me whom I disliked or envied I could have named none. It was a feeling destined to last until I returned home nearly two years later. Him I would normally have disliked I now only pitied, the wealthy in their homes or yachts I no longer envied, but once evening fell I uneasily needed to return to my boat. Money, of course, would have helped me to do more for *Solitaire*, buy the best antifouling, more sails, charts, pilot books, but I had chosen this life and regular wages would have meant regular commitments. I expected to pay my way, but I wanted to choose the method. My pleasures were cheap: I had never smoked, and drinking was for special occasions. My clothes would consist of shorts and an open-necked shirt, my feet bare.

I felt affection for the people I was meeting; they did not consider the world owed them a living. I would visit their yachts and, if the owner happened to be working, would simply join in. I had boxes of spares left over which always came in useful. My rubber dinghy allowed me to ferry large loads ashore and my 5-gallon containers proved useful for getting water to the other yachts.

Since there was only food to buy, money had little meaning for the natives. *Solitaire* inevitably had more fruit on board than I could ever eat, picked by myself or traded for things I no longer required. Locals would place stands of bananas and the odd fish on deck. It was normal practice to row across to new arrivals and discover what help they required.

The cruising world is both large – meeting people from many countries – and small, particularly when greeting new arrivals and receiving news of old friends. People are like mirrors and reflect what they see: if you are genuinely pleased to meet someone and bubble inside, that feeling will be returned. But if you did not fit in and took advantage of friendships, you would be slowly ignored, wither and fade away.

When subsequently I looked back on the time I spent in the Marquesas Islands I remembered half a dozen eggs. Juli and Dontcho were among my first friends to leave and on their last morning in Hiva Oa I wanted them to breakfast with me, the first time *Solitaire* had guests for a meal. I spent a good deal of time deciding on the menu including pamplemousse for starters, of course. Tinned butter could be obtained in the village, a bit expensive, but a special treat, which would go down well on the crusty rolls from my Chinese countryman. I would buy a couple of eggs each for the three of us, and finish with the marmalade given me by the French couple. All went well until I discovered there was a shortage of eggs on the island. After trying the village store, I chased every cockcrow in the hills. All the other yachts were reduced to powdered eggs and that night I went to sleep knowing that I would have to accept second-best. It was quite late when two strangers in a dinghy woke me: they had just arrived in the lagoon and, having been told by the people on the other yachts of my quest for eggs, they had taken the trouble to bring them over. I think that's what cruising is all about.

It was time to waken *Solitaire* from her slumber. Fatu Hiva, where many of our friends were, would be our next stop, with no navigation problems this time. Although the island was 50 miles away, on a clear day you could see her majestic peaks reaching into the clouds so I decided to sail through the night and arrive at dawn. There were a dozen yachts at anchor when we hove to but not a soul to be seen on the boats or beach. The anchorage is small compared with the size of the bay, which must be one of the most impressive in the world. A shelf extends off the beach for a few hundred feet, then quickly drops away to 15 fathoms. Winds are invariably offshore and now and again blast down between the mountains at 60 miles an hour. For all that, it is a safe and beautiful harbour, once berthed.

Solitaire circled the other craft feeling like a child that had not been invited to her best friend's birthday party. Meanwhile I was blowing on a whistle and shouting. Jeff's trimaran was there; it crossed my mind that he had warned the others of my verbal diarrhoea and I imagined them hiding in their cabins, the locals concealing themselves behind trees, in case this new horror spread to their village. *Solitaire* nudged her way between *Dinks Song* and another yacht as I peered through portholes, expecting beady little eyes to peep back.

When the echo sounder showed less than 20ft, I let go the anchor. *Solitaire* moved slowly astern sulking, as if to say, 'I know when I'm not wanted.' Everything was as dead as a dodo. Had we dragged our anchor, no harm would have been done, as only open waters lay behind us. If *Solitaire* felt she had been cast aside and snuck away in the night, the worst that could happen would be bringing a reluctant child back against wind and tide.

After a cup of tea I put down my head and slept. Jeff woke me the following morning to tell me that one of the village lassies had been married. The yachties had joined in happily, the ladies helping to prepare the bride. *Solitaire* and I fell easily into the life of receiving guests and visiting other craft although most of my time was spent with Jeff and Judy. As there seemed to be a shortage of girls on the island, Jeff arranged to take a dozen of the village boys to another island, which had a similar problem – in reverse. The islands spoke French, which both Jeff and Judy could understand so there would always be a few Polynesian men on *Dinks Song*.

Through whom I was introduced to two new forms of food. When approaching the island, I had seen palm trees perched on the sides of the hills sheltering sloping tables. These were used for drying bananas, which retained their flavour but became quite chewy. I later found them in Tahiti, where they were far more expensive. The second food was a piece of a giant ray that came into the lagoon. Apart from a seat in the front row, we had a running commentary from the boys. With a half dozen lads on the paddles, the chief went out in one of the native canoes, by tradition the only person allowed to harpoon it. We watched him jump from the bow of the boat onto the ray's back, putting the full weight of his body behind a thrust. Then he virtually flew from the water as if dropped into a cauldron of boiling oil. I asked one of the young gentlemen how often the village acquired a new chief.

When the poor ray was dragged ashore it looked more like whale worked on by persistent steamroller. The natives started to hack with meat cleavers and the shoreline reddened with its blood, the sea taking on the appearance of a washing machine that had gone berserk as the sharks came in to feed. The yachties, who for days had swum over to *Solitaire*, started using dinghies, but memories were short-lived and soon Jeff was giving his water skiing lessons again. When he and Judy left with their cargo of amorous young men, it was to be for only a few days. In fact, it was the last time I saw them.

CHAPTER FOUR
Tying the Knot
Fatu Hiva – Lymington
May 1976 – April 1978

In a way Jeff's delayed return turned *Solitaire* into a harvester of yachts. At sunset I would spend my time looking out to sea on the off chance that Jeff's transmitter had broken down. If I saw navigation lights I would switch on *Solitaire*'s powerful 24 watt light at the top of the mast, a beacon in an otherwise dark bay. I caught two beauties this way, one a lovely 48ft Swan with two married couples aboard from the south coast of England, one husband a furniture restorer.

The owner of my second catch was also a furniture manufacturer – from France – and was accompanied by his wife and two paid crew. In the dark they anchored near *Solitaire* and later started swinging into us. Although the bay was still crowded, there was no real reason why I should not shift my berth so I explained my intentions and, despite their protests, moved away. The following morning they came over to thank me and invite me back for a drink, another couple I grew to like. During the war the owner had been a submarine commander in the Free French Navy, an occupation that could be seen in the design of his boat. Virtually you could close yourself below and sail it.

He made quite an occasion of introducing his wife. 'Leslie, I have the pleasure of introducing my charming wife to you...'

I warmed to this old world courtesy, which showed the affection he held for his wife and made me feel important to meet her. They owned a private island and I was invited to call there but alas never did. Instead I decided to sail to Papeete in Tahiti and made plans to lift anchor on June 10th, 1976. Tahiti lay 750 miles to the south-west and again there would be no navigation problems. In fact the island at 7,339ft was twice as high as anything I had seen up to then and also possessed a powerful RDF station and full navigational aids. I expected the winds to be kindly at Force 3 to 4, mostly from the east to south-east.

The quick and the brave sailed a direct course calling at the Tuamotu Islands, which are well worth a visit as the locals are friendly, laying on feasts and dancing. However, the low-lying Tuamotus are surrounded by strong currents and at times a palm tree can be the tallest thing around. I have never taken star sights but, if I did, this would be the locality where I would use them constantly as it is vital to know your position to a tenth of a mile. Over the years their reefs have claimed many fine boats. Climbing high in the rigging is advantageous when passing through these reefs but as a single-hander I could not do that and steer *Solitaire* at the same time. I decided to take no risks and, in golfing terms, made a dog's leg of it, sailing above the islands on a course more like WSW. That way, one arrived with a yacht and not on foot.

After leaving the Tuamotus *Solitaire* made 375 miles in the first three days then the winds fell light with the odd shower. There is a low-lying island 20 miles north of Tahiti called Teriaroa, owned then by the film star Marlon Brando. Although I kept a good look out all day, we must have passed it as I saw nothing and *Solitaire* arrived off Tahiti at nightfall. There is a reef to go through to enter Papeete Harbour, well marked and used by cruise liners, but as I was thinking of navigating it, the last of the sun's rays fell into the sea and went out like a candle. Suddenly Tahiti was a blaze of lights, making jokes of channel markers. *Solitaire* groaned, 'Please, please not again!'

So we turned away and I distinctly heard her give a sigh of

relief. We entered harbour at dawn on June 19th, our log showing 755 miles. As Bastille Day was not far off, the harbour was packed with some 90 boats waiting for the festivities to start. The Bastille was a French prison demolished in the times of the Revolution but, so far as I am aware, the British were never blamed for this.

Solitaire circled the harbour a couple of times, nodding to many of the craft she had met before, the boats anchored stern to shore. I saw a space next to a bright yellow Ericson 36 with an American in his early thirties sitting on the foredeck.

'Is there room for one more?' I asked.

'Are you single-handed?' he replied and, on my reply, waved me in.

In fact I had told a lie because at that stage I was anything but single-handed. We had about six dinghies tied to us. How and where *Solitaire* berthed had been taken out of my hands. I heard the anchor go down, two lines were taken to the shore and she was slowly eased back to lie 20ft off. Remembering our arrival in Fatu Hiva, I could almost hear her saying 'Now, this is more like a welcome.'

Many of our visitors I had met in Panama and they had been concerned by my slow passage to Hiva Oa. After any voyage I enjoyed making physical contact with friends, shaking hands with both of mine, and hugging the ladies. You can say a great deal with the strength of a hand or hug.

As this was a Saturday morning Customs would not re-open until Monday. *Solitaire* spent the rest of the day receiving visitors, which kept me busy making endless cups of tea for her guests. That evening I managed to sneak away to a party on another yacht, after which I found Dontcho and Juli's lifeboat and left a message on its closed hatch.

The following morning my American neighbour came over and introduced himself as Webb Chiles. I have never met a more determined person. Twice he left his home port of San Diego for a single-handed voyage around the world via Cape Horn. On the first attempt he had been forced to turn back before reaching the Cape, leaking badly and with broken rigging. He called in at Tahiti, made repairs and tried again, only to be turned back once more to San Diego. Finally he made the voyage on what was virtually a sinking yacht. He had visited New Zealand and had recently arrived in Papeete where, at the time of our meeting, he was writing his book, *Storm Passage*.

I learned much from Webb, the first true single-hander I had ever met and remember talking to him on the sidewalk when a woman reporter asked if she could visit our boats and interview us. She wondered if we had a death wish, a daft question, particularly when put to someone who had just sailed around Cape Horn fighting for his life. I would have advised anyone with such an outlook not to step into a dinghy, let alone a seagoing yacht, and Webb said much the same thing only more trenchantly.

Although not yet halfway round on my first voyage, I had already committed myself to a second and these chats with Webb dictated the route for my next attempt – around Cape Horn. Always ready to joke about my early navigational mistakes and the Brazilian hospital, I was finding it increasingly difficult to live with my errors. My confidante would forget about it the next day; I would carry it in my mind for the rest of my life and wanted to square the account which made me believe a second voyage around Cape Horn might help.

Later the woman reporter visited *Solitaire*, by which time Webb had sailed for home – just as well, I thought, after reading the story she wrote. Under the headline 'Yachtsman Lucky Les earns his nickname' (I've never been called Lucky Les in my life), it started: 'Les, while sailing here from England, was lost at sea, shipwrecked, hospitalised and suffered from hunger.' As I said at the time, 'I hope my luck never runs out or I'll be in real trouble.' In fact, the story helped in two ways. The paper was given away to all the boats in the harbour, and as a result I was invited aboard many of them. If I was not asked to any I thought looked interesting I would contemplate chipping a golf ball onto their decks to wake 'em up!

Through the same article I met Tim Beckett, fresh from England and who, for some reason, I always thought of as a college student with a delightfully dry sense of humour. With him was the co-owner of *Huzar* and they were waiting for Tim's father to join them before continuing to New Zealand. When visiting him, he would send his ropey rubber inflatable across on a pulley arrangement. Once you were aboard, it would wrap itself around you like a starving octopus. If you survived you were greeted with a chamber-pot of tea. Tim later lost *Huzar* on Lady Elliot Island, 60 miles off the coast of Australia, saving only the engine and his address book.

The morning after my arrival in Tahiti, Dontcho and Juli made their appearance and I spent a week visiting places of interest and working on their boat, always with the movie camera churning away. Then they had to leave for Fiji because of the schedule laid down by their country. I made arrangements to sail for Australia the following day, a schedule dictated not by HM Government but by my pocket; I had less than $30 left. It seemed an age since I had established two rules to govern my life at sea: the first that I would always sail alone, the second that I would never accept payment for working on a friend's boat.

Next to Dontcho's lifeboat was a 45ft steel boat belonging to a French aircraft pilot, Peter, who had a beautiful wife and two lovely blonde children. On the day Juli and Dontcho left, Peter and his wife invited me to a local restaurant and asked if I would stay on for a few weeks to fit out his boat. Since he was working and making good money, he could well afford to pay me. After a long talk I agreed somewhat reluctantly to bend my second rule and accept owners in employment. In Peter's case the pay would be low, the local Tahitian rate for unskilled workers being $4 an hour and, since I had to get used to my new rule, I would take no more than a dollar an hour. During the next few weeks I worked a 60-hour week and, by saving two-thirds of my earnings, pushed my $30 up to nearly $200. Then Peter told me Kodak Laboratories wanted some fibreglassing done and would pay $4 an hour, the outcome of which was that I started on one of the worst and most dangerous jobs in my life.

The Kodak building itself was a modern, single-storey factory with a slightly sloping roof of corrugated aluminium. The maximum space between the roof and the ceiling was 8ft, diminishing to a few inches. To prevent the heat discomforting their employees, rolls of fibreglass had been laid in the loft. Particles of this were now falling through cracks in the ceiling onto the film processing machines so they wanted the fibreglass rolled up and replaced on sheets of plastic. Entering the loft was like stepping into a cauldron and it was impossible to wear a mask to prevent glassfibre being sucked into the lungs. Joists, 4ft apart, were all I had to stand on up there. I would take a gallon of water with me and work through an 8-hour shift. Now and again they would call me down for a break, but I would explain that if I ever left their hellhole during the day I would never go back. Each night they promised me a local worker whom they reckoned would be more accustomed to the heat. Now and then a face would pop through the trap door, the whites of the eyes would start to look like two fried eggs and the face would drop out of sight. Why I carried on with the job, apart from wanting to finish something I had started, I shall never know. The only good thing to say about it was that it was great when you stopped.

The laboratory had some splendidly hot showers, the first I had used since leaving Panama. I would stand under them for ages to open up the pores and rid myself of the itchy dust and glass, and then return to *Solitaire*, knowing that I had more money to spend on her. For three weeks I worked a 45-hour week. Then they asked me to knock two rooms into one. After that, would I build some storage racks? When they suggested building some car ports, I decided I was getting too civilised and left to prepare *Solitaire* for our trip to Australia.

Just before leaving Tahiti a young French couple, who planned to start teaching on one of the nearby islands, came to see me. They had bought a 35ft wooden yacht to use as a home, which they considered a good buy until they discovered Toredo worm in the stern-hung rudder and then could find no one to build them a replacement, so I stayed on two more weeks to do the job. My one regret about sailing was that I had not started when I was a young man, fitter, stronger and able to give *Solitaire* more care. Tahiti strengthened my regrets. I wished I could have seen these islands and met the Polynesian people before 'civilisation' had spoiled them.

Only in smoke-filled night clubs could you watch their beautiful native dancing. If you saw a Polynesian thrusting his canoe through the water with muscle power it simply meant that his outboard had broken down and he was on his way back to the garage to get it fixed. Large white cruise liners would dock and release a flood of even whiter chattering mice, all wearing the same brightly-coloured shirts, hats, sunglasses and cameras. False teeth flashing even falser smiles, they would stream past the dancing girls swaying to Hawaiian guitars. The tide would flood the shops to devour everything in sight, prevented only by pavement vendors holding out armfuls of shell necklaces and beautiful woven straw hats. Cameras would click, click, then their Pied Piper would toot toot on the ship's siren and the tide would reverse. The heavily-laden mice would be sucked back into a hole in the ship's side. A puff of smoke on the horizon, and they were gone. The locals would count their profits and a street cleaner remove the last traces of their presence. Weeks later postcards would arrive in New York, Tokyo and Scunthorpe, 'Having a wonderful time in Tahiti, wish you were here.'

When I recalled Hiva Oa in later years, I remembered the Chinese man who thought he was English. Tahiti, for me, meant a small American boy. The local paper printed my story on a Saturday and next day it was customary for children from the cruising ships to attend Sunday school with the locals. I was walking past the church when an avalanche of these terrors descended. Within seconds I had them climbing over me, one even trying to pull off my shorts, so small I had to get on my knees to hear what he was saying. 'Mister, I'd sure be proud to shake your hand,' he said. It was like holding a butterfly. For days after I would smile when I remembered his serious face. He made me feel good inside, wishing that he would always stay young and innocent and not change with the years like Tahiti.

Sunday was always the best day of the week. Now that I was earning good money I could afford to buy the excellent French wines, the crusty rolls and make crisp, fresh salads. The harbour front was Papeete's main street and *Solitaire* was only a few yards from the sidewalk. Sunday was the day that the visits I had made in the week were returned, a day we all looked forward to.

My last hours on the island were spent scrubbing *Solitaire*'s antifouling, not a particularly pleasant chore as the waste from 90 yachts was dumped in the harbour. The sensible thing would have been to go over to the unspoilt Moorea but there had been too many delays and I had to push on.

Saturday, September 25th, was set for my departure and I had chosen Gladstone, about halfway up the east coast of Australia, as my destination. It was just below the beginning of the Great Barrier Reef, the ideal place from which to start the following stage of the voyage. Another consideration was that I would have to remain in port for five months during the hurricane season and, as Gladstone had a large aluminium plant and was building a power station, I thought it should be possible to find work there. I would have liked to have visited Auckland but New Zealand was further away and had few job prospects. I would make the final choice halfway through the voyage when the current started to swing south towards Auckland.

The first leg would take us just below Rarotonga, 700 miles to the WSW, 200 miles south of Tahiti, which had a strong RDF station to confirm our position. After that our course would be virtually due west, dropping only another 200 miles in the next 3,000. Provided we did not go further south than Gladstone's latitude, we should have a good passage. The pilot charts showed much the same pattern as our previous voyage: winds over our stern from the east to south-east around Force 4, with only three per cent calms and a few gales close to Australia, but no worse than an English summer. In all, a voyage of 4,000 miles, no more than 40 days at sea if the pilot charts were correct.

The most upsetting thing about the trip was the places we would miss: magic islands whose names rolled off the tongue, Moorea, Huahine, Bora Bora, Tahaa, Fiji. Each year that would change as more and more hotels and flats destroyed them. It seemed foolish to be wishing I could have been in the South Pacific 50 years before when they would change that much again in the next five. I was giving up seeing them just to sail around a piece of rock called Cape Horn.

As food in Australia would be cheaper than Tahiti's, I kept my stores to a minimum although the cash situation was quite good: in fact I was richer than when I left England and now had $700 in hand. The tucker I would not be running short of was onions as an Australian yachtsman had asked me if I had plenty on board and was amazed when I told him I had never even considered carrying them. Onions last for months and are full of vitamins, he lectured me, and to make sure I got the message, he turned up with a sackful. He must have told the story to all the other cruising people because *Solitaire* was soon packed with them!

The one thing I did not take was a cockroach, although Tahiti breeds some of the world's finest. After dark you could see whole families of them walking along the sidewalks, every now and then stopping to inspect a yacht before deciding whether or not to make it their new home. I believe every craft suffered from them, certainly all those I ate on. You would be eating dinner when they would walk across your plate, splashing through the gravy without so much as a by-your-leave. Because they were a topic of conversation and, cockroach-less, I could not join in, vicious rumours were spread. It was reported that they had been seen walking up *Solitaire*'s shore lines and that on reading her name on the stern there had been a panic to disembark again. It was also claimed that I spent half the night trying to entice the poor creatures on board with bits of cheese which was a lie since I discovered they did not particularly like it! When *Solitaire* sailed through the reef to start her voyage she had not a single cockroach on board and at the time I was concerned, remembering stories of rats deserting doomed ships.

We had arrived in Tahiti on June 19th and left on September 25th, after *Solitaire* had been rested for more than three months. The early stages of the voyage went well enough with a pleasant sail close to that island paradise, Moorea, but during the night things started to go wrong. We ran into fierce squalls and a batten pierced the mainsail, which meant that the batten pocket could not be used again that trip, and a 5-gallon water container burst – nothing to worry about at that stage since I still had another 25 gallons left.

I picked up Rarotonga's RDF signal on the third day out, 400 miles away! A week from Tahiti and Rarotonga hove in sight 20 miles to our north. The pilot charts had been correct up to that point. From then on had I reversed the information it would have been near enough correct. Instead of stern winds from the east at Force 4, *Solitaire* was pushing into winds from the west dead on her nose, anything from Force 6 to complete calm. Under these conditions we could not sail close to the wind as short, choppy waves kept pushing her bow to one side. *Solitaire*, facing a fighter with a long, left jab, would shake her head to recover and try to move forward, only to be hit again. At the halfway mark, passing under the Tonga Islands, I nearly decided to give up and head for New Zealand, 1,000 miles to the south.

Had I changed course then we would have had a current of 10 to 15 miles a day in our favour and, had the winds stayed constant, we would have been sailing with them abeam. *Solitaire*, staggering like a punch-drunk fighter, refused to give up but carried on for Australia and Gladstone.

We had one particularly bad storm that led me to conclude that I should dispense with battened sails. Battens were forever fouling the shrouds, particularly when running, and if they broke they inevitably damaged the sail. Certainly they allowed a larger sail area with a roach but the increased speed was not worth the trouble as I was racing no one. In future I would have battenless mainsails with a straight leech and would also change my reefing system. Although roller reefing was fitted to the boom, I had never used it, preferring to slab reef since my halyards led back to the cockpit.

For the first time in this particular storm I decided to try the roller reefing. The job was nearly done when a squall strained the leech where it wrapped around the boom. The sail shredded in half, making its repair a lengthy project. For the rest of the trip to Australia I had to tie the main off at its last reefing point, cutting the sail area by more than half!

This was turning out to be another protracted voyage thanks to light winds and a small sail area. We were becalmed a few times and I went over the side in the dinghy to clean the waterline, which was largely unencrusted. Some 700 miles from Australia the split pin holding the self-steering rudder broke and I made the rest of the trip without its help. Normally I would have lost the rudder but since I had never liked this method of attachment, I had drilled it and connected a safety rope. Our landfall was Lady Elliot Island, 60 miles off the Australian mainland, which we passed on November 30th. That night we had an electrical storm and I sat watching the lightning under bare poles as if in daylight.

Next day we drifted by the Bunker reefs, sighting land with the dawn. I motored all that windless day to arrive at six o'clock local time in the broad creek on which Gladstone lies, after the longest time we had spent at sea so far, 69 days, beating our previous record by a day. We had logged 4,212 miles.

Australia is psychotic about the import of animals, plants, seeds or food. Normally when clearing Customs I have been asked if I had drugs, guns or drink but the Australian Customs man who boarded *Solitaire* could not care less if I was head of the Mafia or carrying an atom bomb.

'Right, naaaaa, do you have any pets on board?' is the first question.

'No sir,' I replied, 'not even a cockroach!'

We went through the plant and seed bit.

'Right, sport, I want all your food laid out on deck.'

So I went below and fetched my remaining bag of rice, which I placed in the middle of the deck, and then I stood looking at him with my tail wagging and my tongue out, like a cocker spaniel that's just done its business in the dirt box.

'Maaaaaate, maaaate, aaaaall of it!'

I turned out every locker and cubby hole trying to find something I could give the poor man. I kept inviting him to come below and search *Solitaire*.

'Maaaaaate, I don't want to search your flaming boat.'

At last I found two slices of dried meat in a sealed glass jar, which I think the Americans gave me in Panama. My maaaaaate smiled and locked it in his briefcase.

While this was going on, a tramp had been sitting on the side of the dock taking it all in and swigging from a pint of milk through his matted beard. By the time he had heard my story there were tears in his eyes and he offered me his bottle without a word. I drained it in one gulp and handed back the empty.

Mr Customs asked the question I'd been dreading: 'How long do you plan to stay in Australia?'

During the past two weeks I had been picking up their radio broadcasts and, apart from learning of a shortage of work, it seemed that every disaster that occurred was due entirely to the English or, as he is better known, the Pom. Poms ran the unions and were responsible for the strikes, Poms ran the government and were responsible for the country going to the dogs, they controlled the weather, and that was the reason for all the bush fires. There was a disc jockey I'd been listening to whose pet saying was, 'Punch a Pommie every day!'

By this stage I was thinking I might be allowed to take on water before being set adrift. With the hurricane season coming on, I really needed a visitor's permit for six months and when I explained this, I was told to call at the Customs Office next day to pick up one for a year!

The officer told me about Gladstone and the best places to eat, several times asking if I was all right for Australian currency. In fact I bought myself some fish and chips and ate them in *Solitaire*'s cockpit, during which time I was invited to dinner the following night by one couple and to a barbecue that weekend with another. My mooring problems were solved when an Australian offered to share his berth free of charge. Sometimes I think that certain types of radio broadcasters and newspaper reporters would be better employed collecting garbage rather than dishing it out.

Over the next few days I tried unsuccessfully to find work. I could not be taken on as a skilled electrician because I had no Australian licence and unskilled work was carried out by apprentices, but my luck changed when I called on the local boatyard to buy a shackle. The manager, a Yorkshireman, asked if I needed work and then said I could cut the grass around the boats on hard standing. After that it was making racks to store wood, fibreglassing, painting. In the end I spent all my time working for the boatyard. Sometimes I would help tie up ocean-going cargo ships; my last job was putting the yard's transport in shape and, as in Tahiti, I could have stayed on as the company wanted to build fibreglass dinghies and there were opportunities to work on charter boats. I liked the people who were always more than fair; even grass-cutting carried the same wage as everyone else's in the yard.

I managed to stay in Gladstone for more than five months without getting into serious trouble, although I nearly managed to kill myself when working on a large charter boat that could carry 300 passengers. One lunch time, having just returned from buying some fish and chips, I had reached across and put my meal through a ship's window and, stepping onto a catwalk to board, fell 10ft into the water twixt ship and dock. Luckily I managed to grab a rope and haul myself out before the gap closed.

My first thought was to eat my fish and chips before they grew cold but as I quickly ate, all this funny red stuff began running down my front, re-soaking my shorts and shirt. When my workmates returned I was rushed to hospital.

On the operating table, blood from a gash under my chin was flooding the place and half a dozen pretty nurses gathered round me.

'I'm sorry for being a nuisance and making such a mess,' I apologised.

'We need the practice,' a chippy one replied.

'Lift me off the table and I'll go break a leg,' I offered.

'You do, sport, and we'll break the other one!' Which started me laughing and the blood gushing. Even when they were stitching me up, I was still laughing.

There were few things I disliked about Australia. Food was reasonably priced and for a dollar I could fill my frying pan twice with chops or steak. Flies were a pest, particularly the little sandflies which looked like specks of dust but could bite like tigers.

Terrell Adkisson and I joined up in Gladstone for the first time since Panama. *Altair* was berthed 100 miles down the coast but he spent a week on *Solitaire* and we made arrangements to sail through the Barrier Reef together. While in Gladstone I met *Brolga of Kiama* with Rob and Lyn Brooks who were just about to start their voyage around the world. New arrivals in Gladstone creek were not normally greeted by fellow sailors, but I had always liked the Pacific Islands' friendly customs so, although only a visitor myself, I would always row over to newcomers to see if I could help. Rob and Lyn have always made a point of the fact that in their own country it had been an Englishman who had first enquired.

While in Australia I managed to acquire some new sails from England. I had been well satisfied with my original Lucas sails so I had ordered from them again, including a battenless main with three sets of reefing points as I still had to round the Cape of Good Hope, where it can blow. The last reef would so reduce the main that it would double as a trysail. At the same time I stepped up the weight of cloth from 6 to 8oz, and a new storm jib.

The boatyard let me haul out *Solitaire* free of charge and I had another go at the crack in the hull, although it had not leaked since Panama. The antifouling had vanished so I applied a heavy barrier coat followed by two coats of top-quality finish. I also bolted the self-steering rudder to the drive shaft, thus making it a more permanent fixture. I still had $1,400 (then about £700) left, twice the amount I had left England with, and *Solitaire* in many ways was in better condition than when I had set out, even though she had looked after me for more than 16,000 miles. Now she was taking me home, about the same distance again. I had not yet told *Solitaire* about Cape Horn!

The next leg of our trip would be from Gladstone to Thursday Island in the Terres Straits, 1,000 miles away. We had crossed 8,000 miles of the Pacific Ocean on just two charts and a few sketches. Now I needed 30 charts for our next trip, and a couple of Australian friends, John and Penny Pugh, lent them to me. Often I would go to their house for dinner and a bath and they did most of the chasing around for my supplies. Apart from the food parcel they gave me, they made a going-away present of a heavy fishing line (a life-saver on my second voyage).

The Great Barrier Reef starts about 60 miles offshore at the bottom end, closing to a mile or two at the top. Most of the navigation would be by sight, or, as the Americans call it, eyeball, and for much of the time we would have the mainland and a few islands in sight. I still enjoyed single-handed sailing but if there was ever a time when I would have liked a female crew member aboard, this was it. The Great Barrier Reef must be one of the finest cruising areas in the world, anchoring behind your own private island after a day's sail with plenty of fish in the sea and oysters ashore. The sea, protected by the reef, is shallow and flat.

Terrell came into Gladstone Creek to collect me but as my sails had not arrived, he went on ahead. Before I left, the boatyard threw a party for me where I tried to uphold the best British traditions by keeping up with some of the young bloods. After dinner the party continued at the Pughs', of which I remember nothing. Dawn woke me with a thick head, a foul mouth and to a weird sound. I had been sleeping on somebody's lawn and was covered by every dog in the neighbourhood, snoring their heads off.

Solitaire's mooring lines were cast off on Wednesday, May 18th, 1977, and as I had not let her touch bottom since Grenada (antifouling apart), and my navigation had improved, we both felt more confident. A dozen cars followed us on the shore, blasting their horns as we set off, by far the best farewell we had had and one of the hardest to make.

I caught up with Terrell on Friday, June 3rd, two weeks out from Gladstone. We met in Cairns, about halfway up the Reef, where he had picked out a berth for me alongside the town quay. Cairns was another low-sprawling Australian town, so different from home, where everything seems condensed. Here there were modern supermarkets, a cinema and a heavenly laundry. We spent a few pleasant days there, talking to a good many English people who had settled in the area. Terrell's nephew, Leo, had gone back to the USA and been replaced by an Australian crew member. Things improved once we joined up: with four eyes on the other yacht Terrell always took the path-finding position up front, which allowed me to nip below for the occasional cup of tea without worrying about the constant changing picture of mainland and islands.

Cooktown was quite unlike Cairns. You could walk through it in a few minutes but it was well worth the visit, if only to see the museum. The day we arrived they were to re-enact Captain Cook's first landing and on the jetty a good crowd had turned up for the spectacle. Three men came ashore in a rowing boat and the people promptly started to drift away.

'When's Captain Cook arriving?' I asked.

'He just did, spoooort,' came the reply.

Another advantage of being in company with a cruising yacht is that you can take it in turns to visit and cook dinner. We were having dinner on Terrell's boat where, since it was my turn to play host the following night, I asked, 'How do you fancy fish tomorrow night?' Both seemed enthusiastic, so I asked their preference and was requested to catch a few mackerel.

Next day I took out the line John and Penny had given me. I put the 9in spinner, about the size of any fish I had ever caught, over the side and seconds later it pulled tight with a blooming great mackerel nearly as long as my arm on its end, enough for three people. To make sure, I thought I would catch its smaller sister, which turned out to be twice as fat as the first.

I was concerned about possible waste and as I thought Terrell, who was astern, might also be slaughtering fish, I decided to wait for him. I halted *Solitaire* by luffing into wind and when Terrell came within hailing distance, I stuck two fingers in the air and pointed over the side. The effect on Terrell was instantaneous: he belted off in the other direction and I failed to catch him until much later. When I asked Terrell what his problem had been and why the panic, an argument ensued. Two fingers in the air and pointing over the side means I'm over a reef two fathoms down, Terrell insisted, while I claimed any fool knows it means I've caught two mackerel. Although we stuffed ourselves with fish much was wasted which, coupled with the fact that I had not enjoyed watching a living thing die, made me put the line away, believing they would be the first and last fish I would ever catch at sea.

Thursday Island lies between the most northern part of Australia and New Guinea, where the current can reach 6–7 knots. We anchored 20 miles away, timing our arrival to take advantage of the flow. When we reached our anchorage it was to find marker buoys being pushed under by the force of churning brown waters, the last place to drag or break an anchor chain. Thursday Island, which we reached on June 23rd, after a month's sail inside the Great Barrier, was a disappointment. In the days of sail it was known for its dusky beauties who, it was said, would outswim the fast-flowing current to ravish the poor unsuspecting seamen. After a quick walk through its shantytown of drinking houses, we decided to push on for Darwin. Any dusky maiden would have been repelled with a boat hook, after which I would have called a cop.

Darwin was 700 miles away but wind and current would be mostly with us. Gales were rare in the area but a bad sea could build up quickly in high winds. In company with *Altair* and two other yachts, we left on Monday, June 27th. Although we had our sails up, it would be wrong to say we sailed from the island; it was more like being fired from a cannon and we had to start and run engines flat out to keep control. We shot away like cars on a racetrack, trying to correct for drift, which was great fun while it lasted, and circling the course with three other boats made it that much better. Darwin was approximately halfway across the top of Australia so our course would be due west.

On Friday, July 1st, we ran into a storm off Melville Island with some of the worst waves I had seen, not so much in size as in shape. There was little *Solitaire* could do against them so we dropped sail and lay a-hull until Saturday morning, when the storm died. Until then we had been making good progress, covering 565 miles in just over four days with a best-ever day's run of 149 miles. When I tried the engine I found it had seized and was impossible to turn, even with levers directed onto the flywheel, and this wasn't the best place to have it happen. Melville Island and the 15-mile-wide Dundas Straits protect Darwin in much the same way that the Isle of Wight protects my home port of Lymington. I had in fact to sail between them, which turned out to be terrifyingly difficult, thanks to the speed of the tide.

Approaching from eastwards you pass through the Dundas Straits with its tidal current of 2–3 knots. The land then falls away to form a large bay which curves back to the island 60 miles on, where 12 miles separate mainland from island, those few miles filled with smaller islands and reefs. There is a marked channel on the land side, about one mile across. Once through it, Darwin lies only a few miles further on. As I had no tide tables and no engine, I decided to sail up to the reefs and then anchor for the night.

We passed through Dundas Straits on Saturday night and had a fast sail next morning. By Sunday afternoon we were in sight of the islands and their surrounding reefs, with Darwin's voice, 30 miles away, coming through clearly on the RDF. Having negotiated the reefs we seemed to pick up speed but the land was falling away. *Solitaire* was being driven astern – onto the reefs! The tide had turned.

I let go the 15lb CQR anchor on 50ft of chain plus a good length of strong rope, which thankfully held in coral. The seas, an Amazon in flood, raced past us, the anchor rope vibrating like a bow string forcing me to keep a watch all night, checking the depth from time to time. By Monday morning the tide had slackened, then gathered strength in Darwin's direction. I had missed my chance. Instead of heaving in the anchor during slack water I had to struggle manfully to haul it in against the tide – and failed. So, deciding to wait for the next slack, I slung back what I had retrieved. When the tide eased again I found that the anchor had fouled and would not haul in. We had been there 40 hours and there was only one solution. It broke my heart but I had to do it. I cut the rope and lost the anchor and 50ft of chain.

From then on it was a doddle.

There are two bays in Darwin: the first, big and shallow, houses the yacht club. Next to it is an area for ocean-going ships. You can anchor in either and catch the bus into Darwin. On Tuesday, July 5th, I anchored near the Club after a journey of 753 miles. Our stay in Darwin was marred by engine repairs and the sickly smell of diesel. The final diagnosis was that a sump plate fitted to prevent oil splashing about had broken loose, cracking the main bearing and jamming the reduction gear. Deciding to sail engineless and non-stop to Durban, I cabled Saab, requesting them to send on a new bearing and timing instructions.

Terrell and the other yachts arrived a couple of days after *Solitaire*, having run for shelter during the storm which shows, perhaps, the different thinking between a single-hander and a crewed yacht. In bad weather I would always run from the land, an attitude I was never to change.

When we arrived in Darwin they were sinking piles in front of the Club for members to tie up and antifoul. Terrell and I were among the first to use this facility which, at $5 a time, was much cheaper than being hauled out by a boatyard.

From Darwin I planned to sail to Durban, approximately 5,600 miles away, my longest voyage so far, broad reaching again in the south-east trades. We left Darwin on August 2nd. *Solitaire* was surrounded by other yachts and as there was not a breath of wind, Terrell shouted he would pull us clear. For the first time I accepted a tow. Up to then I had felt lonely only once, when the Canadian yacht left us in the Pacific, but as Terrell let go my lines I felt abandoned. I think it's watching the other yacht pull away that's the problem. During the first 24 hours light winds kept us out of trouble, but the next two days brought variable winds from the west and we found ourselves beating into choppy seas. That first week we covered 596 miles, thereafter we were into true trade wind sailing and logged 884 miles in the second week, followed by 912 in the third.

A thousand miles from South Africa, I started to pick up their radio broadcasts, which is always good for morale. The pilot charts for once had proved accurate and we made good time. I preferred the blue, lively Pacific to the grey, overcast Indian Ocean for things to watch. The seas above Australia had a few surprises: black and brown snakes, giant rays that leapt out of the water only to slam back again, and then, towards the end of the voyage, nightly visits from dolphins, which invariably cheer up life.

Thursday, September 22nd, was our 50th day at sea and, after sailing 5,555 miles, we had another 400 to go. I was trying to make our landfall well north of Durban to allow for the Agulhas Current sweeping us south.

On Monday morning we were nearly run down by a tanker, not in fact one of the super type although I thought it then the largest ship ever built. Because I could not keep my lights on all the time I had been standing in the hatch keeping watch in poor visibility when, hearing nothing, I saw a ghost-like bow loom out of the dawn mist. At first I thought she was cutting across *Solitaire*'s bows but she was already turning. Looking up I could see her two anchors ready to drop on us. A mass of rust and rivets, she swept down our side and back into fog. Never had I been so glad to see a ship disappear. There were many more after that but she was the closest.

We arrived off Durban before first light on Thursday morning and sat watching the traffic signals and flashing neons. Durban has a long finger of land that points north called The Bluff, with a breakwater beside it, the entrance into the outer harbour. It would have been possible to sail through but I could hardly keep my eyes open and the wind was fickle so, when I spotted a charter fishing boat preparing to enter, I beckoned them over and requested a tow. The people on board had a flight to catch but promised they would radio for a police launch to bring me in. After clearing Customs in only a few minutes, a powerboat arrived from the Club to take me in tow.

Solitaire arrived at the Point Yacht Club on Thursday, September 29th, 1977, nine years after her conception there on a Sunday morning in 1968, on the very jetty she was now moored to. Her log showed 5,952 miles, the longest journey so far. One day I would ask her to carry me non-stop nearly five times that distance!

The international jetty lies directly below the clubhouse with its showers, restaurant, lounges and bars. The cruising season had barely started when we arrived. Only four other boats were moored to the jetty, one an old junk owned by a German couple, another an American Choy Lee ketch, and two self-built ferro-cement yachts, one made and sailed by Susan and Graeme from Yarmouth in England, the other owned by a lovely Rhodesian couple with their three young children on board, together with a crew who knew as much about sailing as I had when *Solitaire* first left Lymington.

After a shower in the Club, I was taken to meet the secretary and given a visitor's membership card. Durban must have had a dull week for news because when I returned to *Solitaire*, reporters were waiting to question me about my Brazilian adventures and the voyage from Australia. I was also asked to take part in a broadcast by a chap who ran a navigation school, to which I agreed, provided my talk was based on mistakes so that others could learn from them.

That first night I was too tired to sleep and walked the streets seeing how the other half lived, wandering around in sloppy flip flops, tattered shorts and open shirt, comforted by the knowledge that *Solitaire* was waiting to take me anywhere in the universe I wished to go. Our stay in Durban was a happy one. *Solitaire* had a safe berth, the lights from the surrounding flats sparkling at her as I went to the occasional party. On Sundays the yacht club and several large hotels would put on a self-service meal with a double-feature film show, all for £1. Food was as cheap as we had found anywhere and the local wines were first class and equally inexpensive, so much so that I threw a birthday party for *Solitaire* on October 24th, without considering the cost. We set a new record of 16 guests in the cabin, with Lord knows how many on deck.

These fine wines led me to a brief affair with an Australian lady. I had been invited by a couple of English lads to a party given to celebrate the launch of their 40ft yacht. When I arrived I found their boat had been rafted onto the end of nine others. With a bottle of grog in each hand, it was hard going clambering from one craft to the next. I had nearly reached my goal when I came across a boat turned the opposite way from the rest. Hitherto I had walked over the foredecks in approved social manner; now a cockpit faced me. I should have walked up the deck and crossed in the middle but instead I tripped on the lifelines and fell into the cockpit which is where I made a terrible mistake. It seems that a crowd of hob-nailed boots had already passed that way en route to the orgy. The woman who attacked me came out of the main hatchway like a bull terrier, a fat one. From Australia. Suddenly I was a flaming Pommy trying to kick holes in the side of her flaming boat. Where the flaming hell did I flaming think I was? Flaming Piccadilly Circus? I secured my retreat only by promising never to darken her cockpit again.

The wine flowed freely and things were slightly blurred when I left the party but I managed to remove my flip flops and cross the decks barefooted. When I came to the Australian boat, I remembered my promise and, going forward, fell through a hatchway onto spongy flesh. The sound was reminiscent of the air raid sirens in the last war, low pitched at first but reaching a teeth-shattering screech.

Since the lady appeared not to appreciate my company, I decided to leave. 'We have lift off,' I'm sure I heard as I came back out of the hatch like a Polaris missile leaving a submarine.

Terrell turned up in Durban two weeks later. After letting go my lines at Darwin, he had sailed to the Cocos Islands where he had picked up the crew of a wrecked American boat, which was lucky for him. Halfway across the Indian Ocean, *Altair* was thrown on her side by a rogue wave and Terrell finished up in the sea. He could think of no reason why this wave had formed. The sea was flat and wind moderate and there seemed no reason to wear a life harness. As he lurched overboard he grabbed a yellow seat cushion, which was all the crew could see when later they came on deck. They homed in on it to rescue him.

I wanted to be in Cape Town for Christmas and the jetty, where *Solitaire* had lain snug for two months, was becoming crowded with visiting boats. It was time to move on and I planned to set out for Cape Town on Wednesday, November 23rd.

My biggest regret in Durban was that I had been unable to see Rome, although we kept in contact by mail. He had called his Nor-west 34 *Adhara* and had been given leave from the RAF to compete in the OSTAR single-handed transatlantic race. Having put up a good performance in that, he had been selected to navigate the service entry, *Adventure*, in the Whitbread Round-the-World Race. On completing the first leg to Cape Town, he had been asked to navigate to New Zealand and was now in Cape Town between stops. We tried to arrange a meeting but had to make do with a few phone calls.

Whether a voyage is easy or difficult depends on the yacht's crew and the weather: strong winds from the south combat the Agulhas Current which rushes south at anything up to 5 knots. Gales from the east send waves sweeping across 4,000 miles of Indian Ocean to pile up on the ledge that runs close to the South African coast. With so many super-tankers in the area, a single-hander can never find the voyage hazardless, even in ideal conditions. The 1,000-mile voyage from Durban to Cape Town can be made in stages: East London after 240 miles and Port Elizabeth a further 140 miles, both readily accessible. Thereafter the harbours are more difficult to enter in bad weather. The best plan seemed to be to wait for a settled weather forecast, then sail close to the 100 fathom line, taking advantage of the current, closing ashore at the first signs of bad weather.

Solitaire's motor was still very tight. The new main bearing sent on by Saab had been fitted and the instructions for re-timing carried out. Despite changing the oil a couple of times, small particles from the smashed sump plate were still finding their way into the gears and I could not rely on it to start in an emergency. Fortunately the engine started for our departure. Outside the harbour we found light south-westerlies but after two days we were within sight of East London, having logged 151 miles when our true run was 240 miles. The Agulhas Current had pushed us 45 miles a day. Although we had sailed in strong tidal currents before, this was the fiercest in a constant direction. The afternoon was spent becalmed outside East London. With the setting sun I decided to enter harbour, but it brought up a steady northerly so I ran south intending to go into Port Elizabeth. On reaching there, the winds swung to the south and increased to gale force so that for the first time we were beating into fast seas with three reefs in the mainsail and flying our brand new storm jib.

A week out of Durban and we still had 300 miles to fetch Cape Town but the constant presence of tankers prohibited sleep, even making relaxation difficult. Then the wind rose to storm force, the working jib blew out and I let *Solitaire* lie under bare poles close to shore in shallow water but well away from the steep ledge. I went below for a few minutes for a cup of tea and closed my eyes to rest them. I opened them again after a few minutes and discovered that six hours, with no control over whether I lived or died, had passed. I had been lucky.

My confidence in the ability of tankers to avoid yachts was shattered when I saw two of them wrecked on the beach east of Cape Town, one of which had broken its tow line. I'm not sure why the other was there, maybe because he thought the first was lonely, certainly not from trying to miss a yacht. Our last night at sea was spent becalmed, so we motored the last 35 miles into Cape Town, passing through a mass of lights on what, I think, were local fishing boats. Somehow I managed to lose the log's trailing spinner, possibly taken by one of the fish the locals were trying to catch. It must have had sharp teeth for the line was cleanly cut. I had seen hundreds of seals in the water who liked to play around *Solitaire* but I'm sure they didn't take it, unless they carried razor blades!

Cape Town, with Table Mountain in the background, often wearing her cap of white cloud, is one of the most beautiful and impressive harbours to enter. *Solitaire* passed through the break-water on December 5th, 12 days after leaving Durban and all I wanted to do was sleep for the next 12. A pilot launch led us to the yacht club where the manager, Peter, took our lines. The Royal Cape Yacht Club I will ever remember for its kindness and hospitality. On my arrival I was taken as I was – barefooted, in shorts and tattered shirt – to meet the Commodore and a lady I had heard a good deal about: Joan Fry, the Club Secretary. My apologies were brushed aside and they asked what the weather had been like on the trip down. I said I had run into gusting conditions, which they seemed to find amusing. Gales apparently had been sweeping the coast; the Town Harbour had been closed and one ocean-going ship had been forced to enter with a damaged bridge.

Was there anything I needed? they asked.

'Sleep,' I said.

Other interests besides sailing?

'Golf,' I said.

I went back to tend to *Solitaire*'s needs and, when tidying up, I heard my name being called over the loud speaker to say I was wanted on the phone. Puzzled, because no one knew of my arrival, I picked it up.

'My name's Frank Minnitt, I understand you play golf, Les,' came a strange voice. 'Are you free tomorrow? I'll pick you up at nine o'clock in the morning.'

No yacht club should be without a Joan Fry. Not only did she know all her members and their interests, she took the trouble to make a complete stranger a welcome guest. After arranging my golf game I felt far less tired. Rome had given me the name of a family friend, whom I phoned. Betty was a keen ballroom dancer so I promised to escort her to a Christmas dance. After that I had my first decent sleep in nearly a fortnight.

Frank Minnitt arrived next morning in a white Jaguar. Maybe a little older than I, very pro-British, he had fought with us in the Second World War and was the owner of a Contessa 32 which he had shipped from England. Apart from sailing he would take on anything that had been cast aside as useless and make it work again, his favourites being old British cars and motorbikes. His dog was an English cocker spaniel, which was blind in one eye and inevitably named Nelson. On one occasion when invited to his house for dinner and having had my one suit cleaned, I found myself in his garage helping him to take a car to bits. He had a son in the Navy and a charming wife called Solfrid.

I have often heard yachtsmen talking about the effects of long voyages, some claiming that the land appears to move. I can't say that I had this experience, although my golf seemed to suffer! I would play more for the pleasure of watching other people swing a club correctly and to see beautiful greens set in rolling hills, feeling the lush grass under my feet. On the course I met Neil Nisbet, who became my partner in a four. Later I went back to have dinner with him, meeting his wife, Beverly, and their two teenaged daughters, and ended up spending most of Christmas with them.

Frank Minnitt gave a dinner at his Club on New Year's Eve and I found myself sitting beside another lovely lady, Caryll Holbrow, who had three grown-up sons, one of whom, Andrew, was forever turning up with picnics to help work on *Solitaire*. Caryll's home was in sight of Table Mountain and was as beautiful as its name, Moonrakers. It was not only the hospitality of these people that made Cape Town such a memorable stop. The yacht club was always active. Following the departure of the Whitbread Round-the-World Race they were running the Rothmans Week.

Terrell turned up just after Christmas with a new crew member. Again he had made all the stops from Durban. *Rolling Stone* rolled in with Graeme and Sue. Another ferro-cementer was in Cape Town when I arrived. Her owners, Glen and Norma Harvey, farmers turned sailors whom I had met in Durban, had completed their 45ft craft in nine months. Knowing nothing about sailing they had paid a skipper to bring them down to Cape Town. Their two children accompanied them along with two cats, one of which was blind and was led around by the other. The family were adventurous, hard-working and with a pioneering spirit, characteristics that were missing in some of the older established countries. Eilco Kasimier was a well-known and well-liked Dutch single-hander whose wishbone ketch, *Bylgya*, was alongside *Solitaire*. Eilco had sailed in the single-handed transatlantic race and from America had continued around the world the wrong way via Cape Horn. A Dutch hotelier and an experienced seaman, he taught me much.

I had to tear myself away from Cape Town, where there was always a reason to stay longer: to play another round of golf, go to a party, a concert... *Solitaire* was given her last coat of antifouling before setting off for home. Although the slipway had been heavily booked by the Rothmans racing boats, the club manager had fixed it for me to slip her for eight hours, thus ensuring our departure would be eased by the knowledge that the hull was clean and so speed our trip to St Helena, the next port of call 1,660 miles away.

Our course went north-west. The charts suggested lightish winds over *Solitaire*'s stern from the south-west but as we had a high-pressure area to pass through, there could be a few calm patches. For the first two or three days I could expect little sleep until we cleared the shipping lanes and the area of gales. Navigation would present no problems as St Helena is small but mountainous, and there could be no mistake in recognising it, the nearest neighbour being Ascension Island, 700 miles further on.

After clearing the harbour *Solitaire* found a gentle southerly as we headed north, a broad reach under main and genoa. Table Mountain dropped sadly below the horizon. On the second day out a disturbed sea brought problems in holding a course, with the odd bad broach as the winds did not match wave size. Two slewed us and a third knocked *Solitaire* flat, breaking three of her stanchions.

I dropped all sails – a mistake. I could have continued to run with them but perhaps my judgement was impaired by finding myself with no secure lifelines to starboard. Later, when the winds increased to match the seas, I hauled up the working jib and sailed comfortably. I made an entry in the ship's log next morning and spotted the date, Friday, January 13th. 'No wonder!' I wrote.

On Monday, January 30th, the entry in the log read: '0300 GMT, St Helena sighted'. It always warms me to see land loom out of the dark, particularly when, as with St Helena, there is no lighthouse! I waited until morning before entering harbour, after logging 1,607 miles, which meant we must have had a strong helping current.

St Helena was where Napoleon found himself interred in 1815 after his defeat at Waterloo by the British, since when the island has changed little. Many of the battlements built to prevent any attempted rescue can be seen from the harbour. There is little industry for the 5,000 inhabitants, so many of the young men emigrate to find employment elsewhere, leaving a surplus of attractive ladies with time on their hands. As there is no airfield, the only outsiders who call regularly are yachtsmen.

When the Customs boat came over, I asked them what the main entertainment was or, at least, what the second was. I was told there was a cinema show three times a week. What they neglected to say was that they were the same three films, one of which just consisted of coming attractions that never came.

As soon as practical I rowed ashore, walked through the old town gates and up a sloping cobbled street where the islanders, a friendly lot, crossed the street to greet you. At the local tavern I asked the innkeeper to bring me a tankard of his finest ale and, as I got stuck into this, became aware of a toothless woman weighing close to 18 stone who was sizing me up. She told me that the town was holding a beach barbecue that night, for which I thanked her kindly and promised to attend but, tired from the voyage, I slept and failed to make it. Next day I was talking to some of the local girls and expressed sorrow at missing the big event, whereupon they started to laugh. It seems the only people on the beach that night would have been me and Toothless. She already had 12 children and was trying for a record 13. After that, my stay on St Helena was like having both my mother-in-laws with me. She would swim around *Solitaire*, a cross between a shark and a whale, and I had to keep explaining she could not come aboard because we would sink.

Local dances started at 7.30 but I was warned to stay away because of the danger of being attacked by man-hungry ladies. At seven o'clock I would be at the door trying to start a queue, only to find, once inside, the blight of my life. The night would be spent with her not so much sitting on my lap as flowing over it, every now and then uttering a war cry reminiscent of a Gordon Highlander. On one occasion, when I saw a crowd of yachties and girls leaving early, I asked the reason. They explained that although the beach was of pebble, there were cardboard boxes to lie on and did I want to reserve one? Not bloody likely!

Many of the South African boats came into St Helena while I was there, including Eilco Kasimier on *Bylgya*, later to continue to Holland for a hero's welcome, and Glen and Norma Harvey on *Chummy*, which was to hit a wreck off Brazil and sink. Fortunately all aboard were saved although I'm not sure what happened to the cats. Six boats were lost at sea between leaving Tahiti and reaching England but luckily all my friends survived.

Another boat from South Africa, *Sundance Kid*, came in just before dark one night when I was able to help, an attention they repaid later in spades. Aboard were Doug and Mary Solomon, with two teenage boys and a crew member, John. They had run out of diesel and were coming in under sail. Although Doug was a first class seaman, the light was poor and as St Helena sometimes has a 30ft swell at that time of year, anchoring alone is not particularly healthy. It is far safer to have at least one rope onto a mooring buoy so I rowed out with a torch and directed them to lie alongside *Solitaire*.

Life on this island must be a paradise for any able-bodied seaman but after 10 days I felt as pure and as disappointed as a snowflake falling in summer. Next stop was Ascension Island, 700 miles away. We set sail on Saturday, February 11th, 1978, in company with *Sundance Kid*, only to watch them pull away under poled-out headsails.

The conditions were much the same as before, with following winds from the south-east. The trip passed without incident, apart from the sextant falling to bits, which I soon cured with a few elastic bands. After logging 671 miles we arrived on Saturday, February 18th, quite blasé about our navigation, despite a sick sextant. The island, emerging from the ocean like a dirty grey volcano, I spotted 30 miles away. I was thrown a curving ball in that the powerful RDF transmitter was off air. One would think that when you approach an island that is packed with satellite-tracking equipment, a BBC relaying station and a modern airfield, not to mention their own Russian spy ship, there would be little problem in keeping a simple transmitter serviceable. One would think. I had the confidence not to worry, although I did pray for the sun to come up every morning so that I could take sights. My prayers increased in tempo when I looked into the anchorage.

It is always difficult to judge a breaking wave from the back. Even taking a picture of a really terrifying one from this angle will show only a comparatively flat sea. I could see things were quite interesting by the bashing the sea wall was taking and the puzzling way everything kept disappearing – now you see it, now you don't. One minute there would be landing barges and yachts, the next the anchorage would be empty. Obviously a monster swell was responsible for this illusion so I considered giving it a miss and pushing on to the Azores but, as there were two yachts at anchor and I wanted to post some letters, I decided to take a closer look.

In England I used to watch an American TV show called *Hawaii Five-O*, which always started with some nut on a surfboard inside a wave. During the next few minutes I was to become that nut. I began to enter the harbour under power with sails stowed and conditions looking not too bad. Then, as everything went dark, I looked up, expecting to see a black cloud across the sun: instead I saw water reaching for the top of the mast. We were inside a breaking wave, with no way out. If I tried to turn we would broach, capsize and finish as a wreck on the rock-strewn beach. To do nothing meant surfing in at Lord knows what speed to smash into the harbour wall.

The wave took the decision out of my hands. It fell on us.

Even as the cockpit started to empty I was turning *Solitaire*, bringing her around to face the threatening seas, clawing back out to sea. I could now see where the breakers started and finished so I made for a marker buoy and rounded it to make another attempt but, as we closed, the other craft still kept vanishing, clinging to their mooring buoys. The wind was offshore so that whenever the swell came in, the boats would rear mightily, surge forward, and then be driven back by the wind as the wave passed through. There were no free buoys but I would be unable to leave the tiller long enough to secure a line anyway. The nearest yacht was *Sundance Kid*. I decided my only chance was to get a line onto one of the landing barges and hang off its stern. I went round the nearest a few times but there was no one to take a rope.

I closed Doug's boat intending to shout goodbye before continuing on to the Azores when John, the crew member, dived over the side and started swimming towards me, risking his life. I just could not see how anyone could survive in that sea. Had Lana Turner been alone on the other craft, begging me to step off *Solitaire*, I would not have gone, even after my disappointment in St Helena. In that situation I think I would have gone below and quietly cut my throat. No way would I have left *Solitaire*.

After getting a line to John, he managed to clamber on board. When we had chewed a piece out of the bow and twisted a pulpit, he succeeded in getting a line onto a bollard on the stern of a barge, whereupon I played out as much rope as I could without endangering the craft astern of us. Each time the swell bore in, the rear barge would lift like a bird of prey, come screeching down for the kill and then stop a few yards short of *Solitaire*. Next moment we would be shooting up in the lift, looking down on the craft ahead, before plunging for its decks. My stomach muscles relaxed when I became confident that this vessel would move forward before we struck. It is terrifying to realise you have so little control over the life of your craft and, for that matter, your own.

John told me *Sundance Kid* had arrived the day before. The people on the adjoining boat had gone ashore with Doug's wife and the boys, whereafter the swell had started. Those ashore had been forced to spend the night there with no chance of returning until things eased. In fact it was 48 hours before we could land and the island newspaper reported it was the worst swell, rollers and resultant undertow for years. Concern was felt for the Giant Turtle eggs that were destroyed, Ascension Island being one of their few breeding places. *Sundance Kid* had been watching when I made my first approach and, as the first wave hit *Solitaire*, it seemed she had gone down like a stone. Later some of the Americans and British, who had been standing on the surrounding hills keeping an eye on us, confirmed that even the mast vanished. Having decided that we were lost and that they should start looking for survivors on the beach, *Solitaire*'s bow shot back from her grave to live again. Tongue in cheek they offered to take a collection for a repeat performance!

I told them bluntly what to do with their cameras.

Ascension, in many ways, is the opposite of St Helena, which is green and reasonably fertile with a surplus of girls and little to do, a tired island living in the past and totally isolated from the modern world. Landing on Ascension, in comparison, is like landing on the moon. Barren of greenery, the island is grey and dusty, growing only tracking and transmitting aerials charged with static electricity, a man's island with few spare ladies. Although it is under British control, Ascension depends on the gigantic American airbase for its lifeblood. I have played golf in some unlikely places, in the deserts of South Yemen and Saudi Arabia, and on a beach in Brazil, but Ascension has a golf course which its members describe as the worst this side of hell and, after playing on it, I was forced to agree. It is more like playing on a pinball machine. Having hit your ball you can relax awhile, watching it leap from rock to rock. When it settles, the game turns into hide-and-seek. At this stage you realise that this is also a very expensive course to play since every time you hit a ball you are virtually kissing it goodbye.

Everything possible is done for the servicemen and contracted civilians working there. If you weary of the black and grey landscape or looking out to sea, there are always the latest films to be seen nightly at a variety of clubs. The Air Force base has a fine restaurant that looks as if it has been freshly shipped from Hollywood, the meals cheap, the food fresh. Spending most of my time in the clubs talking to BBC and service personnel, I never did get to see a film.

I cast off from the stern of the landing barge on Friday, February 24th, with England 5,000 miles away and Cape Horn a further 20,000. We left in a mood of uncertainty. If I sailed direct to England, spring would hardly have sprung. Should the weather prove too cold as we pushed north, it might be advisable to stop off in the Azores and wait for a warmer welcome home. There was enough food and water on board for a non-stop voyage. I would play it by ear. *Solitaire* had now sailed close to 30,000 miles since we took our first stumbling steps with Rome in the Solent. Considering the punishment and adventures we had shared, she was still in good health, although her motor gave concern. On top of that, the working jib that had seen us round the world was on its last legs, broken stanchions needed welding, and the sextant was held together by faith and elastic bands. The self-steering needed new nylon bushes but at least it still worked well.

On Tuesday, March 21st, *Solitaire* crossed her outward-bound track, tying the knot and completing her first voyage around the world. In the past I had run the motor every week or two, now I was exercising it every few days, but each time it became more difficult to start. I ran it for long periods to circulate the oil and charge the battery but every mile north the problem increased. As the Atlantic grew colder the seas sucked through the engine froze and thickened the oil, adding more problems to those with which we left Cape Town.

Wednesday, April 5th, found us close to Horta in the Azores after logging 3,330 miles from Ascension. Land's End, England, was approximately only 1,200 miles away. I had heard many heart-warming incidents about the Azores and its people so the temptation to call in was great but, above all, now I wanted to see my family so we sailed on. The waves that broke over *Solitaire*'s decks were touched with ice and her cabin grew cold, damp and dreary. Slowly I increased my clothing, first long trousers and sweater, then heavy socks and sea boots, which I left on for longer periods until finally I slept in them.

The motor grew even harder to start and 900 miles from England it groaned for a few minutes, slowed down and coughed as though it had consumption, exhaled its last breath and died. I performed every operation I could think of to bring it back to life, bleeding its system, stripping it down, taking off its head. Its dismembered body was strewn over a heaving cabin floor and I did everything possible bar give it the kiss of life. I accepted the fact that we would have to sail up the English Channel without its backing, conserving the battery for navigation lights.

The last days of our voyage were insistently cold as we beat up the Channel into wind, rain and fog, tacking back and forth through heavy shipping. At last I heard a faint RDF signal from St Catherine's Point on the Isle of Wight, which grew louder and louder as I turned towards it, the gloom and mist pushed aside. Here at last were England's white cliffs and green fields to welcome home two weary travellers.

Then fate played its last dirty trick. Tacking past the Needles in company with other yachts, we looked into the peaceful Solent anchorage, at which point the wind dropped and the tide turned. The rest of the boats took down their sails and started their engines, leaving *Solitaire* to be swept back to sea. Enviously I watched them leave us for hot meals and baths, soft beds and warm arms. Rejected, we turned away and headed for Christchurch Bay, there to spend another watchful night at anchor.

Although lacking tide tables, I had noted the time the current had turned the night before and I knew that an early start would see us safely home, so we swept past the Needles that Sunday morning, April 30th, on a fast tide. Then the wind dropped again, although the current bore us past Hurst Castle. Lymington River came up to port and I tried to edge over into its mouth but still the tide carried us. After a frantic dash to drop an anchor, a long wait ensued until a zephyr came up in the afternoon, allowing us to start for home. Again it died and left us helpless, drifting towards the mud banks as a motor cruiser closed on us.

'Could you give us a tow into the marina? The motor's packed up.'

'Sure,' they said. 'We'll put down fenders and tie you alongside.' Then: 'You're flying a yellow flag. Where have you come from? France?'

'Ascension Island in the South Atlantic,' I replied proudly. 'I've just sailed around the world.'

The cameras came out. Wine, chicken, chocolates and cups of coffee showered on *Solitaire*. It was the Easter holiday and the marina was full, but we were allowed to tie alongside the wall, *Solitaire* still secured to the cruiser. The Customs launch that had followed us downriver soon cleared us. Standing on top of the wall was John the rigger, the first person to steer *Solitaire* three years before.

'Nice to see you back, Les,' he shouted. 'What kept you?'

PART TWO

squaring the account

CHAPTER FIVE
Land of Hope and Glory
Lymington
1980

The first circumnavigation, leaving Lymington on Monday, August 18th, 1975, and arriving back on Sunday, April 30th, 1978, had taken 12 days under two years and eight months. The east to west voyage had been made far too quickly and I had missed out many of the countries I would have liked to visit. Such an exploration, of self as well as the world, should take a minimum of ten years and anything up to a lifetime. Now my main driving force was to make a fresh start to round Cape Horn.

The distance *Solitaire* covered on that first voyage was roughly 34,000 miles, with a best day's run of around 149 miles. The longest time spent alone at sea was 69 days, with a best non-stop distance of about 6,000 miles. Not that any of this was important. *Solitaire* and I were neither equipped for nor desired to set records. It's what is in your head and heart that's important, not what Joe Soap, who has never stepped on a boat, thinks. Was it a good sail, a warm day, did the sun set in a blaze of colour, did the dolphins visit, were we contented? Those are the questions whose answers matter.

I shall never forget or forgive my first navigation blunders. After the Brazilian disaster I made yet more mistakes but thenceforward I kept a mental note of *Solitaire*'s position, the weather conditions she was in and the dangers she might face. When laying out a course, I would draw lines from point to point, trying to skirt around areas of calms, storms and shelving seabeds, using such charts as I possessed. Sometimes things go wrong and three or four problems are thrown at you together. Then there is no time to think and you must react instinctively, preferably having the cure ready before you catch the disease.

For me the time taken on a voyage was important only as far as food, water and the boat's condition were concerned. If I could make 100 miles a day, I would be content. Had I the funds I would have worked out the stores required, then doubled them, but I was in no position to do this until towards the end of the voyage. The second circumnavigation, this time west to east, broadly speaking depended on three things.

First, my family's reaction. Both parents were now in their 70s. My mother had been in poor health for some time and brother Royston had spent much of his time caring for her and Father while I was gallivanting. If Roy wanted to alter his way of life or the voyage distressed my parents, then it would have to be delayed.

Second, my friends had an influence. Hitherto they had only encouraged me but if they tried to dissuade me I would sail for Cape Horn no matter, although I would be apprehensive, and really alone for the first time on any voyage.

Third, finance. I had to find work quickly. I left England in 1975 with £300 and returned with the same sum, which I had saved in Australia. But to carry out modifications, equip *Solitaire* with new gear and stores would cost at least £2,000. My best way to make this money (and quickly) would be to try for an overseas contract in electronics.

I spent my first night in England with Group Captain Rex Wardman and his wife, Edith, who welcomed me warmly with a hot bath, sizzling steak and a bed, full of sleep. Later that week Rex drove me home to Birmingham, where the news was good.

If my family, who had moved into a small, semi-detached house, did not exactly encourage, they certainly made no attempt to discourage me, their attitude being that the sea was my life and

I would be off again. On my arrival I found a couple of reporters. In writing to my family I had omitted or glossed over the bad times but when talking to the press, I forgot this and mentioned some of the sailing's gorier aspects, which caused the newspapermen and my family to blanch. My photograph duly appeared in the papers, not that that means anything, but parents like this sort of thing, provided it's not just before they hang you!

Three days later Rex drove me back to Lymington, whereafter I spent a week with Rome and his mother, catching up on my writing. I contacted Saab who told me to take my engine to Savage Engineering in Southampton, where the motor was stripped, cleaned and serviced and the fuel pump attended to for an all-in charge of £20! After that I had no further trouble, making up for all the problems I had experienced after leaving Australia.

Most of the remainder of my time was spent talking to Rome about the modifications I wanted. The major task was to change *Solitaire* from sloop to cutter rig and perhaps add a bowsprit, which would put her headsails further forward and thus prevent her broaching when on a run. Cutter rig would also give me a bigger choice of sails. When beating into storms I could get a better slot effect with the main by using a small staysail, which would also serve as a backup for self-steering. The one objection against the mod was that I might have to fit running backstays which did not appeal. When Rome sailed his transatlantic race, he fitted an unsupported inner forestay on his boat but agreed it was not worth the risk in the Southern Ocean. Having experienced the Roaring Forties on *Adventure* in the Whitbread race, he told me about the conditions, explaining the problems in his quiet, precise manner, never discouragingly. Later Brian Gibbons came to see me and designed a new mast support, then Rex Wardman joined in. I was no longer alone.

My stay in Lymington had been a good one. I had overcome the initial problems on my list and *Solitaire*'s engine was in perfect condition. All that was left was finance, and that was tricky as the work situation boded ill. I had no luck with my old firms, most of whom were cutting back on staff, and the Job Centre could offer nothing. The public moorings cost £10 a week and the £300 with which I'd arrived home was shrinking, so I decided to take *Solitaire* to Dartmouth and anchor in the river. Although an overnight stay was prohibitively expensive, it was possible to pay by the season, which was comparatively cheap, and the plus point was that I had friends there I wanted to see, and could spend the rest of my time writing.

Rome said he would sail as far as Poole with me whereupon I suggested we tack there.

'What do you mean by a tack, Les?'

'How about Cherbourg and back?'

The tack to France was 120 miles and so, for the first time in her life, *Solitaire* made a voyage with a crew of more than one. Since a boat can have only one skipper aboard, Rome got the job and I dropped a rank to first mate.

After anchoring at Dartmouth, I contacted Anne and her daughter, Susan, who had moved there soon after I had set off on my first trip. I stayed with them and Richard Hayworth, a quietly spoken man, forever throwing bones at me to growl over while he sat back with a twinkle in his eye. A fighter of lost causes with the tenacity of a bulldog but as gentle as a lamb, he was English to the core.

John and Diana Lock invited me to dinner at their beautiful home. John was a retired RN commander whose name had been given me by Caryll Holbrow in Cape Town. Later I helped crew his boat in a race but I'm afraid the round-the-world sailor impressed no one. When asked how to make the boat go faster, I said, 'Start the engine.' One night when I was dining with the Locks I had opposite me a very young man whom I imagined was probably still at university. He produced some cheese, which he said he had bought in France that morning. I could not work out what form of transport he had used: the time he gave for the journey was too slow for an aircraft, too fast for a yacht. Allen turned out to be the captain of the warship that had escorted Naomi James home the previous week. As a result of this fortuitous meeting, I was invited to a cocktail party aboard his ship, then the petty officers had me back next day for dinner.

In turn this led to an experience which, at the time, disturbed me. After my visit to Allen's ship, one of his officers invited me to spend the day at the Naval College with his sister, her husband and their three children, one a baby. Despite being embarrassed by their praise of *Solitaire*'s voyages, I enjoyed my time with them and played a good deal with the baby whose tiny hands clung to my fingers. I started laughing.

'She's a beautiful baby but if she doesn't let go of me you'll have to take me home with you.'

The mother's face glowed. 'Do you really think she's beautiful?'

'She's lovely,' I replied.

'Oh, I'm so glad. You see, she's mongol.'

For a moment I could not take in what had been said by this young woman with a child she would care for for all its life, a woman with far more guts than those who get their names splashed in the papers.

Because I had no work, my financial situation was worsening daily. I was now pushing 53, an age which, in the electronics field, made me ancient. Many of the government contracts I tried for were of a secret nature and for a successful response you had to be British and able to prove your movements over the past three years. No employer could be expected to undertake that on my behalf.

I heard there were some mud berths at Cobbs Quay in Poole where, reputedly, the mooring fees were low, but my move there in August 1978 with £100 was to prove my biggest mistake since hitting the reef off Brazil. Not only were there no vacant berths, but those boats already there were being asked to leave because it was an 'unscheduled development'.

Solitaire could be lifted out, her mast dropped and put in a cradle for £60 and I could live on board for two weeks. The fortnight passed without my finding work, apart from a couple of private jobs in the yard. One paid £50 and the second should have been £200 but the owner found it convenient to flit by moonlight without paying me.

In October I saw an advertisement in the local paper asking for electronic wiremen and rang the firm for an appointment. 'I have to tell you I'm 53 years old,' I said, having been turned down so often that I believed I had no chance.

I turned up with my last £10 note in my pocket – and got the job. If the basic wage was unexceptional, there was plenty of over-time and by saving hard I reckoned I could still leave for Cape Horn the following June. I walked and ran the four miles to and from the factory, which helped build up my legs and get me fit for my voyage. *Solitaire* was the one I really felt sorry for, sitting forlornly in her cradle with her mast down, dreaming of her warm bed in Hiva Oa sunshine. As winter progressed, the marina became more like a graveyard, the snow-covered boats so many tombstones.

To save money I spent Christmas in the marina, trying to hide from the manager, but he caught me on Christmas Day before I could dodge behind the tombstones. His weekly enquiry as to when I was going to remove *Solitaire* changed to 'Are you still here?' I remembered vividly my last Christmas which had been spent in Cape Town when it had been, 'Can't you stay longer?' Rome collected me on New Year's Day to spend it with his family and Annegret, a girl he had met in Cape Town, an airhostess with a German airline, who was to play a major role in my second voyage.

Work fell off after the holiday so I moved to Plessey Electronics on a six-month contract with good money and more overtime. For £25 I was offered an old banger that had six months left on its MOT and was taxed for a month. I bandaged the broken silencer but never managed to cure the carburettor, which drank petrol like an alcoholic, so I threw the bum in the dustbin and got another from the scrap yard. I needed a car for work and, more importantly, to start fetching equipment and stores for the voyage.

I drove to Derek Daniels' home to order a second Hydrovane self-steering gear. He would service my old unit free of charge for the feedback information it would provide and I could then use it as a backup. He guaranteed the delivery date on the new one with ten per cent discount. From Kemp Masts I ordered a new Jiffy reefing boom. With this system of slab-reefing I could feed all the down-hauls back to winches in the cockpit and use the old roller boom as a stand-by. Meanwhile I had been buying ship's stores from the supermarket, and the boat's lockers, unlike Mother Hubbard's, were starting to fill.

As the weather warmed I hired an industrial sander and spent my spare time on *Solitaire*'s topsides, finally giving her four coats of International 709 paint. I also bought some antifouling to be applied just before the boat went back in the water. This time I would not risk strangling *Solitaire* as I had in the South Pacific. I splashed out, too, on wet weather gear, having it heavily lined to combat the freezing conditions in the Southern Ocean.

There were changes to make on the rigging for safety's sake. The lower shrouds of 6mm stainless steel wire had to be stepped up to 8mm to match the rest of the rigging. Sails were the major item. It might be possible to pick up some strong second-hand headsails, but I needed two new working jibs and a new mainsail, on which I held very definite views. The mainsail would be similar to the one Lucas had sent me in Australia, with a straight leech, no battens and three reef points, the last reef point to provide a virtual trysail. And I needed a heavy luff rope, not only to give strength but to grip on in icy conditions. The seams had to be wide with three rows of stitching and, had I been able to afford it, all panelling seams would have been taped with further stitching. The sail was to be at least 8oz material and heavily reinforced. All eyes, clews, tacks were to be stitched rather than pressed in position, for in the past such eyes had inevitably pulled out. My old Lucas mainsail was still good enough to serve as a backup. The working jib was to be made to the same specification apart from stainless steel, not rope, in the luffs and the piston hanks had to be heavy duty because on my last journey I had worn out two sets.

I consulted a number of sailmakers, all of whom said they could supply to specification and deliver within ten weeks at prices ranging from £400 to £500. A local sailmaking firm had several advantages: they were only five minutes' walk from where I worked, they claimed to specialise in heavy cruising sails, their price was competitive and there were no transport costs. I called at their office on March 14th, 1979, and we had a long talk about the specifications and my reasons for them. If I paid cash with the order, the price would be £400 with delivery on May 14th.

I handed over a cheque for the £400 within a week, along with my Lucas sails to act as a pattern.

'Do make them strong enough to take me round Cape Horn,' was my last request.

'We will make them strong enough to lift the boat out of the water,' they promised. Later I received confirmation of order and delivery date.

Calling in to pick up the sails on May 14th I was told they would be completed five days later. On May 19th an employee tipped me off that they had not even been started and it was the same story on May 26th. After more phone calls and visits, I was finally told they would be ready on Saturday, June 2nd.

Handed three plastic coated sail bags, I asked to see the mainsail. At first they refused, claiming that they did not allow sails to be removed from their bags and inspected on the premises! Finally they let me pull about 4ft of the sail from its bag. The first thing that came to light was what I thought was a large tack or eyelet which had been pressed in and not stitched as agreed. Then I realised it could not be either since the material was too narrow, but could only be the head of a sail with the headboard missing! The reinforcing was limited, there was no rope in the luff, the cloth merely turned back on itself, small diamond-shaped pieces had been sewn on into which eyelets had been pressed to take the plastic slides, and the seams were too narrow. My first reaction was that I'd been given someone's poorly-made sail by mistake.

'You've given me the wrong sail,' I complained, whereupon they asked if I had paid for the sails in full.

On affirming this I was told, 'In that case the sails are now your property and you have no case.'

I contacted a solicitor who was also a yachtsman. He made an appointment to inspect the sails but the sailmaker failed to keep it. I contacted the Association of Sailmakers but since my sailmaker was a member of theirs, they refused to act as arbitrators. On June 27th my solicitor advised me to contact the Office of Fair Trading, at which stage I knew I had little chance of leaving for Cape Horn that year as *Solitaire* was not fast and we would be unable to reach the Horn before winter set in. I considered all the actions I could take, starting with taking the sails to the nearest rubbish dump and burning them.

To set off on a voyage without first class sails would give concern to my family and would be unfair both to them and *Solitaire*. But to walk away from the legal problem could mean that other yachtsmen would be taken advantage of, so I visited the Office of Fair Trading and stepped onto a merry-go-round until 1982, when I staggered off as sick as any long ride on the legal circuit can make you.

Once more I was to feel as if I were in hospital, this time one for the insane. Three teams of surgeons came to operate. First were the solicitors, talking softly and incomprehensibly; second were the judges, entering your stomach not with scalpels but with bare hands, twisting your guts into knots; and third were the get-on-your-bike-and-look-for-work brigade whose speciality is the heart. They remove you from the operating table and sit you in a small cubicle where a girl, young enough to be your grandchild, asks, 'Have you looked for work? How much money do you have? Prove it!' You are then allowed to leave their hospital, reporting weekly for your dole prescription, wishing you were a thousand miles away and had never heard of British justice.

The Consumer Protection Department advised collecting the sails and having an expert's written report whether or not they were of merchantable quality and fit for their purpose. I was further advised to apply to Poole County Court for a hearing before the registrar, which was arranged for August 4th, 1978. The sailmaker failed to turn up. The case could now go before a judge after I had engaged an expert witness. Then my contract with Plessey's ran out and I could not afford the repairs to get my car through its MOT so I sold it for £18. Meanwhile I had promised to leave the marina by the end of June for Cape Horn and when this fell through, I was put under more pressure. *Solitaire* was put back in the water and I sailed for Lymington in mid-August, entering Lymington Yacht Haven for a winter berth on September 25th. From now on this friendly marina would always be looked on as *Solitaire*'s home.

The court case dragged. First there were problems in finding an expert witness and a sailmaker made it all clear when he said, 'Dog doesn't eat dog.' In other words doctors don't appear against doctors, an outlook shared by solicitors and sailmakers. Since Vectis cloth had been used for the sails, I tried its makers, Ratseys, who used this as a reason for not inspecting the sails! However, they recommended I should contact the chairman of the Association of British Sailmakers, who turned out to be with Bruce Banks Sails and could not help. He recommended a surveyor who, after examining the sails, said, 'Your troubles are over. I'll appear for you in court.' Whereupon he jumped on an aircraft and was never heard from again.

The court case was set for May 5th, 1980. I found another naval architect who inspected the sails and said he would appear for me. The trial went so well that at times I thought the defendant's solicitor was working for me. When I was in the witness box he asked, 'Did you ever write an article for a yachting magazine called "Barbados or Bust"?' I had expected my own solicitor to bring up my past sailing experience, not the opposition.

'Are you the Leslie Powles who sailed from England with only eight hours' sailing experience?'

'Yes, sir.'

'Are you the Leslie Powles who was over 1,000 miles off course?'

'Yes, sir.'

'Are you the Leslie Powles who then came back to England with his tail between his legs to tell my client how to build sails?'

'No, sir,' I replied, 'I'm the Leslie Powles who then sailed 30,000 miles around the world and even managed to find Australia.'

The Australia came out in that country's accent, Austraaaaalia. There was laughter in court, the judge's face reddened, and that line of questioning came to an abrupt halt. It was one of the few enjoyable things about the trial.

The next insinuation infuriated me. They claimed that I had become frightened to make the non-stop attempt and had used the sails as a reason not to go. Finally the judge accepted that the sails were unfit for their purpose and that the sailmaker was in breach of contract. My £400 would be returned and my costs paid, but the expense of bringing *Solitaire* back into a seaworthy condition was refused, the judge taking the view that these costs were in the nature of living expenses and would have been incurred at the end of the voyage.

A second blow came in one of my solicitor's letters: 'The court costs are limited to the appropriate county scale. We will obviously temper the wind to the shorn lamb, but in reality by the time the costs position with the Law Society is resolved you will not get the whole of your £400.'

Shorn lamb! I felt more like a sacrificial goat. By living off *Solitaire*'s round-the-world stores during the winter months, I managed to keep £850 of my savings, but by now we were in a sorry state. The last of the food had gone and *Solitaire*'s hull was covered with weed and had to be taken out of the water for antifouling. Her battery needed replacing, the rigging needed changing, and the fuel tank leaked. Time was running out.

At the age of 55, and for the first time in my life, I wanted to abandon the country of my birth. I had left England a dozen times before but never because I wanted to. Now I wanted to storm out, a spoilt child, the angry husband on the way to the pub to cool down, a feeling, true, which would pass. I was still a free man able to come and go as I pleased but this time go I would, even if it meant rowing my boat down the Channel without her mast.

Once more I started to ready *Solitaire*. Once more I ordered a mainsail and two working jibs, this time from Peter Lucas of Lucas Sails who, after hearing my tale, agreed to help all he could. There would be no problems over the specification; I could even have my stainless steel wire in the luffs of the working jibs. The price was the same as the duff sails, £400, with a couple of bonuses thrown in: my old sails would be checked and reconditioned free of cost and his wife would do all the running about. In fact I received a third bonus. His wife was a lovely Canadian girl, bubbling with encouragement, and I even found myself whistling *Land of Hope and Glory* again!

I gave up the idea of changing *Solitaire* from Bermudan to cutter rig as the cost was too high. The best I could afford was to step up the lower shrouds from 6 to 8mm wire, matching them with the rest of the standard rigging. I had used a local Birmingham firm when I first rigged *Solitaire* in 1975, so I wrote to them asking for a quotation for the stainless steel wire fitted with swaged ends. They answered by return with a price out of my reach. I had just finished reading their letter when there was a knock on *Solitaire*'s hull. The company's representative had called to explain that the price was high because the firm did not do their own swaging. The rep said that since he dealt with local companies doing this kind of work he could put it through at trade cost, and he spent three days chasing back and forth. The modification still cost £85 but what really warmed my heart was that a hometown firm had gone to so much trouble. I still had to change the rigging connections at the top of the mast but that was only a day's work.

A ship's battery, something I could not take chances with, cost £80. *Solitaire*'s motor can be started by hand but only with difficulty, and after months at sea I thought I might be too weak even to try swinging it. New halyards and sheets took another £75. Rome managed to buy charts, almanac, radio and navigation books through the RAF at a discount, but it was still a drain. Some of my original charts could be used again. At one stage Rome pointed out that I had no chart of Australia, which led to our having words. 'Since I've no intention of going within 200 miles of that coast I don't need a chart,' I told him. Rome finally walked away shaking his head after my last remark that it was six months away, and I'd worry about it when I got there.

The problem of lack of money was forever raising its head, not simply because I couldn't afford to buy the things I needed but because I had tried to prevent friends realising just how broke I was. Peter and Fanny Tolputt, who owned a local guest house, took me along to the wholesalers for stores, where I spent £120 buying the cheapest food I could find. They were convinced that I just did not like tinned steak, duck or salmon! At the very least I needed to buy double the amount of food already on *Solitaire*, the eight connections on the mast's top rigging had to be changed (say £60 for that) and I had to buy at least one used headsail for running before the winds in the Southern Ocean.

Each day I rang my solicitor's secretary (her boss had long since stopped talking to me). On June 10th, with less than £100 in my pocket and two weeks to *Solitaire*'s departure, he wrote me from his office in outer space and I stopped whistling *Land of Hope and Glory*.

'Dear Mr Powles,' he wrote. 'I refer to my secretary's recent call from which I gather that you are not minded to return the sails until the question of costs is resolved.' Then came the body blow. 'Unhappily I have to report that the other side have not been prepared to agree costs which will therefore have to be taxed by the court. This process will take at least three months and there is not the slightest prospect of resolving this matter before your intended departure this month.'

I was no longer the angry husband slamming out of the house. Since I had been rejected I would look around for other attractive company with whom to have an affair. I remembered all my American friends and the kindnesses they had shown me on my first voyage. July 4th was their Day of Independence so it would be mine, too, mine and *Solitaire*'s, the day we would sail.

Perhaps at this stage a normal individual would have considered finding a sponsor, but I was dead against it, my feelings stemming, perhaps, from my working-class background. With a sponsor's money I could have a yacht built with electric self-reefing sails, sensors that would record any strain and reef the sails while I stayed below watching the latest video, relaxed in the knowledge that our satellite navigation aid was keeping us on course for Cape Horn. Without a commercial sponsor I would be cold, hungry and afraid, but I would be using the gifts given to me by the only sponsor I was responsible to.

The closest I came to being caught in this rat race was when I met Dr Herbert Ochs, who came to see me about using a new antifouling he had invented. A chubby, jolly man, he must have been a bit older than me. I liked him on sight, a down-to-earth character I could have spent days talking to, a man I could trust to keep his word. When I told him my feelings about sponsors he said, 'There's no question of your considering me a backer. I simply want you to put a gallon of my concoction on *Solitaire*'s hull, take it round the world non-stop and let me inspect the results. Er, should you hit a reef, run aground or sink I'd be grateful for any last minute photos you manage to take.'

While we talked in the cabin I worked on my old plastic sextant, which still had the handbag mirrors I had stuck on in Panama. The adjuster had been held together by elastic bands, now perished, and I was replacing them with the finest money could buy.

Dr Ochs, or Herbert as he had become, grew more and more agitated. Unable to contain his curiosity any longer he asked what I was doing.

'Getting my sextant ready for this trip,' I replied, whereupon he turned a lovely shade of green.

'Not with my .... antifouling you're not!' he exclaimed. He promised to replace the sextant and a week later turned up with a beautiful Zeiss product. After much discussion I agreed to accept it on the understanding that when I returned, *Solitaire* would be taken out of the water to have her hull inspected but that I would not be required to express an opinion. I felt thoroughly ungrateful but I did not want to be obligated.

Lymington Yacht Marina allowed me to haul *Solitaire* out of the water early on Saturday morning and leave her in slings until Monday. This kept down the costs and was far more efficient than rushing the antifouling on a six-hour tide at the Town Quay.

Rex drove me to Birmingham to farewell my family and leave the duff sails with Tony and Irene Marshall. If they had heard nothing from me after a year the sails were to be sent to my solicitor, otherwise I'd deliver them myself when I returned and carry on with the court case.

Driving back to *Solitaire* all I could remember was my father's big, rough hands, my mother's frightened eyes and her last words, 'Keep warm and be sure to have plenty to eat.' I would remember those words later!

On my return to *Solitaire* I entered the half world that I knew well from past voyages. Normally the transition was made one or two days before sailing; this time I had been slipping in and out of it for two years. I badly wanted to hold on to what people said to me, record them on tapes in my mind to be taken out in the months ahead to be used, gone over slowly and to enjoy when I had more time to think. But life became more and more difficult as there seemed so much to do in so little time and questions merely served to trigger more problems.

The July 4th departure had to be postponed. Keith Parris became my unpaid, uncomplaining press agent. He and Anne were two people who sneaked up on me and I can't now remember when I first met them. Both were schoolteachers who owned a boat in the marina, Keith with time on his hands. Without really being aware of it I began to rely on them more and more as my sailing date neared.

A couple of nights before I sailed, Rome and Annegret threw a party for me at which were his mother Grace, his sister Terry and her husband Martin. All had presents for me which, since it was late, Rome would bring to *Solitaire* the next morning. Sure enough

Rome and Annegret turned up and loaded an unending stream of parcels. I could not really appreciate it all, staggering over water containers and trying to store the presents on top of the bunks. Annegret excitedly tried to explain that for weeks Rome and she had been making ten of the parcels, which were to be opened at different stages of the voyage. One was marked 'Crossing the Equator', another 'My birthday', besides 'Rounding the Five Southern Capes', 'Christmas', and so on. Over the coming months I tried to log just what these parcels meant to me. At one stage tears of frustration streamed down my cheeks, unable to transcribe my feelings into words. In the end all that would be written was, 'God bless them'.

On my last day there was another rush of gifts, mostly paperbacks and food. A parcel from Peter and Fanny included a tin of salmon and a bottle of champagne for rounding Cape Horn, and two fruitcakes, ideal for the early days at sea. A Dutch friend had somehow obtained ten boxes of NATO army rations, each box supposed to last 24 hours. From the local bakery I had bought 70lb of flour housed in two 5-gallon sealed containers. Another container held 5 gallons of sugar! A last minute purchase of 30lb of onions, another of potatoes. Fanny gave me three dozen fresh farmhouse eggs. I had food enough for a six-month voyage. With help from my guardian angel I would be at sea for nine months... I was saying ten, by the end of which I would surely end up looking like Twiggy.

The morning of July 9th, 1980, brought light northerlies and a few scattered clouds in an otherwise clear blue sky. I had been up since dawn, *Solitaire* becoming the stage for a farce I played every time we sailed. Before learning this game I would get into all kinds of trouble trying to do three things at once while carrying on as many conversations. The engine had been run and was still hot, but this did not prevent my remarking, 'I hope the motor starts, otherwise you've come for nothing.'

Rigging, halyards, sheets and sails had been checked a dozen times but I still walked the decks, pulling and kicking things as though seeing them for the first time, allowing me to concentrate on the things that really mattered. Will the wind push *Solitaire* onto the berth or away? How will the current affect her until she attains speed and can be steered? I wanted to say nothing that would leave behind a bad impression because the next day I would not be there to say I was sorry.

In Tahiti I became close to an American family whose daughter would row over each day while I was at work and put a letter on the chart table for me to find when I arrived home. On the morning I sailed she was there with a garland of island flowers. As I put out to sea I turned for a last wave, the flowers still around my neck, and remembered that today was her seventh birthday. I had planned it for ages but at the last moment had forgotten. I could not turn back, too many people had come to see me off. The voyage to Australia lasted 69 days and that's a long time to be sorry.

After preparing *Solitaire* for her departure it was the crew's turn, another ritual carried out before each voyage. My thinning ginger hair had given up the ghost the night before when Annegret had butchered it in (what else?) a crew cut. The pasty white body scaled a grossly overweight 14 stone – for the first time something to be pleased about since it could live off its own blubber during the early stages of the voyage. And it had delighted in its last soaking in fresh hot water, where pores had opened and been cleaned. From now on there would be showers direct from the sky but the pores would always contain salt. I dressed in clean clothes. The day before, my laundry had been done. I wore my oldest gear, keeping the best for the long months ahead.

At 8.30am on July 9th, I walked down the pontoon to *Solitaire*. All I had in my pocket (in fact all I had in the world) was £60, of which £40 had been given by a TV company a few days before. They had promised £20 at first but after the recording had doubled the amount. With a few violins it might have been further increased. On my return I learned that they had interviewed another single-hander at the same time and put us both on the same show. The difference was that the other chappie was sponsored. His yacht had cost £350,000 and a further £40,000 a year to run but the funny thing was that after all the money and shouting he never even sailed!

Solitaire waited for me to step aboard, her old red ensign now a faded orange, her spray dodgers dirty and rust-streaked, her new golden boom with an unused mainsail, her old number two genoa hanked on to one forestay, the new working jib on the other.

These I could see as the visitors saw them, perhaps shaking their heads, believing me foolish to set out on such a voyage so ill-equipped. It was what they could not see that would have convinced them I was mad, the equipment I lacked that most sane yachtsmen would require for a voyage across the Channel, let alone around the world: liferaft, radio transmitter, barometer, flares, charts, wind speed indicator. The list was endless. A sane person would work out stores he needed, then double them. I had worked it out and halved it, not from choice, but because I had stopped being rational after depending on others for justice and fair play.

Aboard *Solitaire* things speeded up. A quick interview with a TV crew, Keith Parris saying they would follow me downriver in the marina launch for last pictures, them asking if I would put full sails up to leave the mooring, and I explaining that I would have a following wind and could not. Once clear of the berth I would put up the genoa, leaving down the mainsail until we reached the Solent.

I looked for people I could trust to let go and spotted Peter Tolputt and Margaret Brown. A shout to Peter, 'Will you take in my fenders?' then to Margaret, 'Please take in our springs.' A dash to start the motor. Back on deck, collect the fenders, drop them below. 'Peter, the motor's on slow ahead. Will you let go our bow line then come back for the stern?'

At 9.15 *Solitaire* severed her links with land for 329 days. A quick wave to Rex and Grace. 'Tell Rome I'll see him in ten months' time.' (He had a flying detail that morning and could not be present.) Hard over with the rudder to pass between the other row of berths, then heave up the genoa which, with my excess weight, went up easily without need of a winch handle. A quick chase up deck when its sheet snagged. Waving to friends on other yachts then into the river, pursued by the Yarmouth Ferry and the TV crowd, trying to take instructions from one while not being sucked into the other.

Then my own request to Keith, the last for 329 days: 'Phone Mom and Dad and say I'm on TV tonight.' Their shouts of 'Good luck', before they turned back to their safe homes.

CHAPTER SIX
Feeling the Old Freedom

Lymington – South Atlantic
July – September 1980

Solitaire cleared Lymington River into a surprisingly empty Solent and headed for the Needles. Her new self-steering gear had its bright red wind vane set for the first time, already proving it was more sensitive than its predecessor. The trailing log's spinner was put over the side, registering more miles to add to the 34,000 already recorded. Our new mainsail was hauled up, the reefing ropes passing through eyes on the leech of the sail then back through the boom to a block on the foot of the mast, thence to a winch in the cockpit, all designed to make reefing easy. It snagged but needed only a small adjustment. Nevertheless I was glad I hadn't tried to be too clever while friends were around. With the main up more contrasts: pure white against patched grey.

The lines that had tied *Solitaire* to shore now secured me to her, as a priority on leaving harbour was to run them from cleats in the stern along the deck to a bollard in the bow. In the old days I would step into the cockpit and secure my lifeline, but for this trip I had taken another precaution: a large U-bolt had been put within reach of the main hatch so that I could fasten on to this in rough weather before leaving the cabin.

Approaching Hurst Castle there was time to nip below to check for leaks, grab my wet weather gear and get back to the cockpit with a few minutes to relax and catch my breath. Broad reaching up the Needles Channel to the Fairway buoy, I eased *Solitaire* onto 254° by adjusting the self-steering vane and hauling in the sails as we came onto a spanking reach, day and wind both perfect. I should have stopped the motor and used the large genoa but decided to leave well alone. Maybe I was lazy, but the number one genoa would have restricted my forward vision, and anyway it was best kept for future use. There was a good reason for running the engine: I needed a fully-charged battery to power my navigation lights and give me a better chance of dodging shipping. But the main reason was to reach the open sea. Already I was feeling the old freedom and no longer responsible to the laws of the land. There were no courts of law out here, and if I made mistakes they would be mine with no one else to sit in judgement. Just God, *Solitaire* and me.

Every voyage consists of steps. A year before, when I believed we would be making the voyage fairly well equipped, there had been only two: England to Cape Horn, then an easy step home. Now the steps had become more of a drunken stagger to provide for possible trouble. First, clear the English Channel, then cross the Equator to Ascension Island where, if the rigging broke, the Americans would help. On to Cape Town and the Royal Cape Yacht Club where I could carry out repairs. In Australia, if I had to, I could buy more food and still round Cape Horn. The Falkland Islands, even if I arrived under jury-rig, would allow me to fix up something to get us home. All vague thoughts. Privately I intended sailing around Cape Horn non-stop even if I finished up eating stewed boots and barnacles. *Solitaire* might have to give up if the rigging broke, but as long as she kept going I would not be the first to throw in the towel. Not that she had any thoughts of giving up: romping along, throwing spray in all directions, alive for the first time in months, her joy was infectious.

I started to straighten up the cabin. The two bunks looked like a double bed, singles joined by the water containers, so I completed the picture by spreading my sleeping bags across them.

At the back of the containers was about a yard-and-a-half of floor space, enough for a bit of disco dancing but a tango was surely out. For a moment I was taken back to South Africa and my first thoughts about sailing when I had told people I wanted a boat to carry me, my suitcase and a set of golf clubs around the world, although then I had not meant non-stop. Here I was setting up another record: the first round-the-world non-stop yachtsman to carry golf clubs.

Back in the cockpit with tea and cake I watched a coastal steamer change direction to head towards us, the crew lining the decks and cheering. After waving back with the tattered remains of my red ensign I decided to stow it away and bring it out only for important occasions. The day stayed warm and pleasant, the land standing out clearly but in my wet weather gear I became tired, hot and happy, and to the slow beat of *Solitaire*'s motor drifted in and out of sleep. By early afternoon we were 6 miles south of Portland Bill, 34 miles in five hours, not bad going considering the weighty stores on board. Start Point light came in view at 12.10 Thursday morning, July 10th, our last view of England for nearly 11 months.

In the first 24 hours we knocked off 125 miles en route to Ushant; it was 75 miles away and took another 12 hours. At first I thought our navigation had been spot on. I had intended passing no closer than 5 miles then to bring *Solitaire* hard on the wind to cut through the shipping lanes out into the Atlantic before coming onto our southerly course, but the land drew closer and buildings, including the lighthouse, came into sight. Blast, I thought, annoyed with myself. This was downright lazy sailing, dozing when one should have been taking RDF bearings. Ushant was sighted at 9.15pm that Thursday, 36 hours out of Lymington, the last land I would see for 326 days. As darkness fell, coded flashing lights from the lighthouse slowly worked their way to *Solitaire*'s stern, then became just a loom on the clouds as man-made lights disappeared, to be replaced by nature's.

Heavy shipping cut off our retreat from the possible storms in Biscay to the open Atlantic, their steady stream of lights making our sail more like a quick dash across a motorway than a safe withdrawal from danger. A ledge runs around the Bay of Biscay and when seas hit it terrifying waves can build up. The quickest way to get off this ledge was to cut straight across. With constant winds from the present westerly direction we would have them just forward of the mast, making for a fast passage, but it meant staying inside the shipping lanes. Even so I could still snatch a few hours' sleep in reasonable safety. I set *Solitaire*'s self-steering to head us 50 miles west of Cape Finisterre, 360 miles across the Bay, and slowly the lights of the ocean-going ships dropped below the horizon. After seeing nothing for an hour I went below to eat, and then to lie on my bunk to think of family and friends.

It has always amused me that on my return from a long voyage I am an immediate expert on loneliness, which bears no relationship at all to being alone. Loneliness is caused by people and places and the real experts are the old-age pensioners who wonder why the children call only once a fortnight and then can't wait to leave; the people with families who wake up one morning to find they have nothing, not even each other. Loneliness is staring into other people's windows at Christmas time, and thrives in railway stations, in airports and divorce courts, but you are never lonely because you are alone. How little people know about themselves surprises me. Few have been alone for more than a few hours, and yet they claim they could never survive so many weeks by themselves at sea because they confuse missing someone with being alone and lonely. I did not miss my family and friends because I simply took them with me and had time to remember them and what they had said, which is no different from re-reading a good book. Indeed in some strange way I became even closer to them at sea.

I had known the other side of the coin: leaving my family to join the RAF, for instance, and a railway station in Toronto when my first wife returned to England. Perhaps the loneliest experience of all is being with someone who no longer wants to be with you.

Friday morning found us 250 miles from our home port ploughing into a choppy sea in a light drizzle with poor visibility. I was still using local time in the log, navigating with RDF bearings on Cape Finisterre and dead reckoning. Once the weather cleared I would change to Greenwich Mean Time, take my sun sights and log our position every noon. The day was spent sorting out food, which even now seemed to be shrinking as I stored it away. Even the number of paperbacks diminished as I sorted them into boxes. When they had been given to me I had said, 'I hope you won't mind if once I've read your book I dump it overboard.' As I normally read a book a day the idea of dumping was already forgotten. I planned to read the best first and keep them for an encore towards the end of the voyage.

The food situation was far worse than I had imagined, even though before leaving Lymington I had estimated that the stores would have to be doubled to ensure a non-stop voyage. When I started to receive presents of food, things began to look up and by sailing time I reckoned I had enough to provide a meal a day for nine months. Only when everything was listed and stored did I realise how serious the food problem would become after reaching Australian waters.

Stews 15.3oz tins

Chicken	12
Beef	12
Steak and kidney	12
Savoury mince	12
Minced beef	12
Total	60

Baked beans 8oz	48
Spam	24
Sardines	12
Marmite 1lb	2
Bovril 1lb	2
Jam, small jars	12

Greens 10oz tins

String beans	12
Peas	12
Mixed vegetables	12
Total	36

Fruit, small tins

Fruit salad	12
Grapefruit	12
Total	24

Flour 70lb in two 5-gallon plastic containers
Sugar 60lb in one 5-gallon plastic container
Rice 60lb in sealed buckets
Eggs 36, onions 36lb, potatoes 20lb

Coffee and tea posed no problems, because at worst tea bags could be used twice. I had ten food parcels from Rome and Annegret, ten NATO 24-hour rations from my Dutch friend, two fruit cakes and other bits and pieces for special treats.

My diet would be easy to work out, prescribed as it was by the provisions themselves and the time they would last. In the past I had baked six bread rolls every three days. Until we were halfway round, say five months, I could carry on doing that, but after five months at sea the yeast would be useless. So bread would be a basic food until Australia when any remaining flour could be used for pancakes. On the other hand rice would last for ever so it had to be kept for the second half of the voyage. The voyage's first turning point would be when we passed under the Cape of Good Hope, 65 days away if we averaged 100 miles every 24 hours. Meanwhile I could have an egg every other day! Onions last well and make spicy sandwiches with Marmite or Bovril. I intended using the NATO rations early on, since they were a bonus, and the first of Rome's parcels on crossing the Equator. Rivers of rain water, running down the mainsail to cascade off the boom end like a broken house guttering, would ensure a water supply. As we carried nearly 80 gallons there was no need to replenish until we were homeward-bound.

The winds were from the west just forward of the beam across a flat sea as we approached the middle of Biscay Bay with 2,000 fathoms of water beneath us. Saturday, July 12th, our third day at sea, I spent adjusting the rigging and making up a new kicking strap. I had Peter and Fanny's salmon for dinner that night accompanied by onions and boiled potatoes.

On Sunday the weather brightened and I brought *Solitaire* hard onto a light Force 3. I should have hoisted the number one genoa but there are times when things are so perfect that you hardly breathe lest you spoil the balance and speed seems of no importance. For the first time I removed my wet weather gear and shoes and socks. Freedom! I changed the ship's clock to GMT and at 7am took my first sun sight for a position line and made a cross on it after my noon sight for latitude. Thanks to my new sextant I had no more worries about loose handbag mirrors or whether the elastic bands would hold long enough for me to take a sight. More freedom! Catching the sun in its flight and controlling it in a slow descent onto the horizon I turned the delicate micro adjuster with reference, like a jewel thief about to break into a safe. A perfect day with a perfect end: stew with extra potatoes for dinner.

I was wary of saying in the log how well things were going because when you are on top of the world, and start shouting about it, someone inevitably comes along to knock you off, but my extended stay ashore had made me forget that lesson. My feet started to slip early on Monday morning after I had woken to find strengthening wind, breaking seas and poor visibility. By noon we had two reefs in the main with the wind backing south-west, and were being pushed towards the land 30 miles away, *Solitaire* taking punishment as she tried to smash through fast-breaking waves. If we continued on our present course we would soon be in the shallower seas around Cape Finisterre. When night fell phosphorescent seas continuously buried the boat, allowing her only seconds to clear herself and gasp for breath.

Her surrender, when it came, was not because of any lack of determination on her part. On a brief visit below I found seawater streaming down the mast support and believed that the deck had cracked. It was my first panic of the voyage. I had to take the pressure off her but as I dropped her reefed sails she came beam-on to the seas, which slammed into her side. She rode the blows, giving ground and heeling to protect decks. With *Solitaire* looking after herself I made a closer inspection of the damage by torchlight. The mast is deck-stepped into a shoe secured by six bolts through the deck onto a steel plate and the top of the keel. After wasting time trying to find the source of the trouble I pumped out the bilges and lay down to sort out my thoughts. Had I put sealant on the securing bolts?

With dawn on Tuesday, July 15th, came light and lovely north-westerlies. I discovered that the mast shoe itself had cracked, but by making a plate to fit over it I felt confident we would see the last of the leaks from that direction. I was unable to get a morning sight due to overcast skies, but by noon they had cleared and the latitude taken put us approximately 60 miles west of Cape Finisterre. My log for the first six days showed 632 miles, despite making only 35 in the last 24 hours thanks to the storm but we were still ahead of our 100 miles a day target to the Cape of Good Hope.

That night I wore pyjamas for the first time on the trip. When a few gusts of wind threw *Solitaire* off course, I removed them to go on deck wearing just a safety harness. Having dropped the mainsail, I replaced the pyjamas and snuggled back into my sleeping bag listening to the contented murmurs of my faithful companion no longer fighting the sea but living with it in peace.

Our first week at sea ended on Wednesday, July 16th. By noon we had logged 750 miles. I should have reset the main, but on broad reach, with just the number two genoa up, it would have blanketed the jenny as I had no whisker pole to hold the headsail in position and it would have slammed every time a wave passed under us. Normally this is acceptable but as the genoa was already weakened I did not want it to take too much punishment. I started to realise how different things would have been with a new number two jenny. Ah, well!

For all that, I was happier than I had been since completing my first voyage. *Solitaire* bubbled along, sharing a contentment that came from doing what you wanted to do in ideal surroundings. At the day's end a simple meal. Margaret had given me bread rolls that could be popped in the oven and baked, and as each NATO pack contained a small tin of cheese, hot baked bread, cheese and onion followed by delicious coffee, it provided all I needed. As I watched the sun set, my cup and belly were full. Deep satisfying sleep!

In our second week we covered 780 miles and the log is full of contented entries. It was not simply finding one's sea legs, the pleasure went deeper than that: it was a feeling of belonging, of walking into a strange room and knowing that you have been there before, of meeting a stranger and recognising a mutual bond without a word being spoken. To have taken me from the sea and placed me in a square box miles inland would have brought as much confusion as if you'd done the same thing to *Solitaire* herself. That week's log read:

Thursday, July 17th. Eighth day at sea, good night's sleep. Not a cloud in the sky. Winds light from north-east 3 to 4. Number two genoa only as, with main up, it is blanketed causing it to slam and wear. I'm not complaining, guardian angel working well. Distance last 24 hours, 124 miles.

Friday, July 18th. Ninth day at sea. Wind about 25° off the stern, should do more sail-adjusting but content to read, eat and sleep. Logged 986 miles, 112 miles in last 24 hours. Position for the amateur yachtsman, 170 miles due west of Lisbon. Big head!

Saturday, July 19th. Tenth day at sea. First 5 gallons of water used. Winds becoming lighter. Have hoisted main and tried to use the heavy aluminium pole to hold out the genoa but too much strain on the sail. Lovely warm conditions. Winds from the east, Force 3. Few scattered clouds. On book five. Very happy. Logged 104 miles in past 24 hours.

Tuesday, July 22nd. Thirteenth day at sea. 0915 Madeira approximately 35 miles to port side. Starting to warm up, could be changing to shorts tomorrow. On my sixth book.

Wednesday, July 23rd. Fourteenth day at sea, 1,530 miles travelled, 109 miles a day average, better than expected. Celebrated by using two cups of water to shave and trim my beard and wash all over. Basked in the sun in shorts with a cup of delicious coffee.

The following week brought sunburn, progress and setbacks: the first because I spent too much time in the cockpit wearing only shorts; the second when we passed 110 miles west of the Canaries; and the third started on Saturday, July 26th. First the skies turned grey, giving the impression an atomic war had just finished. For a while we had a milkily faint sun, then the wind started to increase, gusting from Force 6 to 8 with *Solitaire* surfing on a broad reach, the odd wave breaking over her. I should have changed down to the working jib, but I thought I'd try for a fast sail to make up for two days' lack of wind. And make up for it *Solitaire* surely did with a run of 141 miles. Sunday night was a bit hairy with *Solitaire* still going like a dingbat, the old genoa straining out its heart to keep ahead of breaking seas.

I had been checking the sails during the night with a torch, but when dawn broke on Sunday I saw that the 2-inch seam along the bottom of the genoa had ripped and was trailing over the side: I replaced it with the working jib and hoisted the main when the wind abated. The rest of the morning was spent repairing the genoa by folding the seam twice and wrapping it in the first panel of the sail. The log, however, showed that our mad ride through the night had given us a run of 121 miles, a ride I was to spend two days paying for, sewing sails until Monday night. From now on I would treat the number two genoa as though it were spun from pure gold for use in ultra-light winds only. On Tuesday, July 20th, I started to record the sails I should have had, with a feeling of having let down *Solitaire*, asking too much of her without giving her a fair chance. By noon that day the log read 2,175 miles, 86 miles in the past 24 hours:

Conditions a little better. Hazy sky. Pretty good sights. Will continue heading westerly to clear Cape Verde Islands. Number two genoa in use with main. I'm afraid we have little chance of establishing any records thanks to our lack of sails, poles, etc., but happy to potter along in my own sweet way. Still not eating much, but thirst back with a vengeance. So far have eaten four tins of fruit and have been swilling down Margaret's fresh fruit drinks. Antifouling coming off self-steering blade. No undercoat applied could be the reason.

Wednesday, July 30th. *Despite the ripped sail we have still managed 760 miles this week. Have cleared Cape Verde Islands,* *and now on course 220°, blue skies, lovely weather. Solitaire broad-reaching well. Genoa seems OK after repair. Will not mess about with poles any more but keep them for jury-rigging (I hope not!). Still not eating well, another tin of stew yesterday followed by tinned grapefruit. I should be baking bread but the thought turns me off. I can't understand my lack of appetite. It could be the 25,000 miles still to travel, missing friends, concern for Solitaire and her lack of equipment. Perhaps it's reaction to delay in starting the voyage, or just my oversize waistline bouncing about. I'm even worried it might mean the start of appendicitis. I'm not lonely, I'm enjoying the voyage. Maybe with a few more miles under our belt I'll start eating. We have RDF signals from Cape Verde Islands so no navigation problems. New sextant works like a dream. 1340 GMT: noon position 31°N 24°50'W, log reading 2,291 miles, 116 miles in 24 hours, which could have been much better with decent off-wind sails. Will bake bread for the first time, lovely with sandwich spread and fresh onion. We are 250 miles due north of Santa Antao, Cape Verde Islands. Should clear on this tack with luck. Going well. Good old Solitaire.*

This was one of the longest entries I have ever made in the log. I was confused by my feelings and thoughts but by putting them into words they would perhaps sort themselves out. When I lived in Canada I had a similar experience and went off my food for no reason at all. On my return to England I found that my mother had been seriously ill then; I had not been told to save distressing me.

The damage to our only reasonable running sail was a setback. If we had nothing bigger than a working jib in the Southern Ocean we would be cutting speed by a third, but none of this accounted for my unease. Before setting out I had estimated my chances on a voyage of some 28,000 miles. I believed that with the strong winds in the Southern Ocean pushing us along we should make our 100 miles a day, say 270 to 290 days at sea. The difference between a broad reach in Force 5 to 6 using a genoa (140 miles on a good day) and smaller working jib (95 miles a day) was 45 miles. But the longer we spent at sea the more chances there were of the rigging going and I was uncertain how long the masthead connections would last. From the records of other Cape Horners I knew I could expect at least one roll over; one roll over *Solitaire* might survive, but not two or three. I had known this before leaving and accepted the risk, so I could not understand my new apprehensions, or why I had become so finicky over food, eating tinned stews and fruit, which should have been kept for the later stages of the voyage.

July 31st, saw the start of the fourth week at sea, with flying fish rising from under our bow. I have no idea why they were so called as they don't flap wings but simply leap along the tops of waves to get up speed, then launch themselves into the air to glide on delicately transparent wings. There's intense pleasure in watching them, particularly when a setting sun showers them with colour, and I felt like apologising as *Solitaire*'s eager surge displaces them in a shower of noise and panic. By night they flew into the sails. In our early days I would crawl about in the dark trying to reunite them with their families but they damaged their wings too badly to return them to the jungle that is the sea. I remember holding one, its eyes popping, gasping for breath, or should that be water? I heard a voice say quite clearly, 'Don't just lie there, say something', and was even more surprised to realise the voice was mine. I believe they lock away people who talk to fish. That Thursday there were six on deck, a record. I have read of seamen breakfasting off them, the fish fried in butter with browned potatoes and onions to accompany them. Had they been served that way I would have eaten them with relish, but having heard their death struggles my entry in the log simply read, 'Six large flying fish came on board during the night. Very sorry, I hate to see anything die.'

By that point I was on my eighth book, *The Master Mariner*, one of the finest books I have ever read. Its pages would become worn as I read and re-read it.

'Friday, August 1st. Grey skies, sun about to pass directly over my head', was all I noted. It would be two or three days before we could get a decent sight for latitude. We would then be facing north when we took our noon sight instead of south, which I would have to watch out for when applying declination, remembering my first boob and my subsequent appearance in a Brazilian maternity hospital. I made a large note of the change in the ship's log.

Next day *Solitaire* was approximately 100 miles west of Santo Antao in the Cape Verde Islands. Because the noon sun was still above us I did not try to pinpoint our latitude. What interested me was *Solitaire*'s longitude, 27°45′W. After leaving England *Solitaire* had headed south in a gentle westerly curve to sweep around the tip of Africa and the Cape Verde Islands. Now that we were well clear, we could start to swing back for our first major turning point, the Cape of Good Hope.

On Sunday, August 3rd, the sailing was marvellous, with Force 3 easterlies, the waves small compared with the past weeks perhaps due to their coming from the coast of Africa and feeling its protection. Blue skies with a few scattered clouds to make it interesting, but no dolphins. I remembered reading that Japanese fishermen were killing them off by driving them ashore. Bloody fishermen, I muttered. I started drinking tea again after two weeks of not being able to stand the stuff. And a further note, 'Remember, clown, that the sun is now north of us.'

Next day, calm conditions gave me a chance to lean over the side and check the antifouling. There was no slime or growth, although the paint had changed in colour from a reddy brown to light fawn, the seas having stripped the topcoats. I checked the motor, sprayed it with oil and turned it by hand for the first time in three weeks. I was saving it for the doldrums we would soon be entering. As I was taking my noon sight my old pals, the dolphins, showed up for the first time, so the bloody fishermen had not killed them off after all. To prove the point they came back again that night to put on a special performance. The last two days of our fourth week brought lighter winds and slamming sails in a high swell, a final day's run of only 44 miles. Nevertheless we still managed to make good 692 miles for the week, 2,983 miles in 28 days. Not bad going.

On the last day of our fourth week something terrifying happened. We sighted our first ship for two weeks, not that that scared me. I started the engine and the fan belt broke. That did not worry me either as I soon fitted a spare. By afternoon the wind had dropped completely and I was forced to lower all sails. Then I found that I had read 19 of my supply of books. None of these things caused much concern. But what did petrify me was that I nearly committed hara-kiri by ripping open my belly. It was one of those stupid things you do when not concentrating on your job. I had been trying to cut a piece of canvas with a particularly sharp knife and, like a fool, was cutting towards me. The knife slipped and next second I was looking at a 6-inch pocket I had made in my shorts. When I removed them I found I had blood running down my stomach. Fortunately it was only a scratch, but half-an-inch deeper and I could have been in real trouble. Three inches lower and I would have been the laughing stock of Birmingham.

'Why did you give up sailing round the world, Les?'

'Well, I cut my thing off!'

Perhaps one should not curse the Japanese, even if they are slaughtering your friends.

We had now reached the stage in the voyage when life began to speed up. I'm often asked how it is possible to spend week after week living in boredom. Most people on holiday find that, although the first week goes fairly slowly, the longer they are away the faster the time flies, particularly if they are enjoying themselves. It's the same with sailing. You wake and perhaps bake bread, take the morning sight, have a coffee, read a book. After noon sights, the main meal. More reading in the afternoon followed maybe by a bit of a snooze. Watch the dolphins play with a last coffee. Another day has passed. Work and storms interfere with this fast-moving clock. In moments of danger it stops to freeze you in a lifetime's terror.

Wednesday, August 6th. The start of our fifth week at sea, our latitude 12° north of the Equator and longitude 27°W. Another 720 miles to Rome's first parcel for crossing the line. We start edging to the east to sail down the middle of the South Atlantic, reducing the longitude to around 20°W. No point in heading for the Cape of Good Hope because a large, high-pressure area lies off the coast of South Africa. Better to stay clear of its calms, not that there would be much chance of a direct passage anyway. Since leaving England the winds had started from the west and slowly veered, moving clockwise to north then north-east, giving lazy days of sailing with stern winds. Now they were blowing from the east. The doldrums would bring confusion to the winds. It would be possible to have days, even weeks, of calms to be broken by squalls, short sharp gales from every point of the compass. Flat seas, angry seas. You paid your money and took your chances. Once through the doldrums the wind should settle, blowing constantly from the south-east, and the Cape of Good Hope, our next turning point.

Whenever I think or write about the weather my thoughts seem always to affect it. After writing in the log that we would soon be in the doldrums we lay in a sea of grey steel. Every now and then someone would shake its corner, making it swell and ripple. We spent the night with just the reefed mainsail up. Even so there was much slamming and banging, and for all the noise we covered only 4 miles, and lost two of our three buckets. How I could be so stupid as to lose two buckets one after another I have little idea. The handle came off one as I was trying to bring seawater on deck and fell like a leaf through the transparent blue water. Without more ado I tied a second bucket to a rope and dropped it over the side with the same effect. Neptune must have thought it was raining buckets but at least he had a matching pair. The last bucket now took on a new importance. Although I had a flush toilet on board, once in the Southern Ocean, with its high seas, it would be more sensible to close it down at its seacocks and use a bucket. Fortunately the remaining bucket was stronger than its companions so I thought it should render valiant service.

Thursday night brought a vicious electrical storm with black, racing clouds, breaking waves, skin-smarting driven rain... and our first visitor, an unwelcome one: a butterfly, in the middle of an ocean, bringing only sadness with it for its certain death. As with land birds they last only a day or two as you try to feed them, but they always die. Sometimes you wake in the morning and they are lying stiff on the cabin floor. At other times they disappear and you feel thankful. Days later you move a book or a chart and you find their lonely grave. It's difficult for people living ashore to understand the effect of such a loss. Unlike the human race a single small bird becomes your responsibility; you share in its suffering, it's the only living thing with you.

We had been in the storm for some time. Angry seas tore furiously towards us, breaking over *Solitaire*'s bow and flooding her decks. The night sky, lit by a full moon and hundreds of bright stars, was brilliant. It is only when you watch awhile and notice how quickly moon and stars are being switched on and off by racing clouds, fronts rushing through like stampeding herds, that you understand. I reduced to two reefs in the main with working jib and decided that before enjoying a hot drink below I would first clear up the tangled mess of halyards and sheets in the cockpit.

I bent to pick up the ropes and came up with a screaming monster in my hands. Jesus Christ! I flung it as hard as I could. Only when it hit the boom and its wings splayed out did I realise it had been a storm petrel. I watched it fall into the sea with horror. I had committed murder and the loss of this bird was to stay with me for the rest of the voyage. I would be reminded of it every time I saw other birds gliding past *Solitaire*'s white hull or landing in her sheltered wake.

Saturday, August 9th. One calendar month out of Lymington. Still making progress in squalls and confused sea with runs of 60 to 100 miles a day. Hard on the wind most of the time with plenty of tacking back and forth.

One night when we were hard-pressed I heard two loud bangs like a gun going off. I dashed on deck thinking the rigging had parted. By the time I had reached the cockpit, the thing I used for a brain had already accepted the fact and was calculating how to reach Ascension Island under jury-rig. The rigging still stood and I could find no reason for the double bangs. I had heard aircraft flying through the sound barrier and this had sounded much like that – a cannon exploding followed by its echo. Possibly it was a high-flying jet or even a satellite passing overhead at 100 miles a minute, making unflattering comments as we crawled across the planet trying to make the same distance in a full day.

At this point in my log I made a remark about Francis Chichester. To be honest I've never been a lover of your conventional hero. My type is like Rome's sister, Terry, who had a cancerous breast removed just before I sailed. That did not stop her walking down to *Solitaire* or laughing at the party. During the Second World War I wanted to be a pilot and envied those I saw walking the streets, wings on their breasts, popsies on their arms – the Few who saved the country. But the real heroes for me were the poor devils who spent year after year in mud, covered in lice, until one day some idiot told them to stick their heads up and get them blown off. They received no medals, were never called 'heroes' but only because they were not of the few, but the many. Bloody millions of them.

Chichester, Robin Knox-Johnston, Alex Rose were people I admired for living full lives. Apart from Slocum I had read only one of their books but because I found Chichester's *Gypsy Moth Circles The World* among my paperbacks, I read it to check my positions and times for different stages of the voyage against his. In the ship's log that day I noted that it had taken Chichester only 22 days to reach my position against *Solitaire*'s 32. No way could *Solitaire* equal *Gypsy Moth*'s times. We would set no records; our satisfaction would come from finishing something we had started.

Solitaire continued south through confused seas and grey, overcast skies, tacking back and forth, dropping off the top of waves, decks awash. Concerned half the time because we carried so little sail, worried the next because of sea falling from under us, an anxious eye on the weakened, straining rigging.

For a few days the sun sulked behind heavy layers of mist and clouds, the odd smile it managed so fleeting that it could have been imagined. Dead reckoning put us 300 miles above the equator. Since leaving England I had used one chart only to cover the 3,500 miles we had logged, one of the luxuries I had indulged in! It would have been safer to have had charts of the islands we passed, but a chart of even a harbour will cost as much as one covering several thousand miles. Chart two would have brought looks of disbelief from any self-respecting yachtsman. While in Darwin, Australia, I had photocopied one of Terrell's charts covering the Atlantic from 10°N to 37°S, say 2,820 miles. It was in two pieces as it was too large for the machine in one go and made of thin, coffee-stained, pencil-marked paper. Alas, it did not even cover the 200 miles below the Cape of Good Hope, which I needed to help avoid the fast-flowing Agulhas Current that sweeps from east to west under South Africa. The lack of food, equipment, sails and charts I had accepted before starting out. My log complained constantly about this, but it was only my way of letting off steam.

In the heavy seas, *Solitaire* had started taking on water from the forward compartment and I needed to pump out her bilges twice a day. Once through the doldrums, with their squalls and confused seas, things would improve, but I felt useless as I watched the boat try so hard for so little progress, one working her heart out while the other sat around long-faced and complaining. That apart, my health was good. I still worried about small things like appendicitis, breaking a leg or simply needing a heart transplant. That's another thing I find amusing, being asked if it would not be safer to have two aboard for such emergencies. In fact all you do is double the chances of trouble.

The end of our fifth week found us 296 miles above the Equator, 18°24'W. We had just finished one long tack to the east. Our next would take us back to around 20°W. That week we logged 632 miles which sounds pretty fair until you look at the chart and find that all you have made good in the last 24 hours is 90 miles due east when you want to be sailing south! After 35 days we had travelled 3,615 miles, still holding onto our 100 miles a day, but only just.

In week six more living things, sea birds, started to join us, this time brown in colour. They needed constant winds for survival; perhaps, soon, we would be out of the doldrums, I thought. I

Right The author, Leslie Powles.

Below Starting to show her beauty; *Solitaire* in the final stages of construction, 1975.

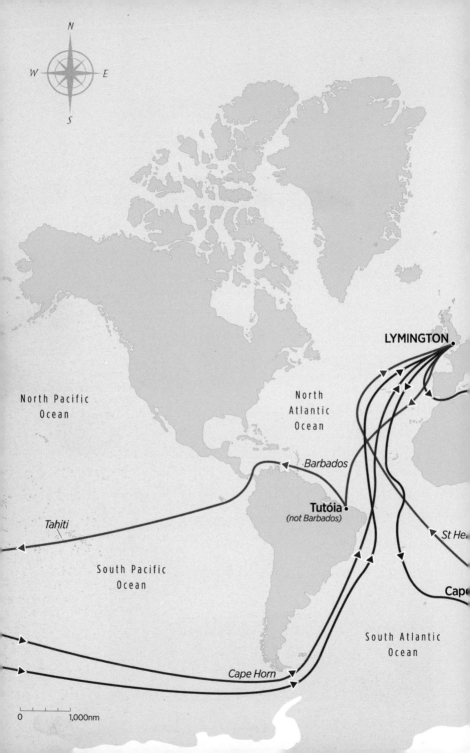

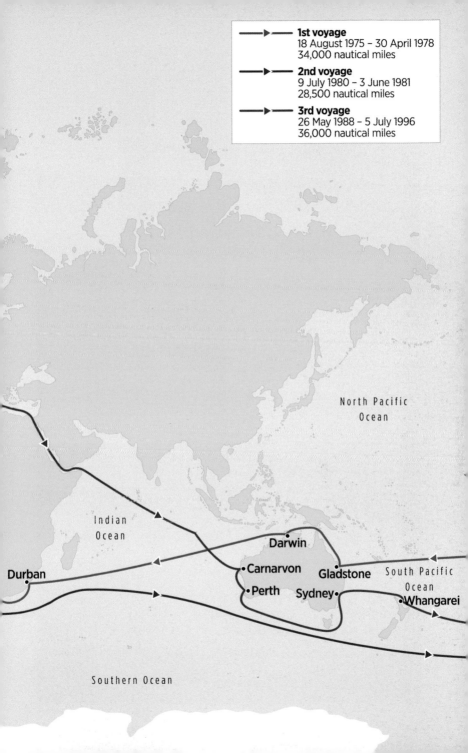

1st voyage
18 August 1975 – 30 April 1978
34,000 nautical miles

2nd voyage
9 July 1980 – 3 June 1981
28,500 nautical miles

3rd voyage
26 May 1988 – 5 July 1996
36,000 nautical miles

North Pacific
Ocean

Indian
Ocean

Darwin

Durban

Carnarvon

Gladstone

South Pacific
Ocean

Perth

Sydney

Whangarei

Southern Ocean

Above *Solitaire* at rest off Tutóia.

Right Running in the screaming winds of the Southern Ocean.

Below Taking advantage of low tide to antifoul the hull. *Solitaire* is leaning against a beached wartime landing barge.

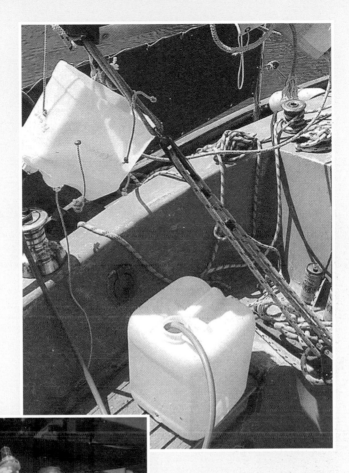

Above One way of getting a supply of water – catch it off the mainsail!

Left Yachtsman of the Year, 1981, as awarded at the London Boat Show.

Above Return to Lymington, half starved, after Les's third circumnavigation.

Below Safe and sound and no longer starving. A very happy man!

Above Flight Lieutenant Rome Ryott, top aerobatic pilot, and friend.

Right Les with Annegret recently. She became a close friend after she and Rome gave Les food parcels in 1980.

A home afloat; *Solitaire*'s cabin then…

…and now. Les checking his emails.

Les on *Solitaire*'s deck in their permanent berth, Lymington Yacht Haven, 2011.

was fitter than I had been for two years and my spare tyre had been worn away by *Solitaire*'s constant movement. My skin had toughened so that I no longer worried about sunburn, and I had settled to my planned diet, baking bread every third day to accompany the eggs and onions. I was conscientiously leaving the food that would last until the end of the voyage.

The biggest lift to my spirits was that soon we would cross the Equator and have Ascension Island within easy reach, and Rome and Annegret's first parcel to open. I started to look forward to that day with an enthusiasm I had not experienced since I was a small boy. My log became full of the event. On Monday, August 18th, our noon sight showed us to be just 24 miles north of the Equator. I could have cheated and opened my present then, arguing that with luck we would cross over the line before midnight. However, I had promised myself that no present would be opened until the specified time. Nevertheless it slept with me at the bottom of my bunk. We crossed the line at 10pm GMT. Inside the parcel was a lovely tin of ham, enough for two meals, a tin of fruit, another of coleslaw, a can of beer, chocolates, sweets and a letter from Annegret. My log read:

Just opened my parcel. Over the moon with contents. I've been cutting down on eating my tinned food but tonight a special treat of cooked ham and coleslaw. I'll be drinking to Rome's and Annegret's health with the beer they supplied. Makes me remember the many times they've had me round to dinner. God bless them! Have taken pictures of parcel with Rome's camera.

Rome had lent me his, together with three rolls of 35mm film. Then Peter Tolputt had turned up with another easy-to-use camera and more film. It was one of the things I just had not even considered because of the cost. Later I was to be pleased that my friends had.

At the end of our sixth week we were 4,155 miles out from Lymington (the direct route by chart was more like 3,800). That week we had logged 540 miles, but by direct line, Wednesday to Wednesday, noon to noon, only 440 miles. Despite the lost 100 miles there was much to be grateful for: the winds had settled from the south-east and were allowing *Solitaire* to sail close to them on a southerly heading. During the day I saw my first whales of the voyage, brown monsters that broke the surface half-a-mile away, blowing water vapour, disappearing, reappearing, bothering no one. That day's log finished on a cheerful note, 'Now for fresh bread, the last of yesterday's ham, fresh onion and soup. Blue sky, scattered white clouds, winds south-east. A good book. It can't be bad.'

August 22nd. For the first time in nine days we covered 100 miles in the right direction. Looking at the chart and reading the daily logged distance you would have thought the rest of the seventh week was sailed in the same blissful conditions: our pencilled course flew arrow-straight for 602 miles, never wavering from our intended longitude of 22°W. The noon positions were equally spaced, 86 miles, 81, 87, 87, 85, 77 miles. Only on reading the log do you realise how bad the conditions were. *Solitaire* has sailed in far worse seas – in fact the winds barely blew over Force 8 (39mph). Maybe it was just worry over the gear and the distance still to go, but I have never known my nerves so raw. For the first time I began to wonder what the devil I was doing out here.

It started that Thursday night with the entry, 'Could be past Ascension Island in a few days if sails, gear and guardian angel don't let us down. Winds gusting, *Solitaire* dropping off the odd wave.'

Friday. Changed down to working jib during the night, winds gusting Force 6. Lots of square waves give impression of climbing upstairs. Can't increase sail area because of slamming. All to be expected in this area with its high swells. Still managing to head south (slowly), blue sky, scattered clouds, 86 miles in 24 hours.

Saturday. No sights possible, very rough sea. 81 miles in 24 hours. Still working jib and one reef in mainsail. Charts show Force 4 winds from south-east. Holding approximate course south, but sea throwing Solitaire *all over the ocean. One minute becalmed, next screaming winds. Bilges constantly filling. Very little sleep with all the bouncing. Nerves get on edge when* Solitaire is knocked about. Nothing I can do: if I reduce sail further we won't make any headway.

Sunday. Solitaire *still being thrown about in high angry seas. Very high winds during night with impressive waves. Double-reefed main. Little sleep, moments of fear. Worrying to have* Solitaire *drop from the top of high waves. What will the Southern Ocean bring?*

Monday. *Pram cover over main hatchway broken (can be fixed later). Only making 80 to 90 miles a day. I can't push* Solitaire *harder in these conditions. Panic this morning: one clock was five minutes adrift, the other had stopped. This shaking can't be doing them any good. Changed batteries just to be on the safe side and wrapped them in foam. Thank goodness for the portable radio: at least I can get time checks and reset the clocks. Bilges full of water again. Have not been eating well. Impossible to go in cockpit with these breaking seas. No room to move about below with water containers covering the cabin floor. I spend hours grasping the chart table and looking astern.* Solitaire *feels as if she is smashing through doors without a chance to run at them, a steeplechaser with obstacles too close together. Not being given time to recover from one jump before finding the next racing towards her. It's just bash, bash, bash with no chance to build up speed. Suddenly to find herself plunging down into pits being brought up short with shattering jerks. The sea is shaking with mirth at our confusion. Mast and rigging alternatively slacken and stiffen.*

Tuesday. *High wind squalls started at 0300. Seas high and angry, double-reefed and working jib. Not my idea of sailing, one of the times I'd rather be watching TV. It's three weeks since we had a good day's sail. Anyone who thinks this is pleasant is mad, mad, mad.*

Wednesday, August 27th. *Noon and the end of the worst week at sea for a long time. During the week we passed 500 miles west of Ascension Island. It was while moored to a landing barge in 1978 that I'd been scared by some of the biggest swells in the world. The pilot book puts them at more than 30ft. I'm confident the seas are* *due to similar abnormal conditions. To find such conditions in an area that the chart suggest were reasonable does not augur well for the areas shown as bad! It's difficult to work on deck and gazing over the stern from the cabin for hours hardly helps. Reading makes the time fly and helps shut out unpalatable thoughts, and it's warm.*

When I was not frightening myself looking down at breaking seas I would sit on my bunk with a book or sort out the mysteries of the NATO food parcels. I found some plain chocolate that went down well and suddenly became aware that I was the proud owner of ten tin openers!

The eighth week at sea was a week of contrasts. The southeast winds from the Cape of Good Hope would soon start in a clockwise direction, veering first to south, then south-west, finally becoming the Roaring Forties 1,500 miles to the south. While they made up their minds what to do they swung back and forth, giving beautiful tropical days with time to sort out leaks and damage. I repaired the pram cover and the forward escape hatch, putting a beam underneath it and securing that to its hinges to ensure it would not fly open in a capsize. Anchor and chain were stored in the stern locker, which also contained the exhaust outlet. Were the anchors to smash the exhaust seacock the sea would flood in faster than I could pump it out so I brought the anchor below and secured it under a bunk. Sorted and repacked our supplies, doing everything I could to prepare us for the storms ahead. The end of the week came with one of the trip's biggest surprises.

I was on my bunk with nose stuck in a book, enjoying one of the better days and thinking I might wander on deck for a noon sight, when I heard the most horrible sound as if we were in the middle of a herd of groaning, pregnant elephants. Ye gods, I thought, the nearest elephant should be 2,000 miles away. I threw the book to one side and dashed on deck to find a few 20-ton whales making improper advances. We were in the middle of a school of these magnificent creatures, some so close that I could have jumped on their backs for a free ride. I rushed below for a camera and managed a couple of shots as they departed.

In the eighth week we logged 627 miles, 5,384 miles in 56 days. We had fallen below our 100 miles a day. The Cape of Good Hope lay ESE, 2,220 miles away. The ninth week started well when the winds went round to the north-east. For the first time in weeks we had a free wind blowing at three to four and came onto a broad reach with the poor old number two genoa and a full main. We glided along without the old smashing and banging. Then the sheet broke and the genoa flew free. However, I soon had it repaired and we continued on lazily. Further south, a shirt joined the shorts I had been wearing during the day. At night I no longer lay on top of my sleeping bag but climbed inside for warmth.

On September 9th we celebrated two full calendar months at sea. Back home they would be making ready for an English winter while we sailed into a South African spring. I became more of a crew than skipper, following quietly whispered commands as I soothed *Solitaire*'s occasional displeasures, taking the strain from her weak body. 'I'm hard pressed,' she would complain and I would reduce sail. 'You're driving me too hard.' I would ease the self-steering so she could take the waves on her quarter.

The ship's log grew repetitive: grey sky – grey sea – grey skipper. Breaking into choppy seas, I really am sick, sick, sick of it. But repetition breeds over-confidence and stupidity. Returning from changing a headsail one stormy night I put the kettle on for tea and reached down to remove my safety harness – it wasn't there!

At the end of our ninth week at sea we recorded a distance of 776 miles, but the tenth was far worse, with only 646 miles to show for it. I'm sure the slow progress was mainly my own fault, although the pilot charts did not help too much. Tristan da Cunha now lay 550 miles south of us. The South African high-pressure area with the light winds and calms was still to port. *Solitaire* had started to sweep in a gentle curve to the south-east to pass well under the Cape of Good Hope.

It's a mistake that many people make in life: you see your target and head straight for it. I should have used my golfing experience and made a dog's leg of it, heading further south towards Tristan, perhaps entering the Roaring Forties before turning south and making for Australia. If it was a mistake to take the direct route it was one I could live with. Many better-qualified yachtsmen had made the same mistake in this area. The pilot charts proved unreliable: instead of skirting the high-pressure area we must have sailed into its outer fringes of calms. Well, as Gracie Fields used to sing, every cloud has its silver lining. The silver in our present cloud was that the calms allowed us to do more work sorting things out.

During my tenth week at sea I started to use words in the ship's log that would have been unusual on our first round-the-world voyage – 'nerves' and 'depression':

Engine: Run for one hour, diesel and water containers stowed.

Food and water: Should have enough food to reach New Zealand, a quarter of water used.

Temperature: Now 70°F (90° on the equator), so am wearing sweater in early mornings, and really need sleeping bag at night.

Antifouling: A few goose barnacles, seems to be working well.

Solitaire: *In better shape than when she left England apart from number two genoa.*

Crew: Has moments of deep depression, worrying about Solitaire's *gear and sailing under jury-rig. Although Cape Town is 1,500 miles away and hoped to make it in 70 days, so far we have been lucky and I have no reason to complain of our progress. So why do I feel so depressed?*

The end of her tenth week brought new records for *Solitaire*: on her first voyage her longest time at sea had been 69 days, the greatest distance travelled around 6,000 miles. These had now increased to 70 days and 6,614 miles; not an earth-shattering achievement, but for the speck moving across the oceans it was important. We were sailing into the unknown with new problems that would have to be overcome. Somehow *Solitaire* had to survive the gales of the Southern Ocean, somehow round Cape Horn. If at that stage I had been asked my main concern I would have answered that it was my own part in the voyage, not *Solitaire*'s. The urge to round Cape Horn was as strong as ever and nothing would stop me, but I could not understand my mental condition. Unless I could sort myself out I was likely to end the voyage in some form of mental straitjacket.

A long-distance sailor on his own must be many things: captain, cook, navigator and doctor but, most important of all, he must be able to understand himself and recognise his own limitations, mental and physical. It sounds easy, but people living ashore pay psychiatrists thousands of pounds a year to understand themselves, despite having family and friends with whom to discuss their problems. *Solitaire* and I were cut off from the outside world. We had no transmitter with which to make the odd call, 'I say, old boy, I wonder if you could help me? I'm in the middle of the Pacific Ocean and I've gone off my rocker.'

When I left England everything seemed so straightforward. I would sail around the world for my own satisfaction and would survive for my own love of life, the desire to see family, friends and England again. To make the voyage I would be prepared for tiredness, cold, hunger and long periods of fear. On my first voyage I had been frightened only for short periods, mostly during the Brazilian episode. I believed I could stand this type of fear for five months or so but I felt it would not attack me until I reached the Southern Ocean. But after crossing the Equator and bearing into seas that normally would have given little concern I became frightened, my nerves rubbed raw for no apparent reason. At one stage I thought I knew why: some of Chichester's descriptions of the conditions I could expect were so vivid that I put down the book vowing not to read it again until we were safely home.

Solitaire's rigging might not survive a capsize, but all who had made this voyage had suffered at least one. What then?

I bitterly resented my lost year thanks to the sail manufacturer and the unjust outcome of the court case. That I felt so apprehensive so early in the voyage proved that, at heart, I was not brave. At sea I would turn anything I could to my advantage, not an unusual trait. It's surprising how after spending their lives without a God, many become aware of Him when in need. I used friends: 'What would Rome or Rex do in this situation?' Others had survived, why shouldn't I? Ah, well, time would tell.

Each day brought danger nearer. In the eleventh week we logged 470 miles, six more than the previous week, in the same old mixture of calms and gales. The worst started on Friday, September 19th, when we ran with screaming winds, under working jib only while rogue breaking waves slammed into *Solitaire* ripping one of the heavy canvas spray dodgers in half. What worried me was that I was over-reacting to conditions we had been through a dozen times before. On my first voyage I had been unconcerned, indeed would have listened to the wave's onrush with interest, putting aside my book for a few moments to hold onto the bunk, awaited the impact, then continue reading. If I was reacting in comparatively safe conditions, how would I cope with real danger when it came?

I spent two days repairing the torn dodger. On September 22nd I recorded our longitude as 00°15′E, in other words we were 15 miles east of Greenwich. Once past that date line the working of our navigation would alter. And September 23rd was the anniversary of my Brazilian adventure when I had started to think about a second voyage around the world. This time I would make the correct adjustments when using navigation figures. As yet I had no desire to contemplate a third voyage!

By the end of our eleventh week we had sailed 7,084 miles. As I reported in the log:

We had rode one gale during the week and were becalmed for its last 12 hours. New Zealand will take forever at this rate. Plenty of sea birds about from small petrels to aircraft-sized albatrosses. Visits from my dolphins after staying away for two weeks. Nice to have my friends back. I have been photographing my fellow travellers with Rome's camera. Still managing to read a good deal. Thank goodness I enjoy books so much. Long days in these conditions would seem endless if you could not lose yourself in other times and places. I'm reading one of Annegret's books called Hawaii *by James A Michener. Have hardly put it down for three*

days. Antifouling still working well apart from barnacles on the
rudder, propeller and a few on the topsides. More than satisfied.

The twelfth week started with Cape Town 720 miles to the
east, a good week's sail to safety, steaks, hot baths and warm beds.
We could be tempted only under jury-rig. Once past Cape Agulhas
I could open Rome's second parcel. I planned to round the Cape
300 miles south of Africa for two reasons: to keep well below the
west-flowing 5-knot Agulhas Current, and to avoid the 90 fathoms
continental shelf. The seas, 12,000 deep beyond the shelf, would
be kinder. The problem in sailing so low was that my charts ran
out at 37°S. I covered the extra 180 miles by sticking an odd piece
of paper to the chart and pencilling the lines of longitude and
latitude onto that. *Solitaire* was about to round her first objective
on a scrap of writing paper.

The week was wet and miserable, navigation made difficult by
heavy rain clouds. The winds played tricks. Were the pilot charts
chuckling quietly, having suggested winds from the north to south-
west Force 5 to 6? Any of these would have been acceptable but
Solitaire had to battle against winds on her nose – from the south.
The odd day we had stern winds brought our first thick fog. At
least we knew that no other ship would be within a couple of
hundred miles of us, ghosts of lost square riggers excepted, for
only a pig-headed fool would venture so far south.

It was fitting that the thirteenth week should be the worst I
had ever spent at sea, the week I thought I had lost *Solitaire*, the
week that I lost my affection for England. Since leaving home I
had been bitter, frightened and depressed. The bitterness I could
understand but not the time I was taking to get over it. The court
case had upset me deeply. Weren't the upper classes, the lords of
the manor, supposed to look after the peasants? I could picture
Solitaire beating up the English Channel, her red ensign streaming
in the wind, with a certain pride in completing the long haul. But
after 90 days at sea the picture had started to fade.

And this was the day the storm started.

CHAPTER SEVEN
Screams in the Rigging

South Atlantic – Indian Ocean
September – October 1980

Thursday, September 30th. Our noon sight showed we were about to enter the Roaring Forties, 250 miles below South Africa on latitude 39°S. The morning winds, around Force 4, came from the north and were cold despite my heavy sweater, foul weather gear and sea boots. It was not just the cold that had made me put on the full gear: the day before one of the water containers had burst and soaked both my sleeping bags so that the only way I could sleep on them now was by wearing oilskins.

I had been forced to stop using the old number two genoa a week before as we had been getting the odd gust that would have ripped it in half. We were reaching under working jib and main with one reef, which had gone in when I had started to feel uneasy. Although, cold apart, it seemed a perfect sailing day with a few scattered clouds in an otherwise clear winter sky. A swell started to build up and the hairs at the base of my neck began to stand on end. During the afternoon wind strength remained constant but the sky turned from blue to black in less than two hours as though coats of film, one atop the other, had finally turned sea and sky to jet. There were no breaking waves but the swell increased until the sea rollercoasted.

Normally I would have taken down the main but for weeks I

had been over-reacting. Was I at it again? The only headsail strong enough for these waters was the working jib, which meant I would have to keep the main up for as long as possible or the voyage would last for ever. Apart from running out of food we would be too late this year to round Cape Horn safely.

If we were to have any chance of maintaining schedule the old rules of the game would have to go by the board, starting with the first and oldest: reef or reduce sails as soon as you think about it. That afternoon I was trying to read *Hawaii*, so uneasily that I found I was scanning the same line again and again. Although *Solitaire* carried no wind speed indicator I know that during our first voyage outside Cape Town we survived winds in excess of 100 miles an hour (as later reported by ships damaged in the area). I know what they sound like in the rigging, what effect flying spray has on bare flesh. This storm did not frighten me as it lasted only a few hours and the waves had little time to build up. My main fear was being run down by a tanker.

When the storm struck – without warning – it was with the force of one of these tankers. This was an assassin's bullet hitting before the victim heard the sound of the rifle. You're alive, you're dead, you're upright, you're on your side. There's a whisper in the rigging, then it screams. A panic-stricken dash to the deck to find the mast nearly in the water. Both spray dodgers have gone. The self-steering wind vane is pushed fully over and is vibrating against its stop. Sails are filling with the sea, their seams about to split. Both sheets are released; for a moment part of the boom and main disappear over the side and God knows what's happening to the headsail because I'm blinded by wind and spray.

I clawed my way to the mast and tugged on the main's luff but the bloody thing would not come down. The pressure on the sail was jamming the slides. Finally I succeeded in lowering it. I should have returned to the cockpit and pulled back the boom inside *Solitaire*'s guard-rails but if I didn't do something about the headsail I'd lose it. Quickly I lashed part of the main to the boom, nothing below me but white broken water. Once the jib was safely down I could return to the cockpit and retrieve the boom dangling in the sea. I tied a rope onto the wind vane and around my waist. When I released it from the self-steering unit it tried to take off like a rocket, bearing me with it. I promptly had second thoughts and in the end managed to take it below, where I wrapped it in a protective blanket.

Now I could think about my own needs. Luckily I had been wearing my wet weather gear on deck, the first time I had ever sat around with sea boots on. As I like to feel *Solitaire* moving under my bare feet, wearing sea boots is like going to bed with a woman wearing boxing gloves. I had had no time to put a towel around my neck so my shirt and sweater were saturated and as I realised this my teeth began to chatter. Then the risks I had taken without a safety harness dawned on me and the chattering increased in tempo.

Tea would have tasted like ambrosia, but first I had to fit a shock-cord onto the self-steering rudder to prevent it banging back and forth, and I needed to retrieve the 30ft of line on the log. One spray dodger was again ripped in half, the other hung over the side, held by a few odd ties. Both had to be removed and stowed. At that stage I was merely thinking of just another stormy night at sea. I would put extra lashings on the sails and rubber dinghy, pump out the bilges, then settle down for a night's sleep lying a-hull.

When the storm started I was confident that *Solitaire* and I had all the answers. After all, hadn't we faced every situation, every type of wind, every type of sea? All sails were down. It would be hours before the seas built up and became dangerous. Lord, what poor misguided fools we are!

Without knowing it, everything I had done so far had been wrong. I was working to rules from the first voyage, rules which said that, provided everything was secured and there was a good depth of water, storms were nothing to worry about. There had been exceptions of course, when the storm brought fierce lightning, which I hated, or we lay off a lee shore or in a shipping lane. Then I would prefer to be sitting in front of a roaring fire, a dog at my feet, contemplating a stroll to the local for a pint with the lads. The rules from our first voyage were as outdated as trying to fight an atomic war with conkers.

I was starting to suspect even the preparation for the voyage. Money, or its shortage, decided what we could or could not take with us, apart from my wet weather gear, which was the best I could find, being the type used by Rome on his Whitbread round-the-world voyage. It seemed to have everything I wanted: the jacket heavily quilted for warmth; the double-lined trousers had substantial plastic zips, which in turn were protected by flaps. The trouser tops fitted snugly under armpits and the jacket had a built-in harness on to which the safety line clipped. The outfit cost around £150, it was money well spent. The first problem showed up when I tried to wear sea boots, which I normally don only when close to English waters. Even at night, although my feet would be cold, I felt no pain and certainly had no frostbite worries. In the old days in emergencies I would dash on deck naked apart from the safety harness. Now when I was needed there in a hurry, I first had to tuck my long trousers into my socks, pull on the outer trousers, put on sea boots, then work the trousers back over the boots, tightening the tapes. The linings slowed down the drill.

I hit another snag trying to get back on deck – I could not get through the hatch! In storms I would lock myself below and wait for a lull, then slide back the hatch cover, remove the top board, step out and replace them. It was fairly easy provided you were not wearing padded jackets. After leaving England I had fitted two bolts to the top board to prevent its loss during a capsize. To clip on my safety line I had to lean over the boards to reach the U-bolt. It made me feel sick. *Solitaire*'s movements were so violent and the winds so strong that I had to keep my back to them. So powerful was the spray that I feared for my sight.

It had become very dark and I was becoming painfully aware that my feet were turning to ice. There was more than a foot of water in the cockpit. With the spray-dodgers lost, seawater broke over us more quickly than we could jettison. It forced its way up my wet suit and over the top of my boots, freezing my legs and feet.

Somehow the trailing long line, with its weight and spinners, had wrapped itself around the self-steering gear, and as it was nearest I decided to make a start with this. Waves continued to break over us and an aching body joined my frozen feet. For the first time my body temperature worried me. In winter's seas you might be lucky to last half-an-hour if you fell overboard off the English coast but if I went over in these latitudes I would have only minutes.

For the first time I realised that many of *Solitaire*'s features that had worked perfectly on the shake-down cruise were a disadvantage in these seas. The skirt that ran around the top of the cockpit, 3–9in above the deck, had prevented water streaming into the cockpit. Now it also trapped and held it until *Solitaire* was thrown on her side and the seawater partly spilled out. The cockpit that had been perfect in Tahiti, Australia, and South Africa was far too large. Instead of holding parties of ten or twelve happy guests it was now holding tons of freezing seawater. The cockpit was made from a single moulding with a 14in seat halfway down its side dropping to the cockpit floor. The seats lifted to provide locker space. I had modified the two lockers so that the channels around their covers were self-draining. On the first voyage the covers were held in place only by shock cords since I could not afford anything more expensive. I had attached half-inch ropes onto the hull, fed them through holes in the locker tops and secured them in this Mickey Mouse fashion. When leaving the cabin you stepped onto a centre shelf which held the mainsheet traveller. An adjustable pulley and block ran from the traveller to the end of the boom, holding the latter in place.

The main trouble with leaving the cabin was my heavy clothing coupled with *Solitaire*'s violent pitching and tossing. What I really needed was something to hold onto and use as a lever. The pram cover frame was far too weak to suffice.

I centred the mainsheet traveller, which meant that the ropes to the foot of the boom passed in front of the hatch, giving me room to squeeze by, using them as a handhold. All I wanted now was to strip off my wet clothes and brew tea, but once I had struggled below I remembered I still had to pump out the bilges. So back I went out into the cold, the breaking seas and the howling winds. Then came the bliss of holding the kettle on top of a dancing stove to produce a life-giving, hot, sweet cuppa. When I started to think about changing my wet clothes I realised I had insufficient replacements and those I had were the wrong type for these conditions.

The suitcase I had carried around the world in 1968 now contained one suit, a dozen assorted nylon dress shirts and sports shirts, and five sweaters. Rex Wardman had also given me a lovely thermal jacket for Christmas, and Margaret a pair of quilted trousers. She had driven me to the Surplus Army and Navy stores in Southampton, where they were selling off old ex-navy diving suits for £10. Unfortunately when we arrived they had sold out apart from one moth-eaten suit that was falling to bits. It was a green fur-lined one-piece affair that I tried on and spent an enjoyable half-hour running around like the Incredible Hulk, frightening customers.

On the way back to Lymington I had asked Margaret if I could put it on again and lean out of the car window. At the time we were driving through the Southampton Red Light district.

'You do and I'll throw you out,' was Margaret's reply.

The thought of a green man knocking on doors in that area had me chuckling for days. Funny how the mind wanders when you are cold and tired!

In a storm like that we could be badly damaged at any time so I had to keep my wet weather gear on. Even if I changed my sweater it would be dry only for a few minutes before soaking up the water from my jacket. The best I could do was take off my boots, empty them, and wring out my socks. After that I wedged myself on the floor behind the water containers and pulled a sleeping bag over my head to retain some body heat. At first it was too cold to sleep but, as my clothes reached body temperature, I started to drop off – only to be brought back with a shock to find myself sitting in 2in of water covering the cabin floor. The bilges were full again despite my pumping them dry within the last two hours. We must have taken in well over 100 gallons in that time.

I waited for *Solitaire* to steady herself, slid back the hatch cover and put my head out into a shrieking, screaming world of horror. Massive seas were crashing on my poor boat, trying to bury her alive, giving her no chance to recover, to fight back. The cockpit was full of water. The lockers that I had made self-draining for the odd breaker were under boiling seas that would be gushing under their covers and running forward under the engine mounts to fill the bilges and then, more slowly, the cabin itself.

Given any other choice I would have gladly taken it. Instead I picked up the bilge pump handle and pushed through the hatchway. Timing it wrongly, I dropped up to my waist in freezing water. My boots filled and the seas worked up inside my legs. *Solitaire* rolled and half the water left the cockpit. I banged my face on a winch and started pumping. Mom and Dad would be warm in bed now, I thought. God, I'd love to see them! I kept on pumping. Sometimes I thought I had nearly finished only to have another wave break over us. For all I knew the cabin could now be completely filled with water, the driest place in the boat precisely where I stood. If we were sinking, how long would it take to reach the seabed, 2 miles down? The water grew denser the deeper you went. There were aquatic creatures down there without eyes – would they turn as we slipped past? *Solitaire*'s white shimmering shape, a lonely figure dressed in red still attached by lifeline. How long would it take? Hours? Weeks? Would *Solitaire* blame me for letting her down? Was being tied to your mistakes for eternity a definition of hell?

Once the bilges are dry the pump passes air only and the handle needs little pressure to move it. When I believed I could be no colder, that I could no longer keep my eyes open for another second, the pump started sucking air. I staggered below, took off my boots, wrapped a towel round my feet and boiled a cup of tea, warming my hands over the flame. After squeezing the water out of my socks I put on my boots again, longing for sleep and sank onto the floor behind the water containers – where I found myself in deep water. Two minutes later I was back in the cockpit, pumping.

The night lasted a millennium. Each time I thought I could close my eyes more freezing water streamed through the cabin floor. The seas were replacing the blood that ran in my veins, the heart pumping ice water to the brain faster than I could jettison it over *Solitaire*'s side. It was numbing, stupefying. At times I was unaware whether I was the bent body in the cockpit or the huddled shape on the cabin floor. At last the sky lightened with dawn. After so long in a black, screaming hell, eyes blinded by stinging salt water, I would see again.

I slid back the hatch cover and for a moment wished I had remained blind. This could be no storm, for storms had waves, the stronger the winds the faster the waves, the higher they reached. Waves marched majestically across oceans like regiments of soldiers. But this was no ocean, just a shrieking horror of unmoving mountains reaching up to a black sky. Suddenly in the distance a flock of small grey birds with outstretched wings tried to scramble up the lower slopes, like so many little old ladies with raised skirts splashing through puddles. As we dropped deeper into the valley the howling wind seemed to slacken and *Solitaire* settled onto the sea's green floor. Over there was the perfect setting for a thatched cottage.

The real nightmare was that despite the deafening sound nothing moved. Then the top of a mountain turned white as though covered with snow and an avalanche descended, slowly at first, very slowly, then gathering speed, roaring down on us, trying to kill its trespassers. I slammed the hatch shut, expecting *Solitaire* to be rolled over and over like a puppy at play. When the avalanche reached us there was not the crash I had expected. Instead the sea flowed over us, carrying us sideways for a few hundred yards before it released its grip and promptly ignored us, a matchstick in its path. For a moment *Solitaire* staggered upright in its wake and again I opened the hatch. The air was filled with stinging sleet. *Solitaire* lay buried in the snow, her outline marked only by the stanchions that stood up like sticks on a cold winter's day. *Solitaire* rolled, spilling half the water over her side.

Surely nothing could live in this mad world. Waves would kill us without noticing. Somehow I had to get the boat moving to give her a fighting chance. The first thing was to replace the self-steering wind vane consisting of nylon stretched over aluminium frame, no more than 3ft long. But the screaming wind tried to tear it from me and it was a fight just to hold it. There was no way I could get it working.

I considered putting up a small headsail to try steering myself. But if I was at the helm I would be unable to pump. Even if I managed both, the winds were still from the north so I would have to run south. And land to the north was more than 300 miles away. If I lost the mast it could take weeks to reach land under jury-rig and any attempt to round Cape Horn would have to be put off for a further year.

Suddenly I was aware of something I had been putting off all night. I had to use the lavatory – or rather the bucket, for the lavatory was out of the question since I'd have been thrown around like a pea in a tin whistle. But the bucket and chuck-it method was far too risky. Then I thought of an idea that was to serve me well for the rest of the voyage. Plastic bin liners were the answer. In order not to foul the bucket I used one of these, putting a couple of sheets of newspaper in the bottom for added strength. After sealing the bag I waited my chance and threw it into outer space, assisted by a wind blowing at more than 100 miles an hour. I believe it was the first time this type of payload had been put into orbit.

It was time to look after *Solitaire* again. I went back into the pumping routine, removing boots and socks, a cup of tea, then more pumping. During one of these periods in the flooded cockpit something happened that I would have given anything to reverse. Time seemed to slow. Whether it was the contrast between the howling winds and the stationary mountains I don't know. At times the illusion was so complete that I felt I could step off *Solitaire*, leaving her freezing cockpit, and run down the green valleys, exploring their secrets. The only thing that stopped me was the knowledge that she would not be there awaiting me when I returned.

Another sequence of thoughts started after another wave hit us without the following swell that would have rolled *Solitaire*, partly emptying her. I found myself repeating, 'There was no need for this, no bloody need at all.' A week before leaving England a friend had given me a new bilge pump, which sat in one of the lockers because I had been unable to afford the piping with which to fit it in the cabin. Had it been installed I need never have stepped outside; my clothes would have remained reasonably warm and I would not be standing in misery, tormented by sodden clothes, cold, tired, battered and bruised.

I started to understand the bitterness I'd felt since leaving England, a country I had loved as long as I could remember, when to hear a choir singing *Land of Hope and Glory* would cause tears to spring to my eyes. I'm not sure when I started to lose this feeling for my native land. Perhaps it was the court case. Perhaps it was after watching an Englishman run for his country and collect a contract to sell a product on TV he had never used. Perhaps it was just that I'd grown old, seen too many lands, met so many friendly people. Whatever the reason, the loss was mine and *Solitaire*'s. I regretted it, but the rest of the voyage would be made without the help of patriotic choirs.

At three o'clock on this day we had been storm-wracked for 24 hours. I had been unable to sleep during that time, I was soaking wet, had swallowed a gallon of tea but had eaten nothing. In the past I had survived much longer without food or sleep, but my main worry was the cold, as I had no previous experience to fall back on. There was no point in putting on warm clothing when once in the cockpit I would be as wet as ever. I thought about leaving the stove turned on. We had three 32lb-bottles of gas on board, and, as on the last voyage, I had used only one bottle every six months. So there was some to spare but essentially I wanted to keep the extra gas for rounding Cape Horn. In any case nearly all my time was spent outside the cabin.

After discovering that I could not replace the self-steering vane I started to consider how to live in the Southern Ocean by correcting my mistakes. I should not have tried lying abeam to these seas or removing the self-steering wind vane. I knew I must always keep up enough sail to control our position to the waves. I could have done little with the self-steering gear at the time as the vane was much too big for the wind strength, which demanded smaller, stronger vanes. I had three plywood vanes from the first voyage, which were unusable in their present state. The blade-holder supported only about 4in at the bottom of the vane and pressure had to be distributed, so I cannibalised one to supply feathering pieces for the other two vanes and finished just before dark.

Meanwhile the winds were still coming from the north at hurricane strength. I could only sail south, deeper into the Roaring Forties. All I could think of was getting into the Indian Ocean past the Cape of Good Hope. Once there we would be less restricted and could ease our way out of these howling, desolate seas. With luck we would find warmer weather and give ourselves a chance to dry out and renew our strength for future battles.

I spent another miserable night praying for the winds to abate. If my guardian angel could not arrange that could he please swing them to the west, giving *Solitaire* wings to leave these watery mountains? No craft could continue to take such punishment and I felt like the condemned man waiting for the trap to spring. As I watched the sea break on us I could see the hangman reaching for the lever. Again we were lifted and carried effortlessly on a boiling cloud, and then, after a few hundred yards, released as a cat plays with a mouse. Sometimes I was permitted to pump *Solitaire* dry before it sprang again, sometimes I was halfway through the hatch dreaming of wrapping my hands around a hot cup and rubbing the circulation back into cold feet when there would be a roar and once again we would be buried.

I was reminded of the Germans outside Stalingrad during the Second World War. Ill-clad in their normal dress uniforms they died in a Russian winter. I remember one upright corpse standing frozen, staring through dead eyes. Someone had stretched out his arm and pointed a finger, turning him into a road sign. At least it seemed a useful way to end your life. When I stood in freezing water up to my waist, unable to move my arms or open my eyes, I wondered if my last effort should be to point to Cape Horn as a service to following seamen. Instead I kept pumping.

Dawn came and somehow we struggled through another day. In fact it went better than the first. Although the storm had not abated I felt it could get no worse and as we had survived one day, why not this one? The cat and mouse game the sea played with us was wearing a bit thin. It was not the dying I feared or even the method. I would rather drown than lie for years, suffering without hope, watching my family and friends walk past a shell for which I had no further use, hearing a priest quote from a book as unreliable as yesterday's newspapers. Yet there is some supernatural force, for without it *Solitaire* would have started on her journey to the bottom long ago. I had no wish to die. There were many things I wanted to do, horizons still to be scanned. And I wanted to see my family once more, just once more, so I kept on pumping.

During our third night of storm I realised that with the dawn *Solitaire* would have to take over the responsibility of keeping us alive. In the beginning I had worried that I was not eating. Now nothing mattered but the pumping. Sleep no longer bothered me; sleep was something that happened between life and death. If I closed my eyes now I would die. Dying bothered me but not sleep. All that mattered was the pumping.

With the dawn I would fit a new wind vane and hoist a head-sail. It would make no difference if the winds failed to drop or if they still blew from the north. It was all I could do, my last card. All that mattered was the pumping, but tomorrow I would be able to pump no more. Most of that night I spent in the cockpit, no longer crouching to avoid the breaking seas. *Solitaire* and I became one, moving in a numb stupor, beaten to our knees. *Solitaire* staggered defiantly while I worked the pump, readying her for more punishment. My *Solitaire* had started as an idea in South

Africa, something I would use as a common prostitute for my own pleasures, after which I would pass her on to the highest bidder. My love affair with her started on a reef off the Brazilian coast and our courtship had been long and happy. For two days we had celebrated our marriage, a ceremony far more binding than the others I had been party to. In sickness and in health, that was true, but till death us do part, never. We would survive or die together. I would never leave her.

Dawn arrived with no drop in the wind's strength, the sky still black although I could see over the mountain peaks to the limited horizon. Without their protection the wind screamed in the rigging, a loose halyard vibrating against the mast like a runaway machine gun. In the valleys I fooled myself into thinking the storm was tiring, then *Solitaire* would rise to the sound of the stuttering gun.

When I had pumped her dry again I started to fit the small plywood vane drilled with an extra hole to take a rope, which I tied round my wrist. I waited my chance and fell into the cockpit with it pressed to my chest. I gripped the pushpit and started to straighten up and for a moment thought I was in a January sale with a mass of bargain-mad housewives tearing at me as though I held the crown jewels. After nearly being swept over the side I managed to rope myself close enough to the self-steering to use both hands to slot in the vane. The blade was adjusted so that its edge faced into wind. The shock cords were taken off its rudder and I freed the locking device. After more than 50 defenceless hours at last we had a means of fighting back.

By this time *Solitaire* badly needed pumping out again, but bloated by our small victory I decided to haul up a headsail. Both working and storm jibs were already hanked onto the twin forestay. The problem was which was the better to use.

When *Solitaire* left her home port she had been very much like a five-year-old family car entered for a round-the-world rally. Since sails take the place of a gearbox in a car we could claim she had a five-gear box. First and second gears were new but the third and fourth gears had been used already in one 34,000-mile rally and both were damaged. As *Solitaire* had no large running sails perhaps you could claim she had no fifth gear. The bolts that held the gearbox in place – the rigging holding the mast – were the wrong type and had been used already on one world trip. And we were about to try to drive out of a land that existed only in a madman's nightmares. The trouble was the mountains were ice-covered and the screaming winds would try to push the car sideways. Our tyres were bald and we had no brakes. Any car driver would say the answer was simple: at the top of the mountain change into bottom gear to control the descent; at the bottom change into second and drive yourself back into position ready for the next mountain. But even in perfect conditions, with both sails in position, it would take me around ten minutes to make the change. With waves continuously breaking over the decks I would be lucky to hoist a sail in half an hour.

If I used the bigger working jib there was a chance it would rip to pieces on the exposed summits or the rigging, and then the mast would go over the side. If I used the small storm jib there would be no power to control *Solitaire* in the calmer valleys. I had heard of yachtsmen running under bare poles in storm conditions but had been unable to understand how it was possible in a rough sea. I had heard of running with twin-head storm jibs poled out, but in these conditions it would have been highly dangerous to dive down one of these mountains. At the bottom of the valley the yacht's bow would dig in and the stern would come over like a pole thrown at the Highland Games. If you came off the dead run and the wind moved from over the stern, one of the running sails would back. Heaven alone knew how long it would take to get sailing again, not to mention possible damage. I decided to use the bigger working headsail. True, it might blow out, I thought, but far better that that happen than be rolled out of control in the troughs.

The 30 minutes I reckoned it would take to hoist the working jib turned into an hour and was completed in an air of misery and bad language. At one interesting stage three waves buried *Solitaire* one after the other. The position I took up while this was happening was flat across the deck, my hand grasping a safety rope on the side over which the seas were breaking. Both legs had gone through the lines on the other side and were hanging in space. Over the past three days I thought I had experienced every possible way seawater could enter my sea boots. The new method was more complicated and took a little longer, but its route was ingenious. It entered by a hosepipe forced up my sleeve, went over the top of my trousers and down my leg.

After scrambling back to the cockpit I slackened the sheet and hauled up the sail. At first I thought it would tear itself to shreds, but after adjusting the sheets the sail, its seams straining, started to pull *Solitaire* stern to wind. Then I adjusted the self-steering and main rudder to hold us on a broad reach, the only possible way I can sail *Solitaire* in such conditions. The main idea is to go down the waves much like a surfboarder, at an angle. The self-steering rudder is not always strong enough to control this type of sailing as the waves take over, trying to push the stern around until the boat lies beam on to the waves. I used the main rudder to control this, its power holding the skid. At the bottom of a run the main rudder helps bring the yacht back onto course ready for the next breaking sea but every manoeuvre has to be just right. Too much correction with the main rudder puts you on the other tack. Usually then the backed sail will tack you again, but the strain on the sails and the forestay sets teeth on edge. Getting it right took frightening minutes whereas normally the time taken is minimal. Of course, *Solitaire* had never tried to sail down the side of a mountain before.

Things looked up. Seas that had broken over us now pushed us forward in wild breath-taking surges. For minutes we would race in spray and a tumbling mass of white water. Advancing cliffs lifted us like a soaring eagle and we balanced above their snow-capped peaks before plunging down into emerald green fields, often out of control. *Solitaire* rushed forward, anxious to find peace and lick her wounds.

I fitted the trailing log line, which curved in a half circle, the weight and spinner like so many flying fish skipping over the ocean's surface. The plastic compass was returned to its cockpit holder, our course south-east. The northern winds drove us deeper into the Roaring Forties, but we were clawing our way east, working our way around South Africa and its Cape of Storms. Dead on my feet I went back to pumping the bilges. Over the past three days I had often thought that I was finished, that I could pump no more, that I could no longer survive without sleep. The seconds had turned into minutes, to hours, to days. Now if something went wrong I felt I could still carry on. I just hoped to God I didn't have to prove it.

When I started this voyage I thought that I could stand being afraid for five weeks and that at the end of that time I would still be sane and able to carry out normal everyday functions. It was a thought based on my past experience. I had not anticipated a situation when for three days I would believe every moment, every breath, could be my last. Oh well, three days gone!

After a while *Solitaire* settled down to look after us both. A few rogue waves still struck our beam. Now and again we would have 6 or 9in of water on the cockpit floor, but no longer were the seas flooding the lockers. Below, I stripped off every stitch and felt the glory of rubbing myself down with a dry towel, putting on a clean shirt, trousers and sweater and, for a special treat, donned Rex's thermal jacket. My wet weather gear I turned inside out to drip dry, had a cup of sweet tea and found some chocolate which I ate at the chart table with my head in my arms.

My mother was shaking me. I was 14 years old and it was time to get up, go downstairs and eat my morning porridge, time to put on my overalls and join the bus with half-asleep men, nodding, coughing, grey-faced men moving through their lives like zombies. I did not want to leave my bed to live this nightmare, tried to pull my legs into my chest to squeeze so small I would never be found, but my mother was banging my head. My mother never bangs my head.

I shocked awake, moving through 40 years in a second, exchanging one nightmare for another. *Solitaire* was in the teeth of a wild beast viciously shaking her from side to side, and she was leaning the wrong way. On this new tack I had slipped sideways. My legs had jammed under the chart table and my head was beating itself to death on the engine cover. When I had freed myself I stood on weak legs, trying to take in through blurred eyes what was happening. I slid back the hatch cover and looked into the face of a breaking wave, slammed the hatch shut and staggered back, only to fall on top of the water containers. From there I heard the wave hit and saw jets of water penetrating the hatch boards.

I threw off my jacket and sweater, for there was no point in getting them wet. It was then that I felt *Solitaire* start to swing onto her correct heading. Her backed headsail and the self-steering were striving to bring the wind on the right side of her stern while the main rudder that had been set to prevent her skidding and broaching would be working to keep the wind on the wrong side.

For a lifetime she seemed to balance on a knife-edge, rolling from side to side. I watched the breaking seas through her windows, first on one side, then on the other, feeling like a gambler who had bet his last dollar on the turn of a card. If she fell one way I would not have to go on deck but could have a hot meal. If she fell the wrong way I would have to put on wet storm clothes and return to hell.

If *Solitaire* could correct a backed headsail on her own it would mean I could sleep knowing she would take care of us. I tried to hedge my bet by throwing my weight behind it, bouncing off the starboard side as if I was trying to drive a hole through it. The bet paid off and *Solitaire* came back on course. The working jib swung across the deck with a shuddering whack whose vibrations ran through us for a full 60 seconds.

It was nearly noon so I must have been asleep for some four hours. I quickly inspected the deck and headsail by holding on to the mainsheet and popping my head around the pram cover. All seemed in order, although the sail looked as if it might rip at any second. The storm jib was still tied securely to the pulpit. The ropes securing the mainsail to the boom were holding.

But the conditions remained terrifying. Any man who claimed that he was unafraid I would have dismissed as a liar. *Solitaire* still slid down the sides of mountains and at any moment might broach. Once she had rolled on her side at speed she would simply keep rolling. Even if we survived it would be difficult to reach land without a mast. After we had passed South Africa our chances would improve as the motor could then be used to stagger us into port under jury-rig. At the moment if we tried to reach land, the Agulhas Current would sweep us into the South Atlantic.

I was afraid, but that was something I could live with. My fears were less constant than they had been in the past three days, coming and going now like storm clouds. There were even moments of pleasure. Not to be soaked and frozen was a delightful change. There are ways of finding sanity even in a world of horror. You can do normal everyday things, like paying more attention to the trivial than you would at home, despite the fact that your house might turn upside down at any second. Part of this fantasy was the cabin floor carpets. One of life's pleasures is sinking bare feet into a soft pile carpet when you leave your bed, maybe because as a boy it was always cold boards. Carpets can be used as a barometer, to gauge the weather and your own feelings. When they are warm and dry you are in trade winds and spirits are high. When they are damp you have the miseries. When they have 6in of water over them you are scared silly. With 6ft of water your worries are over.

At present there were two pieces of carpet on the cabin floor. One I could do nothing about since it was beneath the water containers. The aft carpet I decided to wring into the bilges, at the same time taking up the inspection cover to see how much water we had taken in the last four or five hours. *Solitaire*'s capacity to hold water before her cabin floor consists of a sump at the back of the keel that extends to its bottom, holding approximately 20 gallons. In normal conditions I pump it out once or twice a week, if only to remove smells and any gas that might have leaked from the stove. There is room for around another 40 gallons on top of the lead keel, bringing the water level to about 5in below the floor.

With this 60 gallons on board the bilges require pumping in any bad weather or it will splash through the inspection panels.

If in the Southern Ocean we took no more than 120 gallons a day we could manage quite well; pumping first thing in the morning and last thing at night would be sufficient. When I checked the bilges I thought we could last another two hours before I had to go on deck. Later I would fibreglass in the lockers, but that task I wanted to leave until as late in the voyage as possible. With both lockers sealed it would be difficult to dismantle the bilge pump to clear the blockages as I was unable to reach the seacock on the exhaust outlet.

For the first time since the storm I started to think of food and decided on a tin of stew with peas, and grapefruit for afters. I used to show my friends the logs of previous voyages, some of whom remarked how strange it was that in storms my writing became so much neater. I think this is similar to wringing out carpets; I try to hide my true feelings even from myself. If I write clearly I'm unafraid.

My log for that day read:

Managed to start sailing at 0500 hours GMT this morning. Working jib. Seas quite high and breaking. Self-steering holding reasonable course. Badly need sights for navigation. I don't want to go too far south because of ice. At the same time am concerned about the Agulhas Current.

After another stormy night the next day's log contained even fewer words: 'Still storm conditions. Rain, high seas. Not very nice.' During the night the winds dropped and dawn saw us becalmed in a massive swell, the sky still hazily grey and suspect. As I started to clean up the mess and dry the carpet I received a kick in the stomach. The ship's log records:

Now for the bad news. Seawater from the exhaust pipe has flooded back into the motor. I have drained the oil from the sump and turned over the motor by hand to try and clear the pistons. No spare engine oil. So in a day or two will use the old oil when it has settled and try to start the engine. This voyage is not going too well at the moment.

In fact I took off the side plate of the motor, first removing the starter. The day was spent turning the engine by hand to wash out the pistons with diesel fuel. As it worked its way through to the sump I cleaned it with toilet paper. I had counted on the engine to carry us at least 100 miles if the rigging gave way! I checked the seacock on the exhaust pipe but it seemed to be tightly closed. By afternoon I felt I had done all I could, so I re-assembled everything hoping that my first voyage experience of having to make do without the motor was not to be repeated.

Soon after I had finished drying the carpet, strong gusting winds returned to confuse us all: the sea, *Solitaire*, and the self-steering. Finally they settled to their old habits and direction, like some monster that had dropped off to sleep for a few hours and had awoken irritably, roaring its displeasure. The heaving seas took fright and ran before it with spray flying. Within a few hours we were back in the same old conditions, chased by white cliffs, surging forward on rolling surf – and I was back to kneeling on the bunks, my head hard against the cabin roof, trying to see the mad outside world. The one consolation was that my constipation was a thing of the past. Now my only concern was that there would be enough plastic bags to last the voyage.

On Tuesday, October 7th, we had been in the storm for nearly a week and *Solitaire* wallowed in high, breaking seas. However, there were a few gaps in the clouds and I managed to log our position, 40°42'S, 23°55'E – 42 miles into the Roaring Forties, 360 miles below Cape Agulhas. The winds had backed from north to west and now before *Solitaire* stretched the Indian Ocean, a pencil mark showing that we had rounded our first Cape.

For some days the thought of opening Rome's second parcel had tantalised me, not just for the goodies inside but for the friendship it represented. Its opening would record another milestone on our journey. I would not cheat, no matter how much I wanted to look inside, because that would mean I was giving way, and as that was not on I spent the day on my bunk with the present, looking at it, touching it. In the afternoon I managed to get a further sight, which proved that we were indeed well past the Cape. So I opened the parcel and used its contents for a special meal, finishing with two squares from a block of chocolate. The card enclosed I pinned above my chart table, the start of a new practice. Henceforward each card or letter stayed on show until replaced by a new one, whereupon the old went into the ship's log.

Our thirteenth week at sea had proved to be our worst. *Solitaire* had been in conditions I would have said no ship, let alone a yacht, could survive. Looking at the chart *Solitaire* had been in the worst possible position when the storm started, with hurricane force winds from the north whose speed increased as they swept down the western coast of South Africa. Off the Cape of Good Hope they would hit the Agulhas Current moving at up to 5 knots in a contrary direction. *Solitaire* had been lying in a massive east-flowing swell when the storm reached her. I can't see what more ingredients could have been added to make a storm worse.

Our survival inspired confidence that we really were going to make the voyage non-stop, that we had learned from my mistakes. The old book of rules for sailing a yacht around the world had been ripped to shreds and tossed over the side, old loyalties being replaced by new. The depression I had felt since leaving home I could at least understand. *Solitaire* and I were not making this voyage with the help of England, but in spite of its laws and bureaucracy.

Week 13 ended with our easing into the Indian Ocean. Our latitude dropped to 40°S, on the very edge of the Roaring Forties, the log showing that we had covered 8,099 miles with no major damage. The log for Thursday, October 9th, read: 'Three calendar months at sea. A good day, in fact one of the best.'

We continued to work our way slowly north, trying to find calmer conditions so that I could work on the motor, dry out *Solitaire* and take a deep breath before the next stage of our voyage.

CHAPTER EIGHT
Christmas Alone

Indian Ocean – Cape Horn
October 1980 – February 1981

Our prayers for calmer seas must have been a bit too strong since we spent the day with virtually no wind in a temperature shooting up to the mid-70s. *Solitaire* rolled, half asleep, her decks decorated by carpets, sleeping bags and wet weather gear. Our spirits went through the roof when, having replaced the sump oil, the motor burst into life. I ran it for an hour, then turned off the engine water intake and allowed it to tick over for a minute to clear the seawater from the block and exhaust pipe. I felt that most of the water had found its way into the cylinders not through the seacock but because the exhaust pipe had not been drained.

All in all it was a red-letter day. One great pleasure at sea is listening to music. The BBC and American Overseas Services play a few hours a day. However, once you are within a few hundred miles of a coast you can pick up local stations. I now had the South African Capital station flooding some old favourites into *Solitaire*. That night another special dinner. I baked bread and covered the crusts with pâté from Rome's parcel, finishing off the menu with sliced onions. They had lasted for three months and I now had only two left, the last of my fresh vegetables.

I lay on top of a dry sleeping bag, wearing dry trousers topped by a dry shirt and sweater, listening to music from another world!

We had retreated from the Roaring Forties and were now 84 miles beyond their reach. Tomorrow, refreshed and rested, we would drop south again not to do battle but to assuage the sea's anger. Never again would *Solitaire* lie helpless without sails or self-steering.

The next cape was Cape Leeuwin on the west coast of Australia, 4,500 miles away. Above latitude 40° the chart indicated westerlies (over our stern) around Force 5 to 6, with seventeen per cent gales indicated. Below 40° gales went up to twenty per cent, although it was not this that decided my sailing above the Roaring Forties; it was that the extreme limit for icebergs during October/November was just below this latitude. I already had experience of sailing in cold seas rounding the Cape of Good Hope and was not keen to repeat that misery.

The man who made the chart must have smuggled it out of a sewer or the Houses of Parliament; had I completely reversed his wild claims for the next 2,000 miles they would have been closer to being right. The projected stern winds of Force 5 to 6 came on our nose, gusting 3 to 4. No calm periods for this area were indicated, yet at least once a week we spent a day bouncing up and down in a 30ft swell completely devoid of wind. The game the charts were about to play started with an innocent log entry:

Grand morning, warm 60°F, clear blue sky. Light winds from the east (the way we want to go). Smashing music still from South Africa and making the most of it before it fades. Some sail repair work this morning. Reading Annegret's book from the parcel, James Michener's The Source. *Winds increased to Force 4. Full main and working jib. Would use number two genoa but must save it for later. Now for spam and tomatoes from the parcel, bread from yesterday.*

Next day a short entry read: 'No sights. Back to beating into steep seas. High wind squalls. Two reefs in the mainsail. Grey sky, raining.' And for week after week that's how it continued. Winds increased to gale force and always from the direction in which we were trying to point. *Solitaire* sailed under grey skies, through drizzle and breaking seas. Now and again she would find a smooth patch of ocean and gather speed only to drop off the top of the next wave, mast and rigging a-shudder.

For days I was unable to get a sun sight. The winds were pushing us north, but with all the Indian Ocean to play in there was no danger from bad navigation. Lack of progress was the main worry. Despite my shortage of sails I had expected to make 100–120 miles a day in following winds, whereas our best run was 80 miles and that not in the right direction. I dared not go too far north as, apart from extending the distance, we could lose a helping current.

Fear was not part of the reason. The waves that came towards us were normal, if high marching; the only problem was dropping down the other side as they went through. We started with full main and working jib heading ENE against a wind from ESE! After three or four days it would increase from Force 3 to 4, which caused us to reef. On the sixth day it would veer for a few hours, and when in the perfect direction for us it would drop altogether, leaving us becalmed in a confused sea. Then, surprise, surprise, it would hit us as a gale from the north-east! Although angry and confused, the seas had no time to attack *Solitaire* in force.

We have three reef points on the mainsail, the third of which I do not use as it turns the canvas into a minute trysail. The slab reefing boom has only two reefing ropes through the boom, so if you want to put in a third reef point you have to release and use one of the other ropes, and standing on deck at night in a gale is not the right time to attempt this operation. Having been caught out once, whenever we became becalmed I would put in the third reef and nine times out of ten it paid off. The self-steering with its small wind vane was always in use and *Solitaire* was happy pointing into waves. The odd one might push over her nose, causing seas to break over her deck, but few entered her cockpit. The temperature was back in the sixties and the cabin, if damp with so much rain, fog and drizzle, was not unbearable. And I no longer had to wear sea boots.

I was back to reading my books and baking bread every third day. Wet weather gear was unnecessary apart from when I went on deck. Most of the time I lay on my bunk, a sleeping bag covering my legs. For hours I would look out of the main hatch watching a variety of sea birds: soaring albatrosses, with their 10ft wing-span, I could enjoy all day. Despite my moans and groans I was satisfied with the voyage so far. I would have liked the wind to have been from over our stern, and I wished we had more sails, and more food... but we were progressing slowly. Life could have been worse.

Week 14 passed like the hands of a faulty clock: *Solitaire* trying to reach 12 o'clock while winds from 2 o'clock meant we could only make 11 o'clock. The hands stuck for four days with winds gusting between Force 3 and 6, then they moved slowly to 6 o'clock and over our stern. Just as *Solitaire* was about to say, 'Thank-you-very-much', they died, leaving us bouncing around in a confused sea after a run of 556 miles. We would curse their sense of humour, to which they would reply angrily from 10 o'clock with racing clouds and screaming breath.

In week 15, time passed by like the seas cascading down our decks. The course adjustment on the self-steering broke, and was mended while the clock ticked on. On Friday, October 17th, its fingers registered our hundredth day at sea.

Week 16 saw 565 miles logged and on Friday, October 24th, the heart that ticked away the seconds of my life celebrated its 55th birthday – sometimes faint, sometimes strong, now it beat with *Solitaire*'s. It slowed and raced and would stop with hers.

Some 1,200 miles from South Africa, in winds gusting up to Force 7, the south-easterlies pushed us further and further north. *Solitaire*, a lonely speck 360 miles above the Roaring Forties, forced her way to Australia, trying to edge back south to pass under its west coast. It was time for Rome's third parcel and I prepared a special dinner on a dancing stove, eating it with a birthday card propped on my knee, dreaming of those at home.

In week 17 we passed the 10,000 miles mark, with 746 miles logged, the best for some time. For a few days the winds behaved as the charts indicated, gusting Force 6 to 7 from the west, showing how badly I needed a big headsail. I had the double-reefed mainsail up as long as I could, but when strong stern winds arrived they overrode the self-steering luffing *Solitaire* off course into them.

We slipped back to 517 miles in week 18, often becalmed, and the winds, when they came, were more from the west. I started to appreciate the height of the Southern Ocean swell. I had regretted not having a new number two genoa but from now on there would be few days when its absence would not be mentioned in the log as we passed our fourth month at sea.

Then I discovered our first crop of goose-barnacles under the stern and found pimples on our white-painted topsides, doubly annoying because I had spent good money I could ill afford repainting *Solitaire*. I could have saved time and labour by buying more sails or food instead. We sailed 200 miles north of the small, uninhabited Amsterdam Islands, which lie just above the Roaring Forties, although I had intended to sail below them. The south-easterlies decided otherwise. Australia was now 1,800 miles away and we started to pick up their broadcasts. On Monday, November 10th, I heard that Ronald Reagan was the new US President. More importantly I found we had used half of the 80 gallons of water with which I had set out.

In week 19 we clocked 746 miles, surpassing the 120-mile mark in a couple of days. For the most part the winds obeyed the charts and came from astern, which meant we could pick our course, so I started to slip south to pass under Cape Leeuwin. The end of the week saw us just 150 miles above latitude 40° where I changed our first gas bottle, which meant we had two left. One worry, now that I was down to my last spinner, were the albatrosses chasing it, trying to take a bite. I threw them some stale bread, which they spat out, screeching that I had tried to poison them, and went back to spinner chasing. The last thing I really wanted was to drive them away, as they were one of my main sources of entertainment. Cape Leeuwin was now some 800 miles away. It was time for another parcel.

As I had no chart of Australia I thought I should do something about it, especially after Rome's concern about my lack of navigational aids when I left England. I had said it was something to worry about tomorrow and tomorrow was now today. So I used the chart of the Indian Ocean, changing the figures of longitude to suit Australia, plotting all the main D/F stations and joining them up to make the coastline. If week 19 was good, week 20 was bad. At the end of it we had been at sea for 140 days, logged 12,616 miles since leaving England and were just about to drop under Australia's western coast. But it was the week in which I found that we had used up more than half of our flour and that 45 of our 80 gallons of water had gone (although I tried catching water off the mainsail in one downpour with some success). All the good books had been read but I started to re-read them for the second time around; what with my marriages and voyages it was something I was making a habit of.

I started to pick up Perth radio station, including their weather forecasts, but they gave little help. Their temperature was in the mid-60s, whereas ours dropped as *Solitaire* was about to enter the Roaring Forties again.

Then we began to pass through areas sown with nine per cent gales on the chart. They were right about the storms if not about their direction (as when we were about to round the Cape of Good Hope), for we had gale force winds from the wrong direction, this time the south-east, at the wrong time.

We were still about 360 miles from Cape Leeuwin, which lay to our north-east. For the last three days we had sailed in rain without sun sights, relying on dead reckoning. At one time I thought the wind was veering and reduced to storm jib and headed directly towards Cape Leeuwin, the best course *Solitaire* could hold. It was a bad storm and we took on a good deal of water from starboard. The cockpit started filling again for the first time since leaving South African waters. There was no panic as only the odd wave broke over us and it was far from freezing. Indeed, on deck I did not even bother to wear sea boots. It was more a case of annoyance than fear.

Weeks earlier I had traced a course to sail under Australia, to re-enter the Forties, and since the middle of the Indian Ocean we had made good this track. Now, at the last minute, we were being pushed north towards land. After two days the storm dropped and we were becalmed 250 miles below the Australian coast with 80 miles to go before I could open my Cape Leeuwin parcel.

Week 21 started with a good heart, Force 2 to 3 winds coming back from the north-west. A warm day with a flat sea – ideal for fibreglassing the cockpit lockers and the bottom board in the main hatch. It was a job I had put off for a variety of reasons. The first and deciding factor was that all across the Indian Ocean I had only to pump out the bilges once or twice in good weather, perhaps three or four times in storms. When I had glassed-in the rear locker permanently it would be difficult to open the exhaust seacock. True, it could be reached from inside the boat, but only with a tight squeeze and wasted time.

The main locker that ran down the side of the cockpit was immediately below where the bilge pump was fitted. To clean the pump the locker cover had to be removed in order to hold a spanner on the inside nuts and turn the screws on the outside at the same time. The pump had jammed often – even a piece of matchstick would do the trick! It could be serviced through a small door by the engine compartment but then you had to clamp vice grips onto the nuts and make your way back to the cockpit, with screwdriver, at least three times. Not something I wanted to try on a roller-coaster. I was thankful it had not jammed during the Cape of Good Hope storm. The hatch bottom board could have been screwed in place and then fibreglassed. With a following sea both boards had to be left in place but one of my pleasures was that on a good day I could remove the two boards and watch the birds perform – in fresh air.

On Thursday, November 27th, I started to turn *Solitaire* into a submarine by spending the day fibreglassing-in the cockpit locker. In future it would be hard to repair the bilge pump, but with the mouth of the bigger in-taker of seawater closed there would be less cause to use it.

At 1am GMT that Friday we were scheduled to be due south of Cape Leeuwin in 38°39'S, 260 miles below the cape and 81 miles above the Roaring Forties. 12,656 miles and 142 days out of Lymington: time to open my next parcel and enjoy a special treat of steak and kidney pie, peas and powdered potato. My friend's letter was ceremoniously pinned above the chart table, replacing the birthday card, which went into the ship's log. The final entry in the log that day read: 'Rome, Annegret. Thank you – God bless.'

Solitaire now dropped south to sail under our next cape, off Tasmania. I wanted to pass approximately 120 miles below the island at latitude 46°S, putting us 360 miles into the Roaring Forties. If yachtsmen had been surprised to see *Solitaire* rounding the Cape of Good Hope on a piece of writing paper they would have been even more confused to see her sailing past a red ink drawing of Australia set in the middle of the Indian Ocean!

My pilot charts were unsuitable for navigation, as a notice at the top of each stated, and a further few words stopped my putting too much trust in them: 'Founded upon the researches made in the early part of the 19th century by Matthew Fontaine Maury, while serving as a lieutenant in the United States Navy.' I felt I owed Matthew an apology for thinking he was a Member of Parliament. I must have had him turning in his grave even if he had been buried for a century or more.

Using such charts is like playing a game of chess with a crooked gambler while blindfolded. They are made up of little squares similar to those on a chessboard, each square containing the percentage of gales and calms, and the force and direction of winds to be expected. Although you know full well there's not a hope in hell of winning the game it's the only one in town to play, jumping from square to square trying to avoid the storms and areas of calm. We started to pick up local radio stations and became part of small communities, sharing their pleasures and tragedies. We sneaked into towns like ghosts, unheard and unseen, and leaving without the occupants ever knowing that we had visited.

Sunday, November 30th. No sights, wind increased last night and moved to south bloody east, right on our course. Finished up with the storm jib and three reefs in the main, slamming into rough seas. Albany Radio, 300 miles to the north, reported winds of 30–40 knots but at sea the gusts are much higher than that. A man and a woman have been swept off a yacht and lost during a race from Perth. Solitaire *and I felt their sorrow but our bowed heads went unnoticed.*

On the morning of Tuesday, December 2nd, we had our first visitor. People often ask me how I keep my mind occupied at sea. 'Do you talk to yourself? What is there to think about?' In fact mind and brain work harder as a storm can present a dozen problems at once. Even a small incident can set you thinking for days. Ideas shoot in all directions like an egg splattering on concrete. On this particular morning I was reading in my bunk when there was a crash at the top of the mast, followed by a squawking and clattering as something fell inside the rigging. The largest and most confused albatross I had ever seen filled the cockpit. We eyed one another cautiously until I realised the bird's wing was caught in the mainsheet.

'Me friend,' I said as I released it. Then I remembered that Christmas was only 23 days away and this bird was ten times larger than any turkey I had ever seen. But there was no way I could kill it. In any case, as every seaman knows, it is bad luck to kill an albatross, and seamen have starved rather than harm one feather of their heads. The creatures of the sea were part of my family. We lived and died together. They entertained me with their beauty and grace. There was nothing on God's earth that would make me kill this bird and eat it. But if it was injured I could make a lead for it and turn it into a pet, taking it for walkies around the deck every morning. Should it die of its injuries I could then eat it for there's nothing in the rules that says you can't eat an albatross that dies from natural causes. Suddenly I became aware how lovely this bird was, with its half-frightened eyes and panting chest. I remembered then how many months it was since I had last seen, let alone spoken to, a woman. If it was bad luck to kill an albatross what would happen if you merely tried to seduce one? Was it a criminal offence? I could see the headline, 'Round-the-world yachtsman accused of screwing albatross'. I would make millions. Newspapers would queue up to buy my story and I might even be able to afford some decent charts. This line of thinking came to an abrupt end when I realised that I hadn't the foggiest idea whether this particular albatross was male or female. A seducer of birds, maybe, gay never.

I went to get a piece of rope so that I could prevent it hurting itself further but he must have misunderstood my intentions and shot over the stern like Concorde. As I watched him circling over *Solitaire* I noticed the yellow superstructure of a ship dropping below the horizon, my first sighting since leaving the Atlantic.

Week 21 saw off 596 miles, my Christmas dinner and what might have turned out to be a long and lasting friendship.

Week 22 went by with old Matthew the crooked gambler up to his tricks. We logged 590 miles through storms where there were supposed to be no storms and calms that should not have been there either. The former did not worry me but the latter did as we were making less than 600 miles a week in areas noted for their constant following winds and where I anticipated covering between 700 and 800 miles.

Week 22 started with *Solitaire* entering the Roaring Forties and ended 240 miles deep into them in latitude 44°S. With a number two genoa we could have made more use of favourable winds. Instead we were running out of time and the voyage was taking much too long. Week 22 ended on December 10th, after five months at sea. We were holding a good course with winds gusting from the north-west around Force 6 under clear blue skies and with a cabin temperature of 66°F. But the crew was worried, very worried.

The day before I had made the first check of food stock since leaving England. Until then I had imagined we were reasonably well off for supplies. True, I had exceeded my ration from time to time, not because I was hungry, for hunger was nothing more than an ache in the tummy. It was the side effects that caused concern, the loss of body weight, of sailing instincts and the will to survive. After five months at sea things were starting to go wrong, thanks to an ill-planned diet. Because I was spending long hours on my bunk, I was developing bedsores which I would bathe with salt water. My teeth and gums had given no trouble in the past; now when I cleaned them the gums bled.

Annegret had given me a bottle of multivitamins from which I was taking one a day. Whether it helped I did not know, nor whether washing my back in seawater and cleaning my teeth twice a day did more harm than good. These were small problems that, ashore, would take only a few days to clear up, a few good meals with fresh vegetables, fruit, eggs and milk. A few hot baths. Nevertheless they were problems that gave me a good deal of concern as the log shows:

0000 GMT, Tuesday, December 9th, 1980. Once more becalmed for 24 hours and concerned by slow progress. Either it is blowing so hard that I have to take down the main to prevent weather helm overriding the self-steering, or there's insufficient wind. Since the Cape of Good Hope I have only been able to use the working and storm jibs. The old number two genoa is far too weak for these gusty, squally seas. We are 600 miles due west of Tasmania with the Australian coast about the same distance north. Have logged 13,601 miles. If we were 1,000 miles further on I should have considered us halfway.

Five months at sea with the worst to come and at our present rate of progress we could be at sea for a further six months. My food list shows that two-thirds of our supplies have been used.

Stews, 15.3 oz tins	**Greens, 10 oz tins**
Chicken, 12 to start, now 6	*String beans, 12, now 4*
Beef, 12, now 4	*Peas, 12, now 5*
Steak and kidney, 12, now 1	*Mixed vegetables, 12, now 5*
Minced beef, 12, now 8	*Started with 36, now 14*
Savoury mince, 12, now 6	
Started with 60, now 25	

Baked beans, 8oz, 48, now 34
Spam, 24, now 6
Sardines, 12, now 6
Marmite, 1lb jars, 2, now 1
Bovril, 1lb jars, 2 now 1
Jam, small jars, 12, now 2

Fruit, small tins
Fruit Salad, 12, now 9
Grapefruit, 12, now 5
Started with 24, now 14

Flour, 70lbs, now 15lbs
Rice, 60lbs, now 50lbs
Water, 80 gallons, now 30 gallons
Eggs, onions, fresh vegetables and yeast: finished
Tea, coffee, sugar, milk: no problems. I still have six of the ten parcels Rome and Annegret gave me.

I'm well into the second time round with my books. Oh well, it will soon be Christmas, with another parcel to open.

Apart from the food I was concerned about my parents, having told them I would be away ten months, fully expecting to take no longer than nine. Over the years I'd caused them quite a few sleepless nights, what with my broken marriages and forever chasing off to strange lands. For the first time at sea I wished I had a transmitter aboard.

Week 23 saw the start of some of the voyage's hardest time en route to Tasmania. Christmas was approaching and every time I turned on the radio they were singing about it, the first Christmas I had ever spent alone. And not just alone, but ignored. The log reveals some of the problems of sailing close to a friendly shore, hearing a woman's voice and longing to be in the same room with her sharing the same music, breathing the same air, to be close to another human being.

Thursday, December 11th. *No sights possible, sea very rough. A good run of 120 miles in 24 hours on a broad reach under storm jib in westerly winds.*

Friday, December 12th. *Latitude 46°19'S. Storms dropped during the night and the day now bright with a few scattered clouds. Swell large and winds light with mini gusts still from the*

west, was soaked when a wave smashed through the main hatch
boards to find me without storm gear on, about to eat my only
meal of the day (rice with two squares of melted chocolate on
top). We both got soaked and meal was ruined. Bilge pump packed
up so spent the morning repairing it with some difficulty as main
locker cover was now glassed-in. Lucky it isn't Friday the 13th!

Saturday, December 13th. *Rain squalls so no sights. Little*
wind during night. The lights of two ships sighted on horizon.
Could have been fishing as they stayed in sight for a long time.
Winds from north-east this morning, anything from Force 3 to 7,
ending with one hell of a squall. After which they started gusting
from south-west. Good show. Now on course with working jib
only as gusts too strong for main. Temperature still in the low 50s.
Nights are a bit cold and seas chilly. Able to go on deck without
sea boots and socks but feet slowly turning blue.

At 8.30am GMT a large white fishing boat cut across *Solitaire*'s
bow, giving me a few grey hairs. I had watched his approach for
some time, waving my red ensign. I thought he was going astern of
me when he suddenly turned and nearly removed *Solitaire*'s bow. I
dropped my camera, with which I was trying to take pictures, and
dashed to release the self-steering. When I straightened up he was
past us showing his stern.

For the first time since leaving England I tried to speak to
someone. 'You bloody bastaaaard,' I called but I don't think that
was his name. On the side of his white hull was HHJE, which was
unpronounceable.

0855 Second fishing boat passed astern, JRIU. I think they
must be Japanese. A few small dolphins, first for months, are
around. Ships are coming from the south. Must be returning to
Australia from fishing grounds.

2200 Sight shows us 141°38'E. Sunday in Australia. Have
just heard Family Favourites *with Pete Murray. Makes one a bit*
homesick.

Sunday, December 14th. *0225 GMT. Noon position, 45°38'S*
142°15'E, 120 miles south of Tasmania.

Monday. *Black sky, storms from south-south-east. Hard on the wind under main with three reefs and storm jib. Melbourne Radio reports a low pressure area over Tasmania. Must keep hard on the wind as I don't want to be pushed north. Bit down last night to see my tri-navigation light hanging over the side at the top of the mast. Not that I've used it much apart from the odd ship.*

Tuesday. *Becalmed for eight hours. Slight breeze from the south-east with a high swell inhibiting progress. Charts show no winds from the east or south-east and no calms. They have been useless since Cape Town. Harry Secombe has just been on Hobart Radio, now 190 miles to the north of us. Seems he is doing a show there. Very tempting to spend Christmas in Hobart after all this bouncing about but I can't let* Solitaire *down with these thoughts. Have just checked the trailing log, three bloody miles in five hours and Hobart Radio forecasts light bloody winds tomorrow from the south bloody east. Blast, blast, bloody blast. I was hoping to be well past New Zealand by Christmas. Now I have no chance and Hobart keeps offering water to a man dying of thirst.*

Wednesday, December 17th. *Hobart's weather report gives temperatures around 50°F with rain to come. At present we have blue skies, scattered clouds and light airs from south bloody east. Full main and working jib as I'm trying to save number two genoa for later. We have now passed under our third cape.* Solitaire *is one of the few to sail so low in this area. Chichester, Alex Rose and Knox-Johnston all sailed above Tasmania. One day we will have to visit this island, which seems to have taken the best that England can offer and improved on it. Hobart's radio broadcasts are some of the friendliest I have ever heard. As I write they are talking about a Christmas tree in Hobart Square and asking for tins of dog food to be put under it for the stray dogs' home. The only thing stopping me from going in is the desire to see family and friends. And I can't let* Solitaire *down because of a mere tug on the heartstrings. This afternoon it's bright and sunny and we have more wind. Strangely although south of Hobart and closer to the icebergs our temperature, 13°C, is higher than theirs. More*

Japanese fishing boats in sight. Week's run 547 miles, can't even break the 600 mark.

Week 24 started with high swells and heaving seas as we dropped south to latitude 49° to round our third cape below New Zealand. The lower reaches of the Tasman Sea have a high percentage of gales. Chichester and my American friend had capsized in the Tasman, both rolled over in hurricane force winds in a sea whose bed alternates between anything from 2,000 to a few hundred fathoms.

Our route would take us between Stewart Island and Auckland Island, 200 miles apart (between them the smaller Snares Island), just below New Zealand. I planned to sail between Snares and Auckland as it seemed the safest way, preferring, as I do, to keep clear of shelving seabeds. Now there was no choice. The waters we would be sailing through drop to 80 fathoms. The chart showed names like Sub Antarctic Slope, Solander Trough, Pukaki Rise, Campbell Plateau... if the beautiful names of the South Pacific islands fell from the tongue like poetry, these belonged to a horror story. That we were sailing through the Roaring Forties, reaching for the Furious Fifties, did nothing to stop the hairs on the back of my neck rising.

Hobart's friendly radio station gave a final warning, gales from Brisbane down to Tasmania, then a last song from Cilla Black, 'Day by Day' from the show *Godspell*. I have never really liked Miss Black's voice, a bit too high and shrill for my taste, but at that moment everything seemed perfect... the fading, friendly island, Christmas shopping, that lovely dog food under the tree, the words of the song, 'Day by day, dear Lord, I pray to see thee more clearly, love thee more dearly.' Someone turned on a tap and tears flooded my eyes while two rivers ran down my face. When the song ended the tap was turned off.

Solitaire rode the Tasman Sea as on a big dipper. Pushing her way through head-on gales she rolled drunkenly in confused swells that were enormous. Despite those seas we received a small Christmas present: we broke the 600-mile barrier with a run of 617 miles for the week ending December 24th and that Christmas Eve I spent listening to New Zealand's local radio. The next day, with the parcel from Rome and Annegret, would certainly prove my big day:

Christmas Day, 1980, the start of my 25th week at sea. Food is now a problem. For two weeks I have been cooking rice to last three days, mixing in a tin of soup or mixed vegetables. My yeast has gone but I still try to bake the flour by itself. Yesterday, for a change, I tried to fry this hard bread with a tin of beans, and finished having to suck the fried bread as if I were eating a stick of rock. The morning is grey and miserable with a faint breeze on our nose from the east, the sails just about filling and the self-steering struggling to hold a course. We are 260 miles west of Snares Island, drifting to pass below this island and New Zealand. I have managed to get a few unreliable sun sights through the misty haze but they do tie up with dead reckoning.

Now for my parcel, after a wash and a change of clothes. Just about to open my present, I heard a splash at *Solitaire*'s stern and found a seal jumping out of the water to reach a flock of small grey birds that were teasing it. The way he snapped and whirled around with just his head out of the water reminded me of my old dog. Then I opened my present and started crying. It was not that my friends had remembered me on the other side of the world – and Lord knows I needed the things inside – it was the caring and effort, the thought behind their gift. There was a Christmas dinner with all the trimmings, pudding, a cake with a candle to put on top, a cracker, a bottle of wine, chocolate, a lovely tin of salmon and, perhaps best of all, a Christmas card. Rome and Annegret apologised for omitting the traditional Christmas tree. What puzzled me was how they managed to find all these things in July when I left.

I cried not because I was lonely, or hurt or sad. I was doing something I had wanted to achieve in life but there are times when people show acts of kindness for which words can express no real gratitude. At such times the only way you can show your feeling is with tears. At that moment I would have given anything to wish another human being, 'Merry Christmas'.

I ate only half my dinner, saving the rest for Boxing Day, then spent the afternoon listening to the New Zealand parties whom I toasted with wine. For tea I had cake, and for supper a few squares of chocolate. I could not remember the last time I had had so many meals in one day. The salmon was something to look forward to in the future and, with rice, it would last for two days. *Solitaire* had a holiday, too. The wind died completely. As we both slept, dreaming of the future and Cape Horn, the current carried us three miles in 12 hours.

Boxing Day, 1980. The weatherman gave me a late Christmas present with a clear blue sky for 30 minutes, sufficient to obtain some good sights after three days of fog and drizzle. There are less than 200 miles to Snares and Auckland Islands, which lie some 150 miles apart. After months of sailing in open seas I feel Solitaire *is trying to thread a needle.*

We threaded it in week 25, a week when more baby black seals came to play around us, and a week when I discovered I had only 22 gallons of fresh water left. I tried to make progress by using the old number two genoa, watching it like a hawk for fear it should split in the breeze. It was also the week in which we picked up a new radio station, Dunedin, our nearest possible port, where I heard of the murder of a young girl by five boys. Several weapons had been used, including a cricket bat. It seemed particularly horrible that something that can give so much pleasure should be used in this way, and to kill at a time when the human race was giving thanks. A tragedy for the victim's parents and for the boys as well. *Solitaire* and I often felt that we were from another planet, circling mother earth, puzzled by the means of destruction – planes, tanks, rockets, cricket bats.

Week 25 and 1980 ended on Wednesday, December 31st. I made an entry in the ship's log: '1200 GMT, 2359 New Year's Eve in New Zealand, and spent the night listening to New Zealand welcoming in the New Year. Still 12 hours to go back home. And in large letters I added, "Happy New Year to Folks Back Home".'

If puzzled by the outside world I tried to bring sanity and order into my own by logging our position and objectives on December 30th:

Distance (by Walker trailing log): 15,300 miles.

Time at sea: 175 days.

The four most southerly Capes rounded:

1. October 6th, 1980, week 13, Cape of Good Hope, South Africa.

2. November 28th, 1980, week 21, Cape Leeuwin, Australia.

3. December 17th, 1980, week 23, Tasmania.

4. December 30th, 1980, week 25, Stewart Island, New Zealand.

Cape Horn, 5,000 miles to the east, will be the fifth and last.

Yacht Solitaire: *At present in good shape, her hull clean apart from barnacles on her stern and weed trailing from around her propeller and the bottom of her skeg. I can't be sure of the keel's condition. This is better than I could have expected and I'm pleased with Herbert Ochs' antifoul paint. It is possible the hull will clean when in southern ice.*

Rigging: Always a worry, but no problems so far.

Sails: Very good. Have used only the mainsail, working jib and storm jib since the Cape of Good Hope. Shortage of sails a major problem. My old number two genoa is in reserve for the return trip from Cape Horn.

Self-steering: Good at present, if a bit noisy. Have not had to waste time at tiller.

Food: Have cut down over past weeks. Rome's food parcels have been a godsend. Should be OK.

Water: My main worry at present as I have only 22 gallons left out of the original 80 and still 5,500 miles to go to next possible port, Falkland Islands. Hope to catch rainwater off mainsail before then.

Weather so far: Surprised by winds from east and south-east. From Equator to halfway across the Indian Ocean pilot charts hideously wrong, but pleased with temperature, never much below 50°F. And I'm still not wearing sea boots. Sweaters and trousers worn in sleeping bag.

Crew: His worst time was in Cape of Good Hope storm. Feels his slow progress has let down friends. Keenly anticipating rounding Cape Horn to be on the home straight. Worried about mother and father, having had no contact for six months.

Week 26, Thursday, January 1st, 1981 found *Solitaire* sailing away from the east coast of New Zealand with only two small islands, Antipodes and Bounty (90 miles apart and some 250 miles dead ahead), separating her from her goal, Cape Horn. The islands themselves posed no navigational problems, and at worst I could sail above Bounty Island into the Pacific. But they were the last land before Cape Horn, the point where the shelf that extends around New Zealand with its shallows would end, the seas dropping from a mere 200 to around 2,500 fathoms.

With the start of the New Year we had to change over to our 1981 Almanac, which Rome had managed to buy at a reduced price along with my few charts. The parcel he had given me for rounding the bottom of New Zealand was still in reserve. If this was cheating at least it was cheating on the right side. The problem was that it came too close to the Christmas present. Food, or the lack of it, was becoming more and more of a worry. First it had been my bleeding gums, then back sores, now I was noticing more bodily changes. My knee bones and hips were starting to project, and using *Solitaire*'s winches was proving an increasing strain. When I noticed a new symptom I tended to eat more than my official ration and next day would examine my arms, expecting to see developing layers of fat. Alas, it made no difference. All that happened was the loss of another tin of stew or fruit.

The parcel for rounding New Zealand was opened as we passed 35 miles below Bounty Island, with one more present, the Cold Weather Parcel, to open before Cape Horn.

The biggest bonus on the voyage so far had been how much warmer it had been than I had anticipated. During the Cape of Good Hope storm I froze, and firmly expected something similar of the Southern Ocean. In fact, off South Africa had proved the coldest part of the voyage to date. Now we were sailing at latitude 49°S, well below the iceberg limit, although the seas were bitterly cold. To have fallen over the side would have meant death in minutes, but the cabin temperature was still around 50°F, whereas I had anticipated frost on the deck and icicles on the rigging. As it was I was still running around barefoot. *Solitaire* was wet below and a line I had strung to dry my smalls had little effect, but lying under my two sleeping bags was not the teeth-chattering experience I had anticipated.

Soon after passing Bounty Island we crossed longitude 180° and had two Tuesdays in one week. Navigational rules changed again: now the degrees would decrease as we sailed homewards. Entering the deep waters of the Pacific what I had been dreading happened, two bad gales one after the other. Normally they would have given me no concern, coming as they did from the west and over *Solitaire*'s stern. The seas rushing across the shallow banks below New Zealand were neither dangerous nor particularly steep or high, but their speed was phenomenal and the first storm ripped the plastic cover off the self-steering gear. During a brief spell of calm I replaced it and a worn plastic gear selector knob at the same time.

We were thus more or less ready for the second storm, which arrived shortly before dark, the breaking waves coming through so fast that *Solitaire* was for ever pushed beam on to them and without help would so have remained during the night. It was one of those situations you find yourself in now and again, when wave speed seems to be twice as fast as wind speed. I changed into storm gear with extra sweaters and prepared to spend a night, black with racing clouds, in the cockpit. I could hear the seas bearing down on us before I could see the flashing phosphorus of breaking waves rushing *Solitaire* forward. I felt I was walking a tight-rope using the tiller as a balancing pole while I tried to hold *Solitaire* atop a knife-edge and stop her falling on her side. As the waves went through there would be a back-wash when the tiller would lose its grip and I would have to work hard to get back in position for the next. I steered by scattered stars flashing on and off as speeding clouds chased the rollers.

By dawn I needed a rest. I was tired but it was a satisfied tiredness. *Solitaire*, the sea and I had spent an almost enjoyable night, each playing his or her part without taking too many liberties. Politely the seas had kept out of the cockpit and for once *Solitaire* had been glad of my helping hand on her tiller. As for me, well, it's always satisfying to feel needed for something more than a sail change or a bilge pump.

Week 26 ended on a Tuesday and I struggled to work out how I had managed to lose a day. My navigational figures were still coming out correct so I did not worry too much about it. The week's run was 682 miles.

Week 27 passed with no tragedies, although I ruined the film in Rome's camera. I had a choice of keeping the half of film with the whale photos or the half with the photos of the Japanese boats. I plumped for the whales. The sores on my back worsened and I tried washing them with a strong solution of seawater and Dettol. My gums bled even when left uncleaned and new bones I did not even know I had started to develop. I baked golf balls of bread, sawed them into washers and fried them. Spread with a thin film of jam they could be sucked like pebbles and I would enter in the log that I was on the pill. If they provided any nourishment my bones ignored it and stuck out in protest.

On Friday, January 9th, *Solitaire* and I had been alone at sea for six months. The idea of rounding Cape Horn had been born during our stay in Tahiti in 1976. Five years later all that stood between us and our ambition were a few thousand miles of deep water. Thinking of the seas to come I glassed in the lower board of the main hatch, which I hated doing as I was now virtually sealed below. The rear cockpit cover remained to be glassed but that I could leave to the last minute. The week's run was 640 miles, 16,695 in all and 4,000 miles short of Cape Horn.

A week later we were 631 miles closer, still experiencing gales and confused seas, which baffled *Solitaire* and crew. During a heavy rainfall I managed to collect 7 gallons of water via the mainsail. Mostly I complained about my lack of headsails. Often I had to drop the mainsail when the wind increased because of too much weather helm and would have given anything for a strong number two genoa.

Time passed quickly, marked only by pencil on a chart. One day a whale surfaced alongside us as I was putting a reef in the main. One minute the sea was empty (birds apart), the next we had an upside-down super-tanker alongside. It took some moments to appreciate that something so large could be alive. Although there is much that scares the living daylights out of me, creatures of the sea manage only to rouse my intense interest in their activities. I dashed below for a camera but by the time I returned the whale had gone. At no time did I feel it threatened *Solitaire* and for a long time I lingered in the cockpit and felt lonely when it failed to reappear.

We had some vicious storms, during one of which *Solitaire* was knocked on her side and the Bosun compass in the rear of the cockpit leapt out of its plastic holder and finished wedged against a gas bottle. I had to make a dash to retrieve it between breaking waves, minus wet weather gear or harness. There were days when we sailed under clear blue skies, the ocean swell hardly noticed below decks. *Solitaire* snoozed along at 4 knots with no more noise or movement than when sitting in her berth at Lymington.

Then we passed our point of no return, much as jet aircraft do when flying the Atlantic. From now on *Solitaire* would stand a better chance of surviving by rounding Cape Horn rather than returning to New Zealand, and this engendered a great sense of relief. We would round it, possibly without mast or instruments, food or water, but dead or alive we would pass Cape Horn.

In week 29 we recorded 630 miles, and the following week 679 more. I ran the engine for the last time and glassed in the rear cockpit locker, which meant that from now on I would have to crawl through from the cabin to reach the exhaust pipe seacock. There were a hundred things I wished I could have done for *Solitaire* and I hoped she knew this. If I had had the money, I would have given her the finest headsails spun from the finest silks.

Week 31 was the week in which I opened Rome's parcel, and the first week since the Cape of Good Hope storm that I experienced real fear. It had started well enough. Storms had become routine, a quick dash on deck to change down to the storm jib before the feet iced up. The log shows our lack of concern.

Wednesday, February 4th, 1981. No sights thanks to gale conditions with unbelievable squalls. Solitaire *being thrown on her side. The sky keeps changing colour, blue to black to pink. Fantastic. Sailing under the storm jib only.*

Thursday, February 5th. No sights thanks to overcast sky with drizzle. Gales died during night but high seas ran until early this morning. Have changed to working jib and mainsail doubly reefed. Sea not too bad now. Water running off the mainsail but not enough to catch for drinking. We are now deep into the loose ice area and the seas are bitterly cold. I have been wearing the quilted trousers Margaret gave me, another present I can't remember saying thank you for. Margaret said they had belonged to a butcher who spent most of his time in a refrigerated store. I doubt if he ever imagined their being used to keep someone warm off Cape Horn, but a magnificent present for which I'm truly grateful. The height of fashion this season in the Southern Ocean is Rex's thermal jacket with a couple of sweaters and pairs of socks under full storm gear and sea boots.

At night I doze under two wet sleeping bags with the temperature down to 40°F by night and 50°F on warmer days. The main problem is the damp cabin that allows nothing to dry. I can take off my quilted storm jacket below by day, but on deck full gear is needed as the strong winds bite through sweaters and the seas soon freeze hands. Provided you work quickly there's no real problem. Loss of weight still a major worry and my strength is going as well. Very concerned in case I have to climb the mast as I just don't know how I would manage to pull myself up. My back continues to get worse. Most of my shirts have now been worn and are bloodstained. It seems a terrible thing to do but I sorted out the few that seem reasonably free from filth and intend wearing them again inside out. I tried washing one in salt water but it would not dry properly and seemed to irritate my skin. Oh well, Rome's present tomorrow. We are about 1,400 miles from Cape Horn. I'll get sights when the sun pops out.

Friday, February 6th. *Still no sights, winds from west increasing to Force 6 to 7 as a few fierce squalls came through. Visibility down to a few hundred yards. Drizzling with some heavy rain during squalls. Have considered sitting in the cockpit and putting up the main, trebly reefed, to catch fresh water.* Solitaire *swinging about with just working jib so have given the idea a miss.*

At present I have 20 gallons of fresh water left. No worry as far as drinking is concerned but it would have helped hygiene to have washed a few clothes. Opened the parcel from Rome and Annegret marked 'for cold weather sailing'. Everything inside is perfect... and so welcome. The conditions are better than I could have hoped for although below they are pretty foul and the cabin smell must be terrible, but I have to keep the hatch completely closed with these following seas. As I don't expect visitors I'm not worrying too much about spraying air fresheners. Once or twice a week I treat myself to a throat and cheek shave and the lingering smell of soap in my beard gives pleasure for hours. I've now read all my best books through twice but with this parcel Rome has included a new book. The food and chocolate will give me special treats for a week. Without my friends back home I would have still made this voyage but oh how much I owe them. I just hope we can make it back to thank them properly for all their kindness.

Saturday, February 7th. *Sights put us at latitude 50°18'S but it's a bit of a guess as the horizon is so hazy, thanks to the drizzle, but I'm pleased to have anything after five days sailing on dead reckoning. Becalmed during night in fog, winds are now gusting from the west about Force 5 to 6 so working jib only.*

Sunday, February 8th. Solitaire *suffered her worst knockdown since leaving England. For the past few days I have been frightened, not when the wind was screaming but when it suddenly stopped. Without the background of its noise the sound of the breaking seas seemed to increase, and without the wind's controlling hand on* *the self-steering* Solitaire *ran like a child into thundering traffic. If I had to wait too long for the rogue waves and cross-seas to start slamming into* Solitaire *I would sit on the bunk and cover my ears with my hands, singing to drown the silence.*

Problems at dawn this morning. Very bad knockdown, working jib damaged. All the piston hanks are broken and the luff wire has pulled out, halyard parted. I think I can save the sail but regret the loss of the halyard as I have only one left and if that goes it means climbing the mast. Solitaire *is in a mess with bilge water all over the place. At present winds gusting from the west at gale force with cross-seas from the south. Broad reaching with storm jib under a sunny sky, which makes no sense. I will have to be more careful until past Cape Horn. Port Stanley is now our nearest harbour, 1,600 miles away even if I cut in close to the Cape. The bilge pump is U/S so I've plenty of work for next two days. Longitude sight puts us 102°52'W, 25 miles behind our dead reckoning position. The seas have been too bad for sights over past few days. Pleased to get anything. Worked all day on sail which might shape up tomorrow. At least it will make a good spare.*

Monday, February 9th. *Seven months at sea. Rain or drizzle and no visibility. Winds from west. Had spare working jib up until this morning, then changed to storm jib when rogue waves started breaking over* Solitaire. *Cape Horn lies on latitude 56°S, approximately 1,260 miles to the east. I intend to go down to 58°S, putting us 120 miles below and well into the icebergs, much lower than other single-handers. With only one halyard left and my weakening condition I think it's the safest thing to do. I don't want* Solitaire *driven onto a lee shore without the use of her sails to claw her way off. I've cut down further on food: now I boil two cups of rice to last three days but I still believe we can make this voyage non-stop. Working jib not yet mended. I can't be sure how far* Solitaire *went over in her knockdown. It happened so quickly that I didn't wake up until she had started to come up again. When I went on deck the jib was over the side, held only by its sheets and downhaul. Whether the hanks and halyard were broken when the* *waves hit or as she came up is anyone's guess. The jib is covered with antifouling paint but the seams are OK and I have spare piston hanks.*

Tuesday, February 10th. *Week 31's run 614 miles, total 19,249 miles. Good sights in a clear blue sky. Sea is flat with high swell. Winds 3 to 4 from west. A perfect spring day. Temperature up to 51°F so able to dry out. Noon position, 53°51'S 99°34'W with Cape Horn 1,200 miles to the east, only 129 miles south of our latitude.*

In week 32 we covered 643 miles, 45 miles below Cape Horn at 56°45'W. Should we have lost our mast I thought we could jury-rig a headsail and run past the Cape. We would even give the Islands of Diego Ramirez a wide berth, passing 15 miles to their south. *Solitaire* was in good shape again. I had fixed her bilge pump and mended her second working jib and she even looked tidier below. All the water containers that had covered her cabin floor when we left Lymington 224 days before were now empty, and all but four stored in the forward compartment with the spare sails. My disco dancing could have been extended with the extra floor space, not that I felt too much like dancing. No signs of depression in the log although constant complaints about the lack of headsails, particularly a strong number two genoa.

Food was a constant worry. The problems I had faced with my bleeding back and gums had been only the beginning of many problems caused by a lack of fresh food and vitamins. *Solitaire's* movement did more than irritate the sores; it seemed to wear away the flesh. First I noticed my thighs, elbows and knees starting to stand out, then the fat disappeared. I still had muscles but no body weight with which to use them. Side effects included headaches, blurred vision and blackened toenails. I had enough food aboard to gorge myself silly for a few weeks and would often take some of Rome's chocolate and suck it as long as I could make it last, then I would spend the rest of the night with the remains of the bar lying only inches away from my watering mouth, trying to keep my mind on other things, particularly Cape Horn, now only 500 miles ahead.

CHAPTER NINE
Lost

Cape Horn – Lymington
February – June 1981

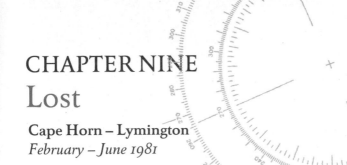

Week 32 saw my dreams of rounding Cape Horn come true, six years after hitting the reef off Brazil, five-and-a-half years after the birth of the idea in Tahiti.

Wednesday, February 18th, 1981. Noon position. 57°30'S, 80°23'W. Sights are not good as sky changes every few seconds. Sun shoots through scurrying grey clouds. Changed up from storm to working jib this morning although winds very strong at times. We don't want to go much further south as we are well into the extreme limit for icebergs. If we could pass Ramirez Island at this latitude all would be fine, 90 miles south of Cape Horn with 2,000 fathoms or more below our keel. Approximately 360 miles to go. Very, very cold on deck. It will be good to sail north into warmer seas.

Thursday, February 19th. Noon position 56°48'S, 77°41'W, some 290 miles from the Cape and 18 miles south of the Diego Ramirez Islands. Log shows 20,061 miles sailed non-stop. Light winds from the south so we have up a full main for the first time in days. Spent last night without my wet weather jacket. Hard to believe we are so close to the desolate Cape Horn in such conditions, with no winds howling in the rigging and the seas flat apart from a constant high swell. Temperatures up to 45°F so we have spent the morning with the carpets drying on the cockpit.

Friday, February 20th. Latitude 57°01'S, 60 miles further south than Cape Horn and we have just spent the night becalmed! I left up the main to stop our swaying in the swells. The chart shows that we have added only 30 miles in the past 24 hours. Now we have gusting southerlies Force 3 to 7 under a main with one reef and working jib. Engine turned by hand seems free enough. A look over our stern for the first time in many a day reveals a crop of goose barnacles that could give trouble. The cold seas are not killing them off as expected.

Saturday, February 21st. Lovely sailing yesterday afternoon on a bright blue sea under a bright blue sky. Winds went to the west Force 5. Gorgeous night with a full low moon, the sky covered with a carpet of stars. Two hours before dawn we ran into our present conditions when the winds died for three hours, then came back gusting from the north to north-east, anything from Force 4 to 7. Reaching under a main with two reefs and working jib occasionally luffing into the gusts on top of the waves. No visibility at times thanks to heavy rain so no sights today so far, but dead reckoning shows us 60 miles below Ramirez Island, with about 200 miles to reach Cape Horn's longitude. And Rome's parcel! Good sight for longitude during afternoon, which confirms our position. Clouds have cleared away. Should not have said anything – we're back to black squalls!

Sunday, February 22nd. Strong squalls through the night reduced us to working jib only. Winds perfect this morning, Force 5 to 6 from the west, for doubly reefed main. Have been taking sights all morning, which confirm that we are still 60 miles clear of Ramirez Island. No noon sight. Winds have dropped and given way to rain and drizzly fog. Would have liked sights but at least we are well clear of land and lee shores. At one time I had considered closing Cape Horn but decided it was asking too much of our guardian angel. I would have welcomed a few photos to replace those I ruined, but Chichester nearly lost his yacht by cutting in too close so it is much safer to stay in these deep waters rather than risk the Horn's shallows just for a few pictures.

1650 GMT. I believe Diego Ramirez is 90 miles and Cape Horn 150 miles north-east of us. With reasonable winds we should have reached Cape Horn's longitude by tomorrow evening. At present becalmed in heavy rain.

1832 GMT. Our position 57°30'S, 70°55'W with winds again gusting from the west Force 5 to 6, higher in squalls. Only 75 miles to Ramirez' longitude of 151°W. Shallow waters extend for 40 miles below these islands so our present position is fine.

Monday, February 23rd. *Lowered main yesterday evening during fierce gusts. Sea remained quite flat so I had a peaceful night after all and winds dropped to Force 3 to 4. Awoke to heavy rain so after hoisting the main with one reef I spent the morning catching rain water for drinking and taking photographs of the operation.*

1640 GMT. Noon position 57°03'S, 68°19'W. Distance run 20,380 miles. We are about 10 miles beyond Ramirez Island with 35 miles to go to reach Cape Horn's longitude. Good conditions at the moment so with luck we should pass soon after dark. I have opened Rome's parcel after cheating a bit. It's such a glorious day I wanted to take some photographs, with their letter attached to the flagstaff. I have included Peter's bottle of champagne by tying it to the pulpit rail.

2100 GMT. Further sight confirms previous position. Now only 16 miles to pass Cape Horn's longitude. Solitaire is pointing due east on latitude 57°S, 60 miles below the Cape in a perfect position with 2,000 fathoms below our keel. Black squalls keep building up astern of us and passing through. How about the navigation? Must have improved since Brazil. Wish the cook could do as well. He dished up Bloody Rice again today.

Tuesday, February 24th. *The end of our 33rd week at sea, 231 days in all. We passed Cape Horn at 0100 GMT this morning, 20,473 miles from home. Yesterday's sunshine has turned into a mixture of gales dying to whispers, rain, fog, drizzle gusting back with squalls then storm force winds again and changing so quickly that I'm leaving up just the storm jib. Below, everything is wet and miserable. I have just taken off my socks for the first time*

in more than a week. My feet look like two dead cods and sur-
prisingly white.

I knew something was missing but could not figure out what until I realised that I was minus my black toenails. When I turned the socks inside out I found them nestling at the bottom. I was now fleshless, toenail-less and my gums bled so badly that I would soon be toothless as well. What else I had to give before this voyage ended I shuddered to think. All I wanted now was to head north and sail into warmer seas, opening hatches and washing myself and clothes if only in boiled sea water. The thought of sitting in a sunny cockpit with cooling breezes that soothed my blistered, itching back was a dream of paradise. I could imagine a shrivelled old man with wrinkles around his eyes eating his daily rice with a gummy smile on his face.

There was no feeling of achievement, only gratitude that the seas had allowed *Solitaire* to pass over them without making too many demands, and relief that the oceans were now open to us. I had my celebration dinner on February 25th, the start of *Solitaire*'s 34th week at sea. We had been becalmed all morning following the previous day's storms. The afternoon was like an English spring day, clear blue skies with a bite in the crystal air. As the carpets dried in the cockpit the temperature went up to 59°F. *Solitaire* started to make her way north with an escort of dolphins to welcome us back into the South Atlantic.

For that night's dinner I reckoned on half a tin of meatballs accompanied by beans and finishing with a third of a tin of sponge cake. Between courses the instructions on the champagne were adhered to: not to be opened until Cape Horn is abaft the beam (although I wasn't too sure what that meant).

The second part of the instructions – 'for internal use only, contents to be consumed in one sitting' – gave no problem. Following these orders I realised how warm and cosy the cabin had become. The saucepan's water had boiled away and my tin of sponge was virtually glowing! In my inebriated condition I forgot about saving some of the sponge for the following day and scoffed the lot, and for a few hours drifted warmly in sleep until a screeching night awoke me. I staggered on deck into biting spume flying from the tops of freezing breaking seas. After reducing to the storm jib I returned to my damp, stinking prison, and lay shivering under a sodden sleeping bag.

With the broad Atlantic stretching ahead navigation was less important. Had I lost the last spinner on my trailing log, or had the portable radio packed up it would not now be too serious. We still had 8,000 miles to go before we reached Lymington, if the charts proved correct and we did not have too many calms. Provided the antifouling prevented our hull from turning into a wet sponge, we would make it home non-stop. All rather iffy.

Two days after rounding Cape Horn we were becalmed again. To sit for hours without movement watching my scant food supplies dwindle was stressful and only partially relieved by my remarks in the log.

It seems hard to believe but we are once more becalmed. Solitaire is lying with just her mainsail and one reef. For the second day we have waves and a high swell but we don't have the most important ingredient, WIND. The red telltales are hanging straight down from the backstays like a girl's skirts, our sails slamming back and forth with frustration. I wonder what the price of property is around here. Might pay us to rent a house while we're sculling about. The log line is visible only for a few feet, dropping out of sight into the sea's black depths. There must be some forward movement as we have progressed two miles in three-and-a-half hours. The Falkland Islands are 230 miles due north so at this speed we could be there next Christmas. After our celebration meal we are back to skipper's choice: half a cup of rice, a third of a tin of peas with curry powder. Sounds bloody delicious. Bet you any money the cook serves up the dish again tomorrow. If we have wind – if – we will soon be sailing over the Burwood Bank where the ocean depth shelves from 2,000 fathoms to 40. Let's hope the winds don't about face. I would not fancy these shallow waters during a storm.

There were good days. On one I was looking over *Solitaire*'s stern when a whale surfaced. A few seconds earlier he would have certainly given us a lift in life. Near the Falklands I picked up some lovely music on the restricted medium wave, probably from Argentina as the announcer appeared to be speaking Spanish. All my old favourites, played by a string orchestra, came across: *Tales from the Vienna Woods*, *Maria*, and what seemed appropriate at the time, *All the Lonely People*.

We were carried over the Burwood Bank shallows by current and wave rather than by wind. At times the boat's forward speed was faster than the following breeze, the mainsail backing itself so that for a few seconds the wind seemed to come over our bow. As we dropped off the shallows into the 1,000 fathom line we ran into a vicious storm and were thankful it had not arrived a day earlier. The rest of the week passed in a mixture of gales, storms and breaking seas, *Solitaire* dragging herself north to break the Southern Ocean's icy grip.

On Monday, March 2nd, *Solitaire* slipped unnoticed past the Falkland Islands, 60 miles to the west. Only their local radio playing request music proved their existence. Next day we ran out of the Furious Fifties and fell off the end of our last decent chart. Now all we had for navigation was a pilot chart, which proved sufficient. The South Atlantic lay before us, its welcoming arms opening wide for a thousand miles.

Week 34 ended with the Falklands 185 miles in our wake, having logged 575 miles despite the calms, 21,117 miles in all, but it would be another week before *Solitaire* cleared the limit of the icebergs and the high storm areas. My log ended with good and bad news. The good news was that the temperature in *Solitaire*'s cabin topped 50°F, the bad was disguised in a few words: 'Checked food supply. Not good'. In fact it was serious. As the food had disappeared from under the bunks the space had been filled by other pieces of equipment. My main food supply, the rice, was kept in a sealed bucket adjoining Rome's last two parcels and such other food as remained was stored behind the main bunks.

Sometimes I failed to understand the speed of its disappearance, as if I were spending £5 notes and finding each was worth only two pence. No sooner had I broken into a fresh cache of food than it seemed to vanish, despite cutting down on my rations so that my bones cried out in protest. At one period I found I had more powdered milk than I needed for tea so I started mixing two spoonfuls of powdered milk, sugar, flour and water which turned out like soft toffee when fried. I would have a little of this at night and cut my rice to half a cup a day.

My last checks on the food supply took no time at all as once I had dropped the bunk backs every morsel of food aboard was in full view. Although we could be at sea for a further three months, hunger was not really all that important. There were millions of people who would have been grateful for a tithe of what I had; it was more a case of wanting to play my part in returning home and not lie on my bunk, too weak to help *Solitaire* on this last stage.

Over the months my attitude had changed frequently. As far as nerves were concerned the worst period had been from England down to the storm off the Cape of Good Hope. In a way I was lucky that it happened so early because, once it was over, it served as a reference point: we survived that one and this is not so bad so we'll survive this one, too.

Week 35 started with a storm that brought some of the worst seas of the last stage. On the first day we had northerlies gusting up and down our nose. *Solitaire* was sailing reasonably into a fairly flat sea with a full main and working jib but just before dark, for no reason that I could explain, I felt uneasy and put two reefs in the main. Much later I awoke to a violent gale which, had I not reefed the mainsail before turning in, would surely have caused us serious damage. Next day the storm increased and I recorded: 'Worst condition since Cape of Good Hope. Severe storm, squalls from the south-west reaching an all-time high. Bad cross-seas. *Solitaire* running on broad reach under storm jib.'

My attitude to this storm is shown by the fact that during its worst period I tied myself to the mast and spent an hour taking photographs. Every now and then I found I was standing without *Solitaire*, clinging to the mast. After an hour I gave up, having failed to take a decent picture. Below, wet sleeping bags and the usual smell of rancid cabbage, dirty clothes, and unwashed bodies greeted me. All I had to write about that was, 'Oh well, things will improve further north'. Although I felt no great achievement in rounding Cape Horn the pressure of passing it before winter set in had disappeared. The worst of the voyage was behind us, the best to come.

By noon next day the gale had dropped and I even wrote about a beautiful afternoon, a clear sky and a sparkling sea with the temperature up to 59°F. For the first time in months I dropped the pram cover from the main hatch and removed stinking sea boots and socks.

Monday, March 9th was probably the best day of the voyage. We had been at sea for eight months covering 21,568 miles. The South American coast was 600 miles to the west. Our latitude was 43°06′S which left us only with 186 miles to go to clear the Roaring Forties. After opening up the forward hatch to flow fresh air through the cabin, I stripped off my filthy bloodstained clothes, boiled some seawater and washed all over, to the instant relief of my itching back. All mildewy or dirty clothing was put into a sealed bucket in which was a mixture of washing-up liquid and scented soap (for good measure).

With ropes attached I tossed the cabin carpets overboard to be washed in the world's largest laundry, their brown water joining the brilliant blue and white one left by *Solitaire*.

The log summed up the voyage so far.

Let's hope the worst is over. We have approximately 7,000 miles to go. The best I can expect is to be in Lymington by the end of May, another 80 days at sea. Solitaire *is not as fast as when she left England. Her hull must be badly fouled and we have the doldrums still to pass through. With just two more strong headsails and the standing rigging reinforced we could have done so much better. The worst part was not, as I had expected, rounding Cape Horn but the storm off the Cape of Good Hope. Rome's parcels have been lifesavers: without them I don't know what I would have done and shall never be able to repay his kindness. I'm just sorry my performance as driver was not up to standard, something like 325 days for the round trip. Might have to emigrate to Brazil to hide my face.*

Tuesday, March 10th saw the end of our 35th week at sea and another 595 miles. Used the number two genoa for the first time without having to watch it hawk-eyed. The log finished on a cheerful note: 'Becalmed at present but having just heard the Budget on the BBC, being becalmed isn't so bad after all!' It was the last cheerful entry I made for some time as the calms continued where perfect sailing conditions were indicated.

Wednesday, March 11th. Dinner was a Roman orgy – tinned lamb stew! Should last two days but food really is a problem. I must start catching fish soon, which should help. No chance for a spinner now that Solitaire is barely moving.

Thursday, March 12th. Slow progress. Swell from the west pushes us forward a few feet now and again but a glorious day with a clear blue sky. Temperature 67°F. Water down to 15 gallons but food still the main problem and leftovers from yesterday's stew will have to last two more days. Now have fishing line trailing over the stern, the last thing I want as I hate the thought of killing anything. Unless we make better progress a non-stop voyage will be difficult. Noon latitude 39°58'S. At last we are out of the Roaring Forties but still becalmed, sails slamming. We haven't had a decent sail for four days.

Friday, March 13th. Becalmed until 0300 but good progress in the last 12 hours. Logged 67 miles.

Saturday March 14th. Becalmed again. I think the idea is to allow me to sail 60 miles a day and no more. Once the daily allowance has been achieved the wind goes on strike. If I don't catch fish I can't see my doing this trip non-stop. Perhaps I can ask a ship for supplies. This morning I inflated the dinghy while becalmed and cleaned the barnacles off Solitaire's hull although the swell made it difficult. We'll try again further north.

Sunday, March 15th. Full gale from the north-east. Reduced to mainsail only with three reefs. Making no headway: we might even be pushed back towards Cape Horn.

Monday, March 16th. Yesterday's storm could have been worse as we lost little ground. Now beating to NNW, Force 5 to 6 and risking our number two genoa in an attempt to make up lost time.

Tuesday, March 17th. Gale conditions have reduced us to working jib and 329 miles this week, the worst since leaving England. Feeling very depressed. I have 12 gallons of water remaining and 60 days' rice allowing half a cup or so a day. I can cut no further and as it is am slowly turning into something dragged in by the cat. Today's main meal will be rice with baked beans; yesterday's was curry powder mixed with Marmite poured over half a cup of rice. Recently I have tried fishing without any luck. In these storms I've had to stay closed in again which doesn't help. If I could catch more drinking water and a fish or two! I will try to pass through the doldrums to the Azores but must reckon on calling at St Helena or Ascension.

During week 37 we still progressed slowly and dinners were not quite up to Queen Elizabeth standards.

Wednesday, March 18th. Skipper's choice: half a cup of rice, half a tin of peas and Marmite mixed with a little flour. Sounds bloody delicious. Bet the cook dishes up the same meal tomorrow. No luck with the fishing.

Thursday, March 19th. Worked on damaged toe rail and washed my smalls in boiled seawater as becalmed, which does allow one to do the odd job like building another yacht or celebrating your 100th birthday. I was right about the flaming cook: curried peas again.

Friday, March 20th. Another 400 miles should see us coming out of the high gale areas. Dinner today: half a small tin of spam, half a cup of rice with mustard. Yuk.

Saturday, March 21st. Dinner: finished the rest of the spam.

Sunday, March 22nd. Dinner: the human skeleton had baked beans and half a cup of rice but it is a glorious day with temper-

*atures up to 76°F. Gorgeous to sit in the cockpit with the hot sun
bleaching your bones. Fishing line out but no luck. Feel content
despite shortages.*

*1500. Nearly caught my first fish, bright green and about 3ft
long. I had it alongside for around ten minutes trying to get a loop
of wire around its tail with a boat hook and pull a sail bag over it
but it broke the hook and escaped. At least it proves my spinner and
tackle work so maybe better luck tomorrow. Whoooopeeee, food!*

Monday, March 23rd. *A few squalls during the night, more
a whisper on black velvet compared with the screams of the
Southern Ocean, forced me to lower the main. No fish so settled
for rice, half a tin of sliced green beans, flour and curry powder.
Maybe cook will give me fish tomorrow... I could use the other
half of the sliced beans.*

Tuesday, March 24th. *The end of week 37 with a run of 486
miles and another glorious day in the low 80s under a clear sky
on a flat sea. A faint westerly barely fills main and genoa. If only
I had food and water, life would be perfect. Solitaire is still the
most beautiful lady in the world but her constant movement over
the last months has worn down my flesh, leaving only muscle and
bone, and I have to keep bracing myself against her movement even
when asleep. A beautiful lady but she's wearing me out. Dinner:
beans, Marmite, curry, flour. And all there is left is hunger!*

In week 38 we logged only 299 miles, the worst this voyage
despite doing everything I could to increase speed. My old number
one genoa I had saved for passing through the doldrums was
hoisted but day after day the sail lay useless on deck. We kept
up the main merely to reduce pitching and tossing. Thoroughly
frustrated, I opened up the rear cockpit locker, breaking my fibreglassing, turned on the seacock and started the motor for the first
time in many weeks. It ran effortlessly to charge the batteries for
a couple of hours, then I switched it off to lie a-hull, rocking back
and forth under a slapping main.

To vary my monotonous rice and curry powder diet I spread
some toothpaste on rice and forced it down as my day's ration;

thereafter each time I cleaned my teeth I felt sick. Then I remembered that Annegret had given me a box of medicines and, sorting through it, found some throat lozenges which I treated myself to at the rate of one a day. Drinking water went down to 8 gallons so I cut my tea ration from three cups a day to three half-cups until I managed to catch 6 gallons, during a rain squall which put a stop to any water rationing. Intermittent calms and squalls gave problems with both old genoas and time after time I was caught with long repair jobs.

In week 39 the winds became more constant from astern and our daily runs increased from 80 to 125 miles, 668 miles in all by the week's end. My spirits rose. Although my trailing line was now constantly in the water, the 9in spinner breaking the surface 100ft astern, I caught no fish. With the high temperatures and crystal waters you would have thought the ocean would be alive with flying fish, dolphins and sea birds but it was empty. Lack of wind could have been the reason for the absence of flying fish since a sea without constant wind is a death trap for them – perhaps they realised that if they dropped on deck I'd have 'em instantly.

Week 40 was one of the best as the winds continued to increase when we reached the south-east trades, and daily runs first touched and then surpassed 100 miles.

On Thursday, April 9th, we recorded our ninth month at sea and 23,638 miles, only another 5,000 to Lymington. On a glorious day with hardly a cloud *Solitaire* stretched her legs as we sailed past another landmark, Ascension Island, 900 miles to our east. Provided there were no major problems we would now reach the Azores, although we still had the doldrums to pass through. And I still had two of Rome's parcels to look forward to. *Solitaire* was in good shape and my own health was not too bad, at least my skin was starting to tan and the blisters on my back had healed. We were progressing.

Friday, April 10th, saw us 600 miles from the Equator, and on my last parcel but one. Winds were a little light but *Solitaire* seemed content as flying fish started to appear, lifting in panic to splash back when their wings failed to gain lift in the zephyrs. Seated in the cockpit, two cushions protecting my fleshless posterior, I willed them to fall into our web of rigging and sails, weary flies for a starving spider. The spinner glinted appetisingly in *Solitaire*'s wake but attracted no takers.

Our radio, however, hauled in its own catch, gorging itself on the BBC's overseas broadcasts. The American space shuttle epic was in progress, reducing *Solitaire*'s efforts to a stroll in the garden, but we shared a common aim: we were both reaching for the impossible and yet making it probable. I was content, despite settling for a dinner of... you guessed it... curry powder, peas and rice.

Next day, Saturday, April 11th, our position was 08°S, 28°53′W (480 miles to the Equator), having sailed 23,862 miles (112 in the past 24 hours). Winds were Force 3 to 4 from the east, and we were under full main and number one genoa. *Solitaire* made 5 to 6 knots on course. Spent morning repairing number two genoa. No luck with fishing so for dinner opened my last tin of sardines and rice, maybe the voyage's last fish dish.

At 6pm I caught and photographed my first fish, a beauty. Food, bloody food! I was resting on my bunk conserving strength when I heard a scraping sound and lay awhile, trying to work out which part of the rigging was causing it, before staggering on deck to investigate. The fishing line was sawing back and forth across the top of the pushpit. The shock cord taking the initial strike was stretched to the limit, so grabbing a pair of heavy rubber gloves I started to haul in the line, which felt as if I had hooked a junior whale. When I had brought it within 20ft or so of the stern, I could see it was 3–4ft long. White and bright emerald green flashed as it twisted and dived, a starving man on one end of the line, a creature fighting for its life on the other. Slowly the hunger of the one overcame the will to live of the other until I had it alongside, holding its massive head out of the rushing water, staring into frightened eyes. How could I kill this beautiful creature, which would surely turn me into a cannibal! I would be eating my own kind and I knew I must not.

My fellow traveller metamorphosed from the most beautiful fish I had ever seen into fry pan potential, and my mouth filled with succulent juices which, overflowing, streamed from my lips. Lacking a gaff I feared he might be too heavy for me to pull on board and that he would escape, but I heaved him out with such force that he shot over my head to the bottom of the cockpit where he flapped and flounced, clinging to life. I grabbed him by the throat to strangle him with hands like claws but in this I failed, so dashed below for the biggest hammer I could find, scattering tools in all directions, before I killed him with one. Remorseless, I sat back as the beautiful greens faded to lifeless greys and learned something about myself: that when the choice lay between my hunger and another creature's life, I would kill unhesitatingly.

Having hung the body on the backstays, I photographed and measured all 46in of it. Lord knows what it weighed as it was as thick as the top of one of my legs – before I started dieting. After removing its head and tail, I cut the rest into steaks, dropped them into buckets of fresh seawater, and selected two pieces, one to be left on deck to dry out for later, the other to fill my frying pan. Slowly it turned from grey to heavenly white food and, as I watched it, saliva streamed down my chin, although I managed to resist the compulsion to eat from the pan. Instead I dusted off my best plate and laid the fish upon it, ignoring the protests of my tormented stomach. The fish required a dressing to bring out its flavour so finding the remnants of some sherry, I splashed a few drops on the fish course and poured the rest into a glass which I topped with water to make a fine wine. The Queen, God bless her! I lifted the glass to check the wine's colour, then smelt and tasted it before declaring it a vintage. Carefully I selected one of the larger flakes of steaming meat, then lay back as it dissolved in my mouth with a flavour never before experienced this side of heaven, the finest banquet, I decided, I would ever have.

For the first time in months I purred contentedly, satiated. One more thing would fill my cup: the aroma and taste of coffee. I had run out some time ago but located a jar with some dark stains in, filled it with boiling water and had my last wish, a delicious cup of coffee-coloured liquid.

The fish should have lasted a week but, fearful that it might go off, I gorged myself for three days, frying, baking and boiling it, and for the first time since leaving England ate three good meals a day. Had I known, I could have made it last longer, for after a few days the pieces I had kept in water grew slimy and started to smell, whereas the chunk left on deck to dry in the sun slowly turned white, looking for all the world as though it were frozen. Best of all there was no smell. Sliced in the frying pan with a tin of tomatoes, my last fish meal proved one of my better recipes.

Back on rice and curry powder I regretted I had not dried out more but, starvation apart, I resolved never to catch a fish again, still remembering the fading colours as the fish died. The smell of death lingered in *Solitaire*'s cockpit and fish scales would turn up in the most unlikely places for days to come. *Solitaire*'s main problem now was her passage through the fickle doldrums: if we were lucky enough to make a fast passage, there would be no need of further mayhem.

The effect of the three days' feeding was dramatic. Bleeding gums, stomach pains, headaches, sore eyes and foul mouth vanished and if my body were still skeletal, at least now it could pull its own weight. With perfect sailing conditions it was bliss to laze in the sunny 80s, cooled by spray.

I had bouts of depression, worrying about my parents and my return to England with nothing in the world but the £60 I had left with, which would not last long as I owed the VAT on my new Lucas sails. Since I would not have spent a full year outside the country, the £60 had to be earmarked to clear that debt. Perhaps I would be allowed to see my family, then sail to the Channel Islands to finish out the year there. Also, I still had a court case awaiting me, the very thought of which sickened me. My chances of finding work would be slim, for who would want a 56-year-old electrical engineer who had spent the last six years at sea? On the dole it would be hard to look after *Solitaire* and get her back to sailing condition. I looked forward to seeing my friends aboard *Solitaire*; perhaps if I were lucky, being invited out to dinner, but that would be the limit of my social life. To go with a crowd to a pub for a drink would be out of the question: I could not stand my round.

England had no place for *Solitaire* and me. Had I been sponsored, things might have been different, but we had left unknown, without fuss, and were returning similarly. I had no yacht club; *Solitaire* and I were working-class misfits, our best hope to settle the court case quickly and sail before debts bogged us down. Some of *Solitaire*'s gear could be sold: I would no longer require two self-steering systems and if the worst came to the worst, I could sell the engine. Yes, I certainly had my moments of depression.

In week 40 we covered 772 miles in all, but the following week would be the important one. With luck it would see us through the dreaded doldrums and across the Equator. Luckless, we would spend days becalmed, watching our stores dwindle. We started well.

On Wednesday, April 15th, the day's run was 120 miles, then the winds swung from south-east to north-east, a sure sign that we were leaving the constant southerlies to enter an area of uncertainty and confusion. My sextant recorded that we were just 29 miles south of the Equator. We must have been passing through one of the main Brazilian shipping lanes for during the day two ships passed down our side. That night one was in sight for hours before slipping astern of us and over the horizon, the thump thump of its engines echoing behind. After that I snuggled down in my sleeping bag for what I hoped would be a long rest, but black clouds racing across the sky brought strong winds and heavy rain.

My main concern was that for some time we had had two small islands, Sao Pedro and Sao Paulo, dancing on our bows. As they were only a few hundred feet high, they were difficult to see, but I was unwilling to spend too much time giving them a wide berth. I changed down to working jib, reefed the main and came hard on the wind.

By Thursday morning we were 40 miles due east of the islands. The wind first dropped (although there was still a sea running after the night's squalls) then went back to the south-east, giving us a broad reach under full main and number two genoa. By noon we were 01°24′N, so despite the squalls we had covered 109 miles and were 84 miles above the Equator, *Solitaire*'s sixth crossing.

Friday, April 17th, was Good Friday. Although it meant opening two parcels close together, I needed to do it and then decide whether to pass through the high-pressure area of the Azores in the hope of stopping a small ship for supplies, or sail west, taking advantage of the current and the lower percentage of calms. I opened Rome's last two parcels, one for crossing the Equator, the second for Easter, and indulged in half a tin of faggots and peas. Having read the letter accompanying the food, I changed it for the Cape Horn message pinned above the chart table, had chocolate for supper and watched the sun set while drinking a tin of Coca Cola, totally content. We had sufficient food to get us back to England non-stop, I reckoned.

By noon we were well and truly in the doldrums, with a hazy grey overcast sky whose light winds died by sunset. We drifted windlessly in to Saturday on a flat sea with the main hard in, not just to cut down our oscillation but also to alert passing ships to our presence.

Traffic grew so dense that I gave up thoughts of sleep and stayed on watch that night. Shortly after midnight a ship zigzagged towards us. Normally I show no lights as they seem to attract super-tankers like moths to a candle, but on this occasion I had no option. The effect of switching on my deck and running lights was instantaneous as the ship promptly turned towards us like a retriever wagging its tail, two searchlights bathing us in their brilliance. It is difficult to know what to do in these conditions: if you wave too much, they may think you need help; if you don't wave at all, they may think you are too weak to do so and try to help anyway. Normally I wave until I'm sure they have seen me, then go below and watch from the porthole. In this case the light went out and the ship pulled away, whereupon I spent the next 30 minutes trying to close my eyes without seeing stars and flashing lights!

On Saturday, when we were 240 miles north of the Equator and becalmed, I sighted a larger vessel on the horizon. For some days I had been making up a chart of the voyage with messages asking that my family be contacted in England. I had tied these onto weighted pieces of rubber tubing in the hope that if I could get close enough to a ship it might be possible to toss them across.

After starting my engine we were spotted and the ship swung in our direction, passing down our port side 100–150 yards away, throwing up a decent bow wave. I held up my red ensign hoping our name would be reported to Lloyd's. When well astern of us she started to turn on to what I assumed was her correct course but, instead, she completed the circle and steamed down our starboard side. When well ahead she swung across our bows and stopped engines. Appropriately enough she was the *Lloyds of Rotterdam*, registered in Rio de Janeiro.

She lay dead in the water, rolling back and forth in a high swell, her hull offering a good windbreak, so I started circling, each time closing the ship. Passengers looked down on us from every vantage point. I went within 40 yards of her then, as we were sucked closer to the towering side of the ship, I realised I could not safely make contact. The spreaders on *Solitaire*'s mast pointed like fingers about to be crushed against steel plates. In panic I pushed the throttle fully open, my heart missing a beat as the engine hesitated before we slowly drew away.

I made a few more passes, showed the flag and pointed to the name on our stern while the sun set in a blaze of colour. With a final wave I resumed course for home, hoping that we would be reported. I would have given much to let my family know I was safe but not at the expense of having *Solitaire* damaged in the process. We motored until dark when, with the ocean to ourselves, I shut down the engine to enjoy a night broken only by the crack of sleeping sails.

Sunday, April 19th, was spent going around in circles, sails constantly backing, the air full of vacuums and bad language. To prevent *Solitaire* running over the non-trailing log I hauled it aboard, but despite this and the confused conditions, we still managed to log 53 miles. Sights gave us a distance of 90 miles with another 300 to go before we cleared the doldrums and sailed into the North Atlantic. With luck we would then have 1,000 miles of easterly trades. That night we surged along under a full main and jenny.

Monday was a great day. With dawn the winds backed to NNE and dropped, enabling me to hoist the big number one genoa. I thought about spending the day fishing but discarded this idea when dancing dolphins surrounded us. Two ships came over to take a look at *Solitaire* and her performing circus, clapped briefly and departed. Having nothing better to do than relax contentedly, I tried to sum up our present position: the Azores were approximately 2,200 miles away and England another 1,800 miles, say 4,000 miles to Lymington. Provided our guardian angel looked after us for a further few weeks, we should make it non-stop. Even if I had to cut down my rations to a mouthful of rice a day we would still carry on, skirting the Azores to the west and leaving their high-pressure area to starboard. Temperatures hit 92°F. Man, *Solitaire* and sea sighed in luxygence, a harmony of luxury and indulgence.

Tuesday, April 21st, brought week 41 to a close. We had sailed 583 miles through the doldrums with far less trouble than I had dared to hope, the nor-nor-easterlies blowing at anything from Force 4 to 6. Still concerned about damage to the worn number two jenny, I tried sailing hard on the wind with reefed main and working jib, but clearly I was under-canvassed and would have to use the genoas even if they were sacrificed in the attempt for more speed to overcome the close chopping waves. *Solitaire*'s staccato steps of the Cha, Cha, Cha turned into a graceful, gliding waltz. Now and again a vicious wave would vent its anger and spray, filled with rainbows of a thousand colours, would shoot up from our bows before cooling the cockpit. At times mast and rigging would vibrate and the leech of the reefed main flutter. *Solitaire* would tremble and shake, matching her movements to the rhythm of wind and sea.

For a week she danced the miles away effortlessly, 878 by the end of week 42, our best run yet. Thanks to our speed through the doldrums, I thought I could risk increasing my third of a tin of soup or greens to half a cup and my rice from a half cup a day to two cups over three days. I had 10 gallons of water left – no worry there.

We still had to pass through the Azores high-pressure area when I could really start thinking ahead. Whether we could reach home by the end of May was a question that could be answered only when we had passed Flores, 1,100 miles to the north. Next day, Wednesday, April 28th, things worsened. I should have learned my lesson by now, not to take too much for granted. The log reports:

Over the past 24 hours our luck has changed. The seam on the leech of the number two genoa has ripped and the bottom piston hank has broken through its holding eye, cutting the luff rope. Islands of yellow and brown Sargasso weed have started to appear, promptly wrapping themselves around the self-steering rudder and forcing me to pull in the trailing log. The winds are still light from the north-east but the occasional squall prohibits our using the large number one genoa, so we ghost through a sea, half blue, half brown, chasing more wind.

I still felt cheerful. The number two jenny had lasted much longer than expected and, if the problem arose, was still repairable. But I would have to cut back to my old food rations, for there was no hope of fishing in this expanse of weed. Thursday was spent working on the jenny and by clearing weed from the self-steering blade, we managed to push 80 miles through the jungle of floating Sargasso.

By Friday morning the headsail was repaired and ready to offer a few more hours of its valuable time, at which point the wind died to a faint breeze, barely giving *Solitaire* steerage way. To make up for the slow progress, I had a celebratory 'parcel' dinner, half a tin each of pilchards and coleslaw, the closest thing I had had to fresh vegetables since South Africa. From the BBC I learned that a certain Bobby Sands was deliberately starving himself to death.

Saturday was gloriously sunny but we made only 16 miles in 24 frustrating hours.

Sunday, May 3rd. We still had 600 miles to go before clearing the high-pressure area. Although supposed to have only two per cent calms, we spent hour after hour rocking in great puddles of flat water, rising and falling with the islands of yellow weed. I started the motor, which at least charged the batteries as we found a path through the islands, jumping from one puddle to the next, the sails still flapping. Once more I cut my ration to half a cup a day, with a small tin of beans for luck today.

Monday, May 4th. In 24 hours *Solitaire* had moved only 10 miles through an oily sea with not a ripple on its surface. I hoisted the sails a dozen times but *Solitaire* was asleep. Dinner was half a tin of mixed vegetables and my rice ration. The entry for the day ended, as had so many, 'Worried about Mom and Dad. I must get word to them somehow.'

Week 43 ended on Tuesday, May 5th, with a mere 395 miles on the clock and with another 670 to the island of Flores in the Azores, plus 1,700 for Lymington. Our chances of being home by the end of the month were fading and food was at a premium. Although I dared not risk losing more weight, I felt reasonably fit and since my fish banquet had no further problems with teeth and eyes. If I did not fancy climbing the mast, at least I felt I could – at a pinch.

Week 43 was depressing. On Wednesday I heard on the radio that the imprisoned Bobby Sands had died and remembered that I had been in Birmingham on the night that the IRA killed 22 young people there. I could feel no sympathy for him. Since the start of my voyage on July 8th, 1980, four leaders in their own fields had reached the top of the tree only to find there a pool of blood: John Lennon, ex-Beatle, shot and killed; President Sadat of Egypt, shot and killed; the Pope, shot; President Reagan, shot.

I had watched nine security guards accompany ex-President Ford around a golf course, condemned, as all presidents are, to being watched over for the rest of his life. Millionaires live in secluded fortresses and spend fortunes protecting their families; bank managers work all their lives to be rewarded with a gold watch and a first-class funeral. I wanted no part of their world, my epitaph read.

Dinner consisted of half a tin of beans with rice and it was while eating it that I heard that Bobby Sands had died of starvation. Bloody amateurs!

That Saturday, May 9th, I celebrated our tenth month at sea, sailing 26,368 miles, by deciding to wash my shoulder-length hair. I remembered that Annegret had been the last person to cut it before I left England and I hoped she might be the first to cut it on my return. With this in mind, as a treat I added tomatoes to the beans and rice before lying on my bunk to hear the Cup Final.

Next day the winds increased at the wrong time from the wrong direction. We were sitting on top of the mid-Atlantic ridge when clouds from the north raced over in evenly spaced banks and as the day wore on, the howling in the rigging started to revive old memories of air-raid warnings in the last war. The storm could not have come at a worse time. The seas that had travelled for a thousand miles now hit the shallow banks surrounding the Azores where *Solitaire* lay, burying her bow and running down her decks in gurgling rivers. I reduced sail first to storm jib with two reefs in the main, then just before dark, when I discovered that we were making no forward progress against advancing seas, to just the mainsail with three reefs, pointing into wind and weather but getting nowhere. Here the current flowed south, trying to take us back over hard-fought ground. Had we been 300 miles further north, we would have been in the homeward-flowing Gulf Stream.

The cook belatedly served up half a tin of chicken soup with rice to a crew close to mutiny. Each wave that slammed the boat was answered by a head thrust out of the hatch and an abusive flow of foul language. When another wave was about to sweep over us, I would hurriedly drop below and carry on the diatribe from the safety of my bunk.

The storm continued throughout Monday and Tuesday, when I managed a few poor sun sights, which indicated that we had been pushed back 31 miles over the last 48 hours. The trailing log for week 44 showed 421 miles covered when in fact we had made good only 390. And the blasted pilot charts showed no gales in our area! That I could live with, but the poor food situation and the beating *Solitaire* was taking were raw salt in my wounds. Not that I felt endangered or even threatened. There was little chance that

Solitaire would capsize so late in our passage or that her equipment would let us down. I could make it non-stop, but my growing concern for my mother and father was rubbing my nerves raw.

Wednesday, May 13th, saw the start of week 45. 'The storms have died down. I changed up to full genoa and main, then the winds fell away altogether to leave us rocking and rolling in a high swell. By noon we had logged 60 miles, which meant that we were precisely where we had been on Monday; time, food and effort wasted for nothing. One good thing about the high winds is that they have blown away most of the Sargasso weed. If we could start sailing again it would be possible to put out a fishing line.

That morning the first big turtle came drifting down *Solitaire*'s side, unaware of the hungry eyes watching it. I could very easily have reached down and patted him on the head, or slipped a rope around his neck. Turtle meat, I'm told, is delicious but as I looked upon its worried, wrinkled brow, I knew I could never kill it. So for dinner I had half a tin of mixed vegetables with rice, after which I wondered if I could catch the damned thing up.

Thursday, May 14th, was no better as we covered only 30 miles in 24 hours. I left up main and number one genoa and sat in the cockpit watching them slam back and forth, oblivious to their wear and tear. What with calms, northerly storms and southerly current, we had made hardly any progress in five days and the food position was now dangerous. I had 14 cups of rice left, which, if I cooked two cups to last three days, meant I would have rations for 21 days. Apart from rice I had six 15oz tins of mince, soup and goulash. A third of a tin a day would feed me for 18 days. Also I had two small tins of mixed fruit that I desperately tried to ignore. They were for emergencies. And I still had 30 tea bags left, with enough sugar and milk.

All in all I felt we could last another 21 days, after which I would have to go without. The sensible thing would be to call into Flores but, having got this far, I put aside the temptation: it had to be England non-stop now, so I would have to put up with starvation.

Friday, May 15th. At noon the Azores were 200 miles to the east and in another 80 miles we would pick up the east-flowing Gulf Stream. If becalmed after that, we would drift towards home and not back to Cape Horn. Dawn's light winds strengthened to a westerly five and *Solitaire* started to stretch her legs with the smaller genoa. My fishing line found no takers although three or four turtles drifted by, looking so contented that I knew I could not hurt their feelings by catching, let alone eating, them. As we had made good 90 miles in the past 24 hours, I celebrated with goulash and rice.

Saturday, May 16th. *Solitaire* had covered 121 miles in the last 24 hours in mixed conditions: heavy rain, drizzle and sunshine. Fortunately the winds that gusted up to Force 7 were from astern and for which I reduced sail to our number two genoa by itself. Flores Island lay 120 miles east of us with Land's End only another 1,500 miles away by crow. Having no wings *Solitaire* would most likely log 1,700 miles but I would pick up BBC local programmes (perhaps Radio Solent with their weather forecasts and lovely, lovely music) after another 1,000 miles or so. I finished off the goulash and rice.

During the night I had to change down to working jib as the fronts passing through were too strong for the weakened jenny, but *Solitaire* still surfed forward on the top of breaking waves. Temperatures were now in the low 60s and I was back to wearing sweaters and quilted trousers which, once more, were keeping my legs hothouse warm. 'As I am on my last 5 gallons of water *Solitaire*'s floor is now unnaturally clear after so many months of clutter.' Sunday night's dinner consisted of a third of a tin of mince with rice.

Monday, May 18th, was bad. The fronts swept through from NNE to north and we made only 63 miles. The waves she rode yesterday now buried her bow with sheets of cold salt as she tried to stagger forward, halting, burying her hull and breaking free only to be submerged again. I had to put three reefs in the main and hoist the storm jib as the BBC reported that gales were sweeping England's south coast. Then my rice deliberately jumped off the stove onto the deck, so dinner had to consist of mince, brown rice and gritty carpet.

We passed over Chaucer Bank on Tuesday when the winds dropped to 5 but with only 15 fathoms under our keel, the sea ran high accompanied by a heavy swell. Week 45 ended with a run of 572 miles.

Land's End was 1,030 miles away on Wednesday, May 20th, but I smelt green fields despite spending the day under a grey overcast sky trying to place a misty sun on an indifferent horizon. As we cleared the shallows, the wind dropped, the sea flattened and *Solitaire* glided through banks of fog, a ghost ship returning from the dead. I started to tidy up, cleaned the cabin and heads, and found some yellow cloth with which to make a Q flag for the Customs man. Able to spare a little sugar and powdered milk, I fried it into a sticky toffee, not my favourite sweet but at least something to suck. For dinner I opened another tin of mince and took out my rationed third. *Solitaire* made 82 miles in silence.

Thursday, May 21st, saw us glide 113 miles, drifting in peace more or less in the middle of the Gulf Stream to Land's End, 1,000 miles ahead. Dinner: mince and rice.

Friday, May 22nd, bit off another 121 miles despite a stormy night when I reduced to working jib only. During the morning the weather cleared, leaving a high swell behind, but the winds stayed around six and seven. I left *Solitaire* to do all the work while I sat contentedly below as we rolled along under the smaller jenny, thankful for the luxury of a following wind. For dinner, the last of the mince with, you guessed it, rice.

Saturday, May 23rd, saw us bowling along in rough seas under broken cloud, content to sit below out of the flying spray while *Solitaire* chopped 130 miles off our voyage under working jib. For dinner I had a change, one third of tinned beef and...

Sunday, May 24th. Gale force winds and high breaking waves made sights impossible but we made good progress with just the working jib on a broad reach. Log shows 125 miles in the last 24 hours. Dinner: guess.

Monday, May 25th. Squally winds from the north as we reached with working jib and three-reefed mainsail. I picked up the BBC last night and for the first time in nearly 11 months, actually heard a local English station. Batteries, like the crew, were nearly worn out. By day I could pick up Irish commercial stations, which proved we were in the right ocean, and managed some sights that confirmed yesterday's dead reckoning. Dinner: minced beef and rice served with curry powder.

Tuesday, May 26th, saw the end of week 46 with 124 miles in the past 24 hours, 801 for the week, 27,856 in all, which *Solitaire* could have bettered with more help from me. We still had the working jib up with three-reefed main as the winds gusted from the north. Were I not so tired we could have been tearing along on a reach with a single reef. I was feeling the cold, perhaps because my blood was so thin. Better that I kept what strength I had for sailing up the English Channel, with its heavy shipping, even if we lost a few miles. Land's End was now only 420 miles away. Soon I'd be with parents and friends, I thought – may they please feed me with anything but rice, bloody rice.

Wednesday, May 27th. The winds died during the night but still we managed 90 miles turning east for the English Channel. When I tried to start the motor that morning, I found the tank had rusted and lost 7 gallons of fuel. Luckily I had 8 gallons of diesel in plastic containers so I disconnected the fuel line from the tank and fed it directly into one container and, after bleeding the system, the motor started without fuss. The sky became hazy with a weak sun apologetically trying to force a way through. Warmly wrapped I settled in the cockpit listening to BBC music before starting my last tin of mince, after which I would have only rice, the chink in my armour.

Thursday, May 28th. Just before dark the wind strengthened and the main started to slam. Instead of dashing on deck I dithered and the sail's seam ripped open just below a reefing point after 28,026 miles of constant use and only a few hundred miles from home. I replaced it with the mainsail from our first world voyage rather than waste time with a repair. Wednesday had not been one of our better days, what with the fuel tank and then the sail. Dinner consisted of curry powder on mince. Land's End was now 240 miles away.

Friday, May 29th. Becalmed since dawn and all I have left is half a gallon of water, half a tin of mince and less than two cups of rice. And, unable to get them out of my thoughts, I'm worried sick about my family. All morning I have been trying to catch the attention of fishing boats for whom I have made up more messages and charts, asking them to contact my family. They come within a few hundred yards but when I start Solitaire's motor and try to close them, they pull away. After a few minutes' chase I lose ground, switch off the engine and lie lonely in a world of mist and lifeless sea.

Dead reckoning shows Land's End approximately 160 miles away bearing 075°, with Bishop Rock in the Scillies on the same bearing 30 miles closer. Had I a good directional radio there would have been no problem pinpointing our position as we were now well within range of British and French stations, but mine was playing up. There was a faint chance it might give some indication when close to the station and assist our Channel passage. For dinner, half a cup of rice with mince-and-curry-powder gravy.

Donning my warmest white sweater I sat in the cockpit while the boat idled on an oily sea, the only sound the faint rattle of her rigging caused by my own movements and disease. I was attracted by movement at the bow which at first I thought was a butterfly but, as it neared, I could see was a small land bird, black in colour with bright blue markings. For a while it performed acrobatics then, having sung for its supper, landed on the foredeck and walked towards me hesitantly, bowing shyly as if unsure of its reception. I slipped below for food, trying not to disturb Solitaire for fear of scaring away our visitor. There was little with which to tempt him but a few grains of rice and sugar, which I put on a piece of paper, filling a saucer with fresh water.

Back in the cockpit I feared it had flown away until its head popped from around the mast as though it had been playing hide and seek. The bird took an age to reach the cockpit, sometimes standing for minutes looking around, ignoring me completely. After gaining a few feet, it would scurry back in panic while I sat motionless. Reaching the cockpit it flew directly onto my knee from where it stared at me, head to one side, then ducked under my sweater and worked its way up until it lay above my heart, its own rapid beats demanding care and protection. Nothing could have made me move, neither storm nor tempest. For hour after hour I sat, unmoving, worried about my family but strangely comforted. For the first time in nearly 11 months, *Solitaire* and I were no longer alone.

Shortly before dark it came out of its hiding place and flew into the cabin. I put on the kettle and worried when the bird settled on its handle, as if still deprived of warmth. I made a nest of cotton wool and placed the food and water beside it.

Then a faint wind sprang up and as I hoisted main and genoa, *Solitaire* started moving, trying to hold a heading for home. With thoughts of more fishing boats in the area I switched on our running light, lay on my bunk and to the faint accompaniment of passing waters, slipped into a restful sleep. I awoke to find *Solitaire*'s cabin pitch black. The wind had strengthened and we were moving quickly but the sea was flat so nothing was straining. I checked our course and looked around for shipping before remembering my new shipmate. Finding a torch I searched the cabin, only to discover a fluffy mound on the chart table, head to one side, its eyes finally closed.

Saturday, May 30th. No noon sights possible. Since raising sail yesterday we have been beating hard on a Force 5 south-easterly through drizzle and fog, trying to head eastwards but slowly being pushed too far north. Despite being becalmed in the early stages, we have managed to log 100 miles in the past 24 hours and have also picked up faint RDF signals putting us 20 miles north-west of Bishop Rock, which means Solitaire *will now have to sail 40 miles south in poorish conditions to round the Scillies. The winds are gusting and swinging a good deal with mist and rain, so visibility is minimal. Instead of cutting through the shipping lanes at right angles, we will be sailing down them. It's going to be a bad night. To prove it, I dine on half a cup of rice and the last of the mince – with curry powder. All I have left now is half a cup of rice.*

__Sunday, May 31st.__ Some 87 miles logged in the past 24 hours but thanks to tacking back and forth, our forward progress has been only 40 miles. At noon we are 30 miles south of the Scilly Isles, becalmed and bewildered, sails sagging under a blanket of drizzle. For dinner, a quarter cup of rice mixed with sugar and powdered milk, which makes two mouthfuls. Thank goodness I can still enjoy a cup of tea.

__Monday, June 1st.__ Logged 81 miles with more tacking into strong gusting winds from the ESE accompanied by heavy rain. Solitaire is sailing as close to the wind as possible but a short, choppy sea sends up sheets of spray. Water is now very short but unless I turn and run with the wind, there's no way I can catch any. Noon position by faint RDF and dead reckoning shows us 10 miles beyond and 30 miles below Lizard Point, with Lymington less than 150 miles away. Both RDF and portable radio have heavy background noise, which suggests there's a storm about. For dinner another quarter cup of rice mixed with curry powder to make a weak soup, a terrible recipe! Wind is still increasing as I try to round Prawle Point but, without tide tables, find it impossible to calculate the current. With luck I'll be with friends and talking on the phone to Mom and Dad very soon. I propose lying alongside Lymington Town Quay until I have talked to Customs about the money I owe them.

__Tuesday, June 2nd.__ At 0400 GMT Prawle Point light is flashing 5 miles due north and with dawn the outline of land appears, the first I have seen for 326 days. Since noon yesterday conditions have been ghastly and the radio is reporting the worst storms for 20 years with lightning turning night into day. Strong winds have died, only to allow heavy downpours of rain. Our deck and running lights vanish as a blinding zigzag flashes across a black sky, destroying my night vision. I imagine Solitaire being found at dawn, *her mast struck by lightning, a burned, shrivelled figure at the tiller. My trailing log line was cut during the night and I had no spare, but we were only 90 miles from Lymington and once past the Portland Bill tide race, we could move inshore and follow the coastline.*

Scenting she was nearly home, *Solitaire* moved effortlessly over a flat sea and as the wind fell, the mist lifted. Then Lyme Bay fell away from us and we could no longer see the land. As we neared Portland, the Royal Navy started to appear and a couple of submarines swept down our side. By noon we were 20 miles from Portland Bill but land was still invisible. Late that afternoon the wind dropped completely, the sun emerged and the mist lifted. For the first and only time in the English Channel I took a sun sight, which put us east of Portland, time to come on course for Lymington.

No matter what happened I wanted to be home the following day. For dinner I had eaten a spoonful of rice with powdered milk and sugar. Now there was nothing. As the sun set we picked up a faint breeze from the west and *Solitaire* crept home like a runaway child, uncertain of its reception.

My own feelings, too, were confused. I dreaded my return to bureaucracy with the problem of deciding how *Solitaire* and I should spend each day. Once alongside, and after phoning my parents, my every move would be controlled by strangers. Customs officials would see a battered salt-encrusted yacht with a skeleton trying to form words for the first time in nearly a year, trying to explain that he had no money with which to pay the duty on torn sails. They might feel sympathetic but, responsible to higher authority and books of rules and regulations, what could they do?

After that I would have to phone the solicitor. Had there been any way of avoiding courts I would have taken it, but I was in too deep. The best I could hope for now was that, since I had sailed non-stop around the world and proved my point about the rejected sails, the manufacturer might wish to settle out of court. If I could get back my money speedily and sell my spare self-steering gear, I could leave England for America in two to three months' time.

By August *Solitaire* and I might be free. Some time before I had decided that for my next voyage I would sail to Newport, Rhode Island, following the course Rome had taken on his transatlantic trip. After that I would sail down the inland waterway and cruise in Chesapeake Bay before setting out for Cape Town and the Christmas tree in Hobart Square.

I started the motor, reduced the throttle until it throbbed in a contented tick-over, and held a close-hauled course for the Needles, 25 miles away. The 3 knots we were making meant a dawn arrival. Perfect. I spent the night in the cockpit watching the shore lights to port and ships' navigation lights to starboard. I was tired and the slow beat of the engine made me feel sufficiently secure to nod off from time to time, only to jerk upright. Just before the dawn I must have drifted into deep slumber for on awakening all signs of life had disappeared. *Solitaire*'s engine still held its constant beat as she pushed through banks of fog but our course had changed slightly, taking us farther south into the shipping lanes. Without a trailing log I had no idea how far we had travelled, but when I tried the RDF I heard a weak signal from St Catherine's Point, halfway down the Isle of Wight, and decided to home in on it.

With dawn the sky lightened and the fog eased. When we broke out of one bank the white cliffs of St Catherine's lay off our bow, and the greens and golds of patchwork fields greeted me for the first time in 329 days. In the small box-like homes ashore well-fed people drank water that flowed from taps, talking together with faces that showed love and kindness and caring. After so long with only the background noise of wind and sea and the expressionless front of a portable radio, we were close to the old sounds, of a footstep, the bark of a dog. When the wind blew, it would no longer start the blood racing; we would hear only the rustle of leaves in bending trees.

I turned *Solitaire* north-west, following the island's shoreline to the Needles Channel 10 miles away. Tipping the last of my water into the kettle, I washed my face with some and boiled the rest to make a final cup of tea with my last tea bag. Now we had neither food nor water, just half a cup of sugar and a quarter tin of condensed milk.

From the Needles I turned into the Channel past Hurst Castle, where I dropped the mainsail and put on its sail cover, then stowed the headsail and sheets, making ready the berthing lines and fenders.

At 9.15am on Wednesday, June 3rd, 1981, *Solitaire* nodded to the line of buoys she had last seen on July 9th, 1980. I intended carrying on to the Town Quay, with its public mooring, but the thought of the people in Lymington Yacht Haven proved too tempting. As I neared the entrance I weakened, pushing over the tiller, and *Solitaire* swept down the lines of moored yachts towards the visitors' berth.

A solitary figure awaited us. Keith Parris had been the last person I had spoken to when I left; it was appropriate he should be the first to welcome me home.

'Where the hell have you been?' was his greeting.

People were lining the upstairs' balcony, many of them old friends. When I arrived in the office, they had already phoned Customs. The good news was that the VAT I had been worrying about since round Cape Horn was payable only on the sails' value and, after a voyage around the world, that was nil.

As soon as practicable I rang my family. My father, over the moon, spoke first, having long since given me up for lost. Then I asked to speak to my mother, only to learn that she had died eight weeks earlier.

Keith gently wondered if there was anything my friends could do. They had all known about Mom, but not how to break the news to me. So I returned to *Solitaire* and made my last entry in the log:

Wednesday, June 3rd, 1981. 0915 GMT. The end of week 47 after 329 days and 28,496 miles at sea. Arrived Lymington Yacht Haven and learned that my mother has died.

Solitaire had shown me the world. Now I was lost.

CHAPTER TEN
Yachtsman of the Year

Lymington
1981–3

When bound for sea, or immediately after returning from it, there is a period of transition between the known hazards of life ashore and the less predictable problems of those afloat. For me the process had reversed: I accepted the solitary life of single-handedness that posed questions without always providing answers, an existence that for me could mean a shortage of food and fresh water, the rancid smell of unwashed clothes, with a circling albatross or a dancing dolphin my only companions. I was less certain of existence back ashore.

On the day I returned from my circumnavigation Keith Parris was the first to greet me. He followed me into the marina toilets where I was anticipating my first hot shower in a year, still questioning me about the voyage. Without thinking I undressed and heard a gasp. Turning, I caught his disbelieving eyes and a quick glimpse in the mirror revealed a horror of skin and bone. I apologised for my thoughtlessness, at which he made a joke about my appearance, said he would fetch his camera and returned instead with a saucepan of vegetable soup. It was the last time I would take off my shirt in public for two weeks, by which time flesh had started to cover the bones and my weight had increased from less than 9 stone towards its normal 13–14 stone.

After an initial hunger for fresh fruit and vegetables, I slipped back naturally into my old life of food and conversation and at a Welcome Home party that first night ashore, I found my verbal diarrhoea had returned with a vengeance. But fresh water I still used sparingly, reluctant even to wash *Solitaire*'s decks with it; to see a running hose untended filled me with a sense of panic.

Next day I phoned my solicitor thinking that I had proved beyond doubt my knowledge of what was required in the way of sails for a non-stop voyage. In the hope that I would soon be off again, I contacted George and his wife, Antje Fisher, whose yacht had lain in the berth next to *Solitaire*'s before we set off. Among their many acts of kindness they had made copies of my first voyage's log. Now I asked if they would make ten copies of the second. Later I put them into folders, together with photographs, for family and friends, in the belief that this would be all I could offer as a memento of our voyage.

Then a visit was made first to the local Job Centre where shrugging shoulders greeted me, followed by the dole office and the searching questions of a girl not yet old enough to vote. For one triumphant moment I brought confusion to calm.

'When did you leave the UK?' she asked. 'And by what means?'

'By sea, eleven months ago,' I replied.

'What countries did you visit?'

'None,' I replied, and brought the system to a grinding halt.

My voyage had attracted little publicity. For anyone seeking fame and fortune from the sea, the first thing you need is a good public relations man who, if he is good at his job, will find the second requisite, a wealthy sponsor. The third essential is a powerful transmitter to keep in touch with the first two. If you progress this far, then it's time to find a suitable craft... Bob Fisher had interviewed me on TV before the voyage and a BBC TV crew had followed me down into the Solent although, to be honest, I have no idea how they discovered I was leaving.

A couple of days after my return Des Sleightholme, editor of *Yachting Monthly*, turned up personally and asked for a couple of articles. *The Observer* newspaper made me Sports Personality of the Week and sent enough champagne to enable me to give a party for the people in the marina. My hometown newspaper kept the story going for a few days and arranged for me to meet the Lord Mayor. Accounts were published in the USA, South Africa and Australia, and within a couple of days I had congratulatory telegrams from friends who had read the story, one of the first from my American pal, Webb Chiles, who had spotted the news in a local paper while sitting in a café in Darwin, Australia.

One lasting friendship emerged from this attention. Dennis Skillicorn had interviewed me for the BBC before my departure and soon after my return arrived on board, where I nearly strangled him. After settling in *Solitaire*'s cabin, the first thing he did was to insult her. Only the twinkle in his eye saved him! Since then I have spent many happy hours with him, his wife Marie and his family. Dennis is one of the very few people allowed to insult *Solitaire*. There was talk between us of a book but this costs time, effort and money, and my real interest was to sail first to America, then to the Christmas tree in Hobart Square, Tasmania.

As so few people knew about the recent voyage, I was surprised to receive a visit that Christmas from Errol Bruce who said I had been nominated by the Yachting Journalists Association for the *Yachtsman of the Year Trophy*. Had it been anyone but Errol, I would have suspected that I was on *Candid Camera*. I had not even heard of the trophy and when I discovered that the previous holders read like a yachtsman's *Who's Who* and included Chichester, Knox-Johnston and Alex Rose, I had even more doubts. Later I was to learn that the choice lay between Chay Blyth and myself. I was selected by a single deciding vote because Chay had won it on a previous occasion. Had this not been the case, I would have been a non-starter. The award gave me a great deal of satisfaction, if only because so many had said I had been fool-hardy and had given sailing a bad name. Like the chappie released from a mental home, I now had a certificate saying I was not completely bonkers.

My departure for America was delayed on three counts, the

first sickening. My solicitor reported that the sailmaker had been unimpressed by my voyage and although the duff sails had been left in England, they were available for use and therefore had been accepted as satisfactory. The firm also claimed that the time allowed for their return had been exceeded. It was to take until early 1982 to have a court hearing, where I was promptly awarded the return of the purchase price with costs which by now were higher than allowed at this court level, the difference to be borne by L Powles Esq. The case had lasted nearly three years and cost Lord knows how much time and money. What really hurt was that if I had left on schedule, I would have been with my mother before she died.

The second reason for the delay was an act of generosity. The Lymington Yacht Haven, learning of my financial problems and in recognition of *Solitaire*'s voyage, gave us a year's free berthing. The third pleased me most. By waiting until the following March, Rome and I could leave together. He had sold *Solitaire*'s sister vessel and bought the hull of a 13-metre Colin Archer sloop. By now Annegret had given up her work as an air hostess and had returned to Germany, but before leaving she had helped to fit out Rome's new boat, *Arolia*, which now lay only yards away from *Solitaire*. The plan was that *Arolia* would cruise in the Mediterranean before setting off for Cape Town, where I would join Rome.

He left on time with a young Australian nurse and Ian Large as crew. *Solitaire* sailed a week later on April 3rd, 1982, just ten months after her circumnavigation. Apart from a new number two genoa from Peter Lucas and an 18-gallon fuel tank made by Brian Gibbons to replace the old 7-gallon container, little had changed. We still had blistered topsides and the worrying rigging connections. Having sold my backup self-steering gear and been paid for my *Yachting Monthly* articles, I had about £600 in the kitty.

My first stop was Dartmouth to visit Richard and Anne Hayworth and to antifoul alongside the harbour wall. A week later I sailed for Newport, skirting the Azores to pick up warmer weather, which I reached on May 20th, 1982, logging 3,775 miles in 39 days. We hit a storm on entering the Gulf Stream and as there was no sense in beating into it with our weak rigging, we lay hove-to for three days.

Peter Dunning, who ran the Goat Island Marina in Newport, and was largely responsible for the success of the transatlantic races, gave me a free berth for the night to allow me to clear Customs and then let me use his own mooring, which lay within a stone's throw of the marina facilities.

Reluctantly *Solitaire* left this hospitable harbour some five weeks later to cruise down Long Island Sound, through the centre of New York itself, her ensign waving at taxi drivers and joggers alike. After passing under the Brooklyn and Manhattan bridges and circling the Statue of Liberty, we made our way to Cape May at the southern tip of New Jersey and turned into Delaware Bay. At its northern end we entered the canal, which links Delaware with Chesapeake Bay, and then joined the intra coast waterway at Norfolk in Virginia to leave it at Beaufort in North Carolina on September 27th, 1982. The hospitality I received throughout was beyond belief. Part of my time was spent giving lectures, the first a few days after my arrival at Goat Island. I had been to a barbecue at the yacht club in time to hear that some interesting character was giving a talk that weekend. Turning to my companion I said I would really like to be there.

'You'd better be, you're giving it!' was his reply.

My last talk was at the Museum in Beaufort. I arrived to find I could not get in and struggled through the crowds, trying to explain that it could not start without me! My cruise down the American east coast had lasted three months.

Rome wrote to me from Gibraltar suggesting we met in Antigua for Christmas and with this in mind, I set sail on October 6th for Bermuda, some 600 miles to the east, and arrived on October 15th. The Sports and Dinghy Club gave me a splendid berth on their pontoon and I received a letter from Rome's mother dated October 24th (my birthday), saying Rome had made a radio link call reporting he was 50 miles off Cape Town, where he would arrive the following day.

On November 3rd Keith Parris rang me from Lymington to say Rome had been missing for eight days. Next day my golf partner in South Africa, Frank Minnitt, sent a telegram from Cape Town to say wreckage had been found but no liferaft, so there was still hope. On November 5th I phoned Rex Wardman to learn the search had been abandoned.

Grace's daughter, Terry, had died of cancer within a month of my circumnavigation. Now Grace had lost Rome too. I thought I could be with her over Christmas and set sail next day but Atlantic winters are always bad and, after a week out, *Solitaire* was pounding through head-on storms. During the night I heard what sounded like guitar strings breaking but, despite searching by torchlight, I could find nothing amiss. Early next morning I found that one of the Talurit connections I had worried about for so long had given way. The forestay in use had shredded at the top of the mast, the strands wrapping around its twin, which I cleared by using a halyard to pull up loops of rope. My worry now was how long the twin forestay would last. There was no way I could reach England before the spring, so reluctantly I turned *Solitaire* before the wind to run to St Martin's in the Caribbean, arriving there on November 29th, 1982.

During the winter I worked on local charter boats before sailing non-stop for England on April 6th to arrive on May 16th, 1983, after logging 3,636 miles.

Rome's body was never found. In his last letter to his mother, sent from the Canary Islands, he sounded confused and undecided, and even talked of sailing to Recife in Brazil. At this stage he was single-handed in a boat designed to carry a crew. A vicious storm had hit the South African coast just after his last broadcast, but what went wrong we shall never know.

On my return to England a large envelope greeted me. On it Rome had written, 'These are all your letters from the first voyage. They might be of use in writing a book...'

PART THREE

third time lucky

CHAPTER ELEVEN
Hands Open

Lymington – Larnaca, Cyprus
May 1988 – May 1990

Full of guilt that I hadn't been with my mother when she died and unable to help my friend when he needed me, I wrote the original version of this book, then called *Hands Open*, which was published during 1987 and dedicated to Rome.

During the years before publication my life seemed to revolve around Rome's mother, Grace. Wednesdays and Saturdays became sticky bun days. Over coffee and buns we would talk about Terry (Rome's sister), and Rome and Grace's home in South Africa. Once a week fresh flowers were taken to Terry's grave. When the loneliness became too great, Grace would turn up at *Solitaire*.

For *Solitaire*, these were bad days. For most of her life she'd sailed the deep blue oceans of the world. Now she was forced to sit and watch as other yachts with far less experience sailed down the English Channel and out into the wild Atlantic. Sometimes she would take our close friends out into the Solent. Tony and Irene and their children Sally and Tracy would spend their summer holidays in Lymington and we would go out most days.

Reluctantly I did make two voyages without *Solitaire*. The first was the delivery of a Rival 41 to Newport, Rhode Island, USA. It was during the time when the dollar was on a par with the British pound. Buying British boats became a good deal for Americans.

I was walking by the offices of a charter company situated in the marina, when the owner, Peter, popped up with the offer. Without a second thought I turned the job down. At that time stony-broke, I was on my way to arrange to tie *Solitaire* alongside the Town Quay for drying out and antifouling. On learning the cost, I sadly made my way back to Peter: 'Er, about that delivery...'

If I were to list my many faults, at the top would be that I'm pig-headed and unable to take on responsibility. This could be proved by the break-up of my two marriages and the promotions I turned down.

The yacht was fitted with an Aries self-steering wind vane plus autopilot. I would have much preferred to have taken the boat on my own, but because of insurance problems, Peter arranged for a crew of two 20-year-old lads, Rob and Angus, to make the crossing with me. Both were strong, fit and experienced yachtsmen.

The trip went reasonably well, I thought. A slow passage with headwinds most of the way. I taught the guys to do astro-navigation. True, we did find our way on course to Brazil a couple of times. I will admit to a bit of back seat driving: 'Watch that squall cloud coming through!' It's a fact that if they were on deck at night and happened to blink, I would go charging up screaming, 'Christ, I thought you'd fallen overboard!'

Later, in a Newport pub and over a celebration pint, I asked for my valiant crew's verdict. They gave it with enthusiasm and in unison: 'Les, you've just sailed that bloody boat over here single-handed.'

No such problems with the second delivery. Bob Livingston was one of the quiet, unassuming New Zealanders that over the years I would grow to respect. Half his time was spent in Egypt running his surveying company, the rest in Lymington with his English-born wife, Sally. With no previous experience in sailing, Bob had bought a first class cruising yacht, a 45ft steel Endurance. While he was away I kept an eye on it for him and ran the engine from time to time. The funny thing about Bob was that although he was much younger and fitter than me, deeply tanned by the desert sun and looking like he belonged at the wheel of a boat, he would never take the helm. Sally, on the other hand, was a natural – you could see and feel it the moment she took the wheel.

When Bob decided to berth the boat in Cyprus to be closer to his work, he asked me to be the skipper. He would join us for different stages of the voyage. For crew I would have Sally and Ian Large, who had crewed for Rome part of his last voyage – by now a close friend of mine. No longer desperate for funds, I turned the offer down. I did say that if they ever became stuck I would fly out and get them to Cyprus. A professional delivery skipper was employed and I shouted, 'Good luck!' as they left the Yacht Haven. Good luck they didn't have...

Three weeks after they had set sail, there was a cry of 'Les!' from the pontoon. Sally had arrived. The delivery skipper had turned out to be a modern-day Captain Bligh. Bob, a man of few words, had, on arrival in Gibraltar, gone straight to the nearest travel agent, bought a ticket and put the chap over the side. When I asked Sally for a few days to clear up my affairs, I was told: 'The taxi has been ordered to take us to Heathrow Airport – we're on the first flight out in the morning.'

The trip through the Med was enjoyable: we made the most of the stops, never at sea for more than two or three days, with relaxed watch-keeping during the days. Never able to sleep at night with other people on board, I would take over when the rest of the crew wanted to turn in for night.

Disaster struck on our very last day in Cyprus. Ian had been the first to leave for home. Bob had returned to Egypt the day before. Sally and I had showered and put on fresh clothes for our flight home. The yacht was moored stern-to on the north pier in Larnaca Marina. We had laid out a couple of bow anchors and a boarding ladder was used. It was while trying to push this plank into the cockpit that I over-balanced and fell into the stagnant oily waters. I came up looking like a drowned rat, blood streaming from a flattened face that had tried to put in the boat's steel stern. All modesty gone, I changed into clean shirt and trousers. There were a few funny looks when we arrived at the airport. Water was still squelching out of the top of my shoes as I climbed on board the jet. During the flight home, Sally tried to hold an intelligent conversation, but every time she looked at me, she burst out laughing. It was to be the last laughter I was to know for some time.

By this time I was just beginning to come into my 60s. Looking back, health-wise I didn't think I was too bad: first voyage around the world at 50, second at 55, the starvation diets I'd put my body through. Despite all these adventures and lack of vitamins, I still had all my own teeth. At a pinch, I could still see without my reading glasses.

The only problem I had was with my breathing. Soon after my return from the Southern Ocean, I developed a very bad hacking cough. At the same time, the passages in my nose seemed to close. To walk up a steep hill or try to run any distance would put me out of breath. To think of my mother or Rome could cause the same effects. The guilt would come flooding back. My doctor's diagnosis was that I had asthma and introduced me to the magic of Ventalin inhalers. One puff and I was running around like a two-year-old. My nose would require an operation, and for this there was a waiting list.

Financially, I was just keeping my head above the water. The British Government was paying my berthing fees with unemployment benefits. I think that anyone who joins a dole queue believes they're losing part of their self respect. To overcome this, I continued to give free talks to schools and charities.

There were two of these talks that I will always remember, the first because it would introduce me to another friend for life and his family. The talk was at the Lymington Civic Centre. A buffet with wine was provided. My glass would be filled every time I managed to empty it. Things began to get a bit hazy. I could clearly remember the first slide being shown; after that I must have been flying on autopilot. I woke up on *Solitaire* the next morning with a terrible head and a large chocolate cake sitting on our chart table.

Frightened even to show my face, I was swilling down aspirins with cups of tea when Ken Swann turned up to say how much everyone had enjoyed the night. Ken was someone I'd known for some time without ever really talking to him. His yacht was parked on a pontoon at the back of *Solitaire*. Always one of the first to arrive in the mornings, there would be shouts and waves, but that's about all the conversation we had. A bit older than me, he reminded me very much of my old friend Rex Wardman. Ken's yacht was called *Cedarwing*. The similarity of the two men became more apparent when I asked where the name came from. Turned out it was his call sign when he'd been a pilot. It took me some time, but I found out that during the war, Ken was in the middle of his second tour of operations over Germany (when you were very lucky to survive one) when the war ended. After that, he'd gone into civil aviation. He started flying clapped-out German Junkers 52 and finished with one of the big Airlines on Boeing 707s. Later I would meet his wife Althea, son Anthony and daughter Caroline, both in their mid twenties.

In a way, that morning I was to suffer two hangovers. When in a crowd of people and someone else was doing the talking, I would much prefer to listen. But after any long voyage, there would be a build up of ideas and it would be hard to shut me up. It was the same when you stuck me in front of an audience. With all the questions I'd answered over the years, the book and articles I'd written, all it would take to set me off would be to put a few slides on a screen and my mouth would slip into gear. The downside of these talks would start the moment they were over. I would start to worry that I'd said too much, that in trying to explain something it had sounded as though I was boasting. The real hangover would normally hit me a few days later when I would be joking with someone, only to find they were waiting to go into hospital for a heart transplant or a close relation was dying of cancer. I would swear that I'd never make a fool of myself again. The promise was never kept.

The second talk was perhaps the best and at the same time the worst I would ever give. It came about from a knock-on effect. John

Bradfield was a quiet, charming, elderly man who ran a private school called Walhampton, situated just outside Lymington. Soon after my return from the non-stop voyage, he called to introduce himself and asked if I would talk to the children. From that I was passed onto another local school for boys and girls from broken homes – their ages running up to 17. Later, two more teachers called from other schools where children had parent problems. This time their ages ranged from 9 to 14. I was told that only the children over the age of 10 would be allowed to attend, since the younger ones would grow restless. I said I would like to talk to them all, but before beginning they should be told that anyone wishing to leave could do so. This was agreed to. However, I was told that there was one boy aged nine who was disruptive and uncontrollable. Johnny would not be allowed to be there.

From the start the talk went well. I got one hell of a lift from the eager young faces. The questions at the end were some of the most intelligent and searching I'd ever been put through. One young boy at the front really tied me up in knots over something I'd said, that 'at times you could feel so tired and miserable, that it would be a pleasure just to go to sleep and never wake up... The thing that stopped you was the hurt you would inflict on family and friends.' I tried to explain but in the end I felt like I was trying to teach a blind man the meaning of colour.

Later, when I was having tea and cakes with the teachers, I said how much I'd learned from being there, but that it was a pity they had kept Johnny away. It turned out that the boy who had listened to every word, who couldn't understand the meaning of love, was Johnny.

Due to giving these talks, Grace and I needed a cheap set of wheels. Apart from visits to Terry's grave, I drove Grace down to Heathrow Airport for flights to South Africa. Terry's husband, Martin Maudling, who had MS and was in a wheelchair, was now living in London and we wanted to pay him calls.

For about a year I'd noticed an old Mini car sitting in the car park like a ruptured duck. On closer inspection I saw that the poor thing couldn't move. The rear sub frame had rusted through and the body was resting on its rubber tyres. When I managed to contact the proud owner, he said I could have it at a give-away price. The sub frame was renewed and I finished up with a car that would last until I was ready to set sail once more. It would cruise at a steady 55 miles an hour, using a gallon of gasoline for 45 miles. I was more than happy.

This happiness was to be short-lived and I was to start on a slow spiral down into depression. In a short space of time I was to lose my father and my friend Rex Wardman. My father died in his sleep, which in a way was a blessing. After we lost Mom, he hardly ever left the house. My brother Roy, who was now living in a council flat, would visit him every day and cook and clean for him. It was my brother who found my father. It was always understood that when we lost Pop, the house would go to Roy. There were too many bad memories with the house, and my brother decided to sell and live off the interest in his council flat.

When Rome died, to give comfort people would say he went the way he would have wanted – at sea with his boat. The same could have been said about Rex Wardman. Rex had raced yachts most of his life, sometimes owning two or three at the same time. A man used to being in command through his service in the RAF and later in his business, a man who never felt the need to raise his voice, and a first class skipper, he died of a heart attack two minutes before the start of another race, his yacht already surging in full flight.

The next two deaths I would never learn to live with; there could never be any words of comfort. During 1986, I had taken *Solitaire* out of the water to allow her to dry out, before giving her three coats of epoxy resin to prevent osmosis of her hull. Early in July 1987, I was in the main marina showers when I was told a policeman was waiting to see me. The conversation was very brief:

'You have a brother called Roy?'

'Yes, officer.'

'He is dead, he hung himself.'

I remember arguing that they had made a mistake, that I loved my brother and he would never do that to me. When I phoned the police station in Birmingham, I was told to report there as soon as possible to identify my brother's body. That weekend I'd promised to drive Grace up to Oxford to visit a distant relation. I told Grace what had happened and promised to pick her up for her return journey.

After I had arranged for my brother's cremation and settled his affairs, I returned to *Solitaire*, hoping that some warmth would come back in our lives. *Solitaire* still sitting on hard standing, it felt like she had died too. As I climbed on board, there were no movements of welcome, no swaying of mast, no slapping of halyards. I was too low and tired to even make a cup of tea. At least things couldn't get worse.

There was a tap on *Solitaire*'s hull. The train journey had proved too much for Grace. She had suffered a bad stroke and was lying paralysed in Oxford's Radcliffe Hospital. I was to take fresh clothes to her. I think from the moment I saw Grace, I knew that we had lost her and that she was already on her way to join her children. The doctors and nurses said the same thing, 'She just wasn't fighting to stay in this world.' I would drive up to Oxford two or three times a week, but when I held her hand, the squeezes became lighter. Finally I had a phone call from one of the nurses to say that if I wanted to say goodbye, I would have to be there that afternoon. There was a last kiss on her cheek. By next morning she'd gone.

The only family I had now were my father's sister Jean, as well as Irene and Tony. There was no longer a reason to remain in England. I started to think about getting *Solitaire* back in the water and making ready for another voyage.

I finally got *Solitaire* back in her berth but it had been a long slow battle. My breathing had become a major problem. The routine in the beginning had been to stay awake all during the day and late into the night. Before going to sleep I would take two or three puffs from my inhaler. This would carry me through until halfway into the night when I'd wake again short of breath. After using the inhaler again I could normally sleep until dawn. Now all this had changed. When I woke now it was to find that I had completely stopped breathing and was in the middle of a nightmare: looking down at my brother's poor body, or terrified to find myself in the water with Rome and watching our boat sail away without us. Having stopped breathing, it would take five or ten minutes to get any benefit from the inhaler. For the rest of the night I would sit upright to get air into my lungs, too frightened even to think about sleep. The doctor gave me tablets to help me relax. But I still had the nightmares.

I wasn't the only one with problems. *Solitaire* was having her own troubles. When she had been taken out of the water, I should have removed her old engine oil and topped up her diesel tank. I'd forgotten to do this. Worse still, the motor was run without changing them and became clogged. Day after day parts were stripped off and cleaned. Other jobs were started and left. The main cabin became a complete shambles. Friends were constantly calling to ask how I was getting on. Tired and covered in dirty oil, I became bad tempered and snappy.

When I finally got the engine to run, I decided to set sail the following day. I paid all my debts. That night I was trying to get our navigation lights to work when my old mate Dennis Skillicorn and his wife Marie turned up. Dennis wanted to do a final tape recording for the BBC. I said it was my intention to sail down to Gibraltar and from there follow Joshua Slocum's route around the world, sailing west about and through the Straits of Magellan. After Dennis and Marie had left, I was too tired to do any more work and spent the rest of the night trying to get through another asthma attack.

The following morning I was standing on the pontoon trying to work out my next move. I wasn't keen on sailing down the English Channel without any navigation lights, but to work on them would mean another day's delay. Brian, another mate of mine, turned up on his way to work to enquire how I was getting on. I can remember snapping back, 'If you bloody people would stop pestering me, I might make some progress.' Without a word, Brian turned and walked away. It seemed at that moment that following Rome's death, I'd been walking down a very long road and it turned into a blind end. I didn't know whether to run after Brian to apologise or to work on *Solitaire*.

There were a couple on a nearby yacht. The day before, the lady had volunteered to give me a pre-sailing haircut. They came over to ask if there was anything they could do. 'Yes, you can let go my lines!' As I started to leave the marina, I saw that they were following me. They passed me in the Solent and started waving, heading towards an anchorage behind Hurst Castle. There they circled and started pointing down, trying to get me to stop as they'd seen I was in no fit state to start the voyage yet. I dropped *Solitaire*'s anchor and, satisfied, they headed back to their berth.

I spent three days there. The first 24 hours were mostly spent sleeping. I finished wiring the electrics and tidied up the main cabin. Feeling much better, I thought about returning to Lymington to say goodbye properly, but in the end decided on running down to Dartmouth where I could write letters and make phone calls. I found that at sea my nose still remained a useless piece of equipment that could neither sniff, smell or blow. However, my breathing improved and with so many things to worry about, the nightmares became less frequent. *Solitaire* spent a week in Dartmouth. Then, with all the wiring sorted out, we set sail for Gibraltar on June 7th, 1988.

Soon all the old sounds returned, the freedom of once more being in the open sea. The trip was to take 13 days. It could have been much quicker if it hadn't been for an unwanted visitor. We were well out to sea and clear of all the shipping lanes when a pigeon came on board. Despite all the pointing he wouldn't leave until we had gone off course and back in sight of land.

Gibraltar was the same dusty, dirty place I had remembered from my previous two visits. When my brother had taken his own life, he left me the money he had inherited from our father. Not a great sum, but enough that, providing that I spent a reasonable time at sea and anchor, I would have an income that would pay for food and cheap marina berths when required. It had been my intention to stay in Gibraltar only long enough to carry out a few repairs and put on stores before setting off to cross the Atlantic. This plan was changed when I received a letter from Tony and Irene, saying the family had booked a holiday on the island of Ibiza in the Balearics for September.

The island was only 400 miles away and I decided to join them. With time to spare, cheap marina fees, and a first class chandlery within walking distance, I decided to fit out *Solitaire*'s forward cabin, and give the main cabin a new headlining. Knowing I could expect fickle winds in the Med and that I would be doing a great deal of motoring, I bought an autopilot to back up the wind vane steering. I spent six weeks in Gibraltar before setting out to cruise along the southern Spanish coast. It was time to leave. When I had first arrived after weeks of fresh sea air, my lungs were much better. The narrow smoky streets and a marina berth next to the airport's main runway were starting to show effects.

The final few days were spent with terrible coughing and sleepless nights. As Gibraltar slipped behind us, I was reminded of the American singer Tony Bennett who had a theme song called *I Left My Heart in San Francisco*. Mine for the future would be, 'I left my lung in Gibraltar.'

After all her long-distance voyages, *Solitaire* set a new record with four stops in the first 50 miles, but we did manage to sail the last part of the trip to San Antonio harbour in Ibiza non-stop. I think I will always remember the voyage for the many contrasts. There was the so-called marina that was a part of a filthy harbour with few berths and one foul-smelling toilet, and the posh place filled with Gin Palaces. When you arrived, they didn't ask the size of your craft, just how many helicopters the deck holds. Then there would be the dozen discos and the howling frustrated Spanish singer, always just out of a stone-throwing distance. But at night I woke to find myself surrounded by magic. There was a piano playing all the old romantic songs: *Stardust, Love Letters, Yesterday*. Then a woman started to sing, switching from English to French, to Italian. I sat in the cockpit until dawn, hardly daring to breathe – MAGIC!

There was the contrast too of a lovely lady's voice in the distance with a naked female only inches away from the end of my nose. Over the years I had got used to the lengths ladies would go to remain cool. In Tahiti during the summer of 1976, going topless had become the fashion. By 1983 in the Caribbean, it had become the norm and men stopped looking. Well, old men anyway. After a sleepless night of being roasted by the heat and deafened by the discos, I staggered into the cockpit to pass another milestone in my life. During the night a German yacht had tied up alongside and a very attractive lady was attempting to stay cool by taking a shower.

Having no hat to raise, I spilt a boiling cup of coffee in my lap. 'Guten Morgen, Fraulein,' I said, which was about all the German I knew. She smiled and I tried to keep the conversation going. At the time she was having trouble with a fly she was trying to swot. I remembered that the German word 'Fledermaus' had something to do with a fly, so said this to her. The smile became a laugh and she disappeared down her own hatchway.

Later, when changing my shorts, I remembered where I'd heard the word. It was from the German opera by Johann Strauss *Die Fledermaus* – The Bat. Telling some naked female that a bat was trying to land on her boobs was not the best chat-up line I've used. But at least it was different, and another contrast.

The holiday with Tony and Irene went as planned. Irene's mom and dad had come along and we enjoyed good sailing weather. I watched two 70-year-olds become teenagers. By the time they left, the first days of October had arrived and it now seemed *Solitaire* would be spending her first winter in the Mediterranean. Irene had always said that one of her dreams was to sail around Greek islands in a yacht. I decided to head in that direction, perhaps spend Christmas in Malta. As we made our way through the

Balearic Islands, the days grew shorter, the nights colder. Yachts started to disappear like flies. The charter boats were the first to go with their darling crews. 'Let the anchor go, darling'; 'Right ho, darling'; 'Has the anchor gone, darling?'; 'Yes, darling, did you want chain on it?'

It was while we were anchored in one of these harbours that I met up with Bob, his wife Liz and his seventeen-year-old son Karl. The family were from Liverpool. Bob was 44 and had spent his working life as an electrician on merchant ships. It had taken seven years to build his steel yacht *Lisarne*. He used the same plans as *Solitaire*'s, but adding two more feet to the length. Liz, a very attractive lady, looked like the American singer Doris Day. She had the same bubbly personality. She would be leaving the following day to be with their second younger son and take up her job in a bank. Bob and Karl on the other hand intended taking *Lisarne* into the port of Mahon in Menorca, leaving her there while they returned home for Christmas. Since we were heading in the same direction, we decided to keep one another company.

We arrived in Mahon on November 17th, 1988. Bob found it difficult to get cheap flights from this island and after a few days returned to the main island of Mallorca. I was having problems of my own. The fuel lift pump went U/S due to faulty valves. I tried to find replacements but without any luck. When I left England I had been given the names of Keith and Liz Trafford, along with their children Hannah and Bradley, as a contact. They had left England seven years before to cruise around the world. Mahon was as far as they got. Starting with only the money from the sale of their boat, they now owned land and villas, which they rented out to holidaymakers. Their own house was in a choice position, built into a cliff overlooking the harbour. They made me feel like one of the family and since they would be returning to England for a Christmas break, they suggested I wait for their return with a complete new pump. Mahon lies at the end of a 3-mile-long fjord. Its beautiful natural harbour is one of the best in the Med. It hasn't changed much since the days Nelson was there with the British fleet.

Keith was partner in a small racing craft with a guy called Fred. The yacht was about half the size of *Solitaire*, but for all that it carried a crew of five, mostly I think to be used as ballast. Whichever tack it was on, the crew would have to sit on that side to prevent the boat rolling over. I still hated racing, but from time to time I would just go along to make up the numbers.

On the day that Fred was skipper we had two new crew members and Fred kept saying that we should go through the man overboard procedure before the race. This normally consists of throwing a fender over the side and turning the boat round to retrieve it. As it happened, there was no time and the next thing I knew, we were tearing down the harbour in the middle of a load of clowns, all under full sail. Just when I thought the boat was about to cartwheel, Fred decided there was something wrong at the top of the mast, put on a harness and got hauled up. At that moment, the yacht did start to roll over. Fred made a majestic descent, still tied to the top of the mast. There was one heck of a splash and all I could see was bubbles.

The two new lads had been hurled over the side and were now standing on the main sail as though they were waiting for a bus. This kept the mast underwater and bubbles continued to break surface. Keith was still in the cockpit but up to his neck in water. As soon as the roll started, I began running in the opposite direction. Perfectly dry, I was now standing on the side of the boat screaming for the lads to get off the sail. There were more bubbles and Fred appeared to join in with me, before once again making more bubbles. Finally Keith managed to release the halyard and our skipper popped up on the stern.

Later, when we were safely back in our berth, Fred asked me how I'd enjoyed the sail. 'Not bad,' I said. 'But I thought your man overboard drill was a bit over the top.' Fortunately, Keith, Liz and the children left soon after that and I spent a quiet Christmas alone on *Solitaire*.

When they arrived back in the middle of January 1989, it was with the news that they had been unable to find the model of pump we required. Without the lift pump it would be possible to run the engine by gravity feed. This meant strapping a container of diesel on the cockpit seat, well above the height of the motor. The process took some time to set up and could only be used for entering or leaving harbour – never in a rough sea. The voyage took seven days, covered 620 miles and we arrived in Malta on January 23rd, 1989. On arrival, I tried to buy a new pump, but the best I could do was to service the old one from a kit.

Food and mooring were reasonably priced, along with a local cinema. It was a popular stopover for the cruising boats. Many of them were trying to book into Larnaca Marina in Cyprus for the following winter. There was a year's waiting list for a berth, but since it would tie up with my holiday in the Greek islands with Tony and Irene, I sent an application form with a cheque.

Bob and his son Karl turned up with *Lisarne*. Liz would be joining them early in May for a week's cruising holiday. After taking on stores, we headed north for the island of Corfu, our first port of entry. April found *Lisarne* and *Solitaire* leisurely cruising the Greek islands in the Ionic Sea. May arrived with Liz. Bob was hoping that she would stay permanently and, to be honest, so was I. Once more I'd become part of a family. For a while, there had been none of the loneliness of arriving in strange harbours, sitting alone in restaurants at tables set for four, trying to ignore waiters with long queues throwing hurrying glances. Unfortunately, there was a home in Liverpool and a young son to look after. Liz flew back. Bob and Karl set sail for England a few days later.

Feeling a bit down, I decided that if I could receive mail from home, it might cheer things up. I headed for the island of Trizonia. Greece is more or less cut in half by the Gulf of Patras and the Gulf of Corinth. Trizonia Island is about halfway down this channel. The pilot guide said it had a yacht club, run by an English actress – another Liz. I had intended to stay only long enough to receive letters, but it was the middle of August before *Solitaire* made her final departure. The food and company were terrific. The view from the balcony at the end of the day, with a cold beer – fantastic!

Irene and Tony arrived for their holiday and we went back into the Ionic Sea, to visit some of its better islands. Once I'd put my sun-tanned crew on a bus for Athens and home, I returned to Trizonia Island, but only long enough for hugs and handshakes and a last goodbye.

As we passed through the 3-mile-long Corinth Canal and out into the islands in the Aegean Sea, it was as though I'd walked through a door and found only an empty room. The islands on this side of Greece I found to be barren and boring, without colour; few trees, little grass, greys and browns of distant mountains, the whites of a few scattered houses. Day after day I seemed to be passing the same island. The deserted anchorages were lonely places.

It was while I was in one of these gloomy moods that I made a stupid mistake that would take me months to correct. At the time I'd fixed a heavy rope under the boat so I could pull myself down to clean the propeller. Just as I was ready to go over the side, a couple arrived in a dinghy to say they were in the next bay and would I join them for dinner. Without thinking, I started the motor. There was a loud thump and sickening jolt. The rope was wrapped around the prop, jamming it in forward gear and breaking the clutch. In future, every time I started the engine, the boat would start to move ahead. Without a reverse, the only way I could stop would be to let a stern anchor go. There was nothing I could do about it until I took *Solitaire* out of the water in Cyprus.

Our last port of call in the Greek islands was Rhodes. It took two days of tiring walking to visit officials for our clearance papers. I filled the fuel tank with diesel. It wasn't until we were well on our way that the engine stopped and I found half the diesel to be water. We arrived in Cyprus to a gentle breeze during September 1989. I had intended to make one or two more passes across the marina entrance, but I could already see yachties watching me from the outer harbour. I sailed straight in to find welcome hands ready to take my lines. This time there were no long walks. In a very short space of time all the friendly officials had visited *Solitaire* and I was cleared to go through the main gate and into the town.

The position of the marina is perfect. There's a long sandy beach running up to its entrance. Cross the road and you have cheap restaurants and modern supermarkets that sell all the British name brands. The Greeks I found to be honest and very friendly. English was their second language. There's a full social life. Apart from the marina, you have the British Army base a few miles away, with its own cinema, restaurants, gliding and golf clubs. With a rented TV set you could pick up their broadcasts to the services. All the news, sport, soaps and films – direct from UK by satellite.

One of the first things I did was to phone Afaf and John Skelton. Ken Swann had given me their names just before I'd left England. John and Afaf had met while employed as teachers in Lebanon. They were now living in the main town of Nicosia. John had his own company as an agent for ship builders. Over the years they were to become part of the group of people I looked on as being family.

To enjoy a full social life I would need a car. A friend of mine said he had a VW Beetle that had been sitting outside his house for months. It seems that an American had run short of cash and had left the car as a deposit against the price of his airfare home. If I would pay the £200 owing I could become the proud owner. Considering the old ruptured duck Mini I'd paid £50 for, this would be a big leap upmarket. As soon as I saw the car I knew I wanted it. In the first place it was a convertible: ideal for the hot Cyprus climate. The sun had already turned the red paintwork to a matt finish of many shades, but the body was sound, without rust. The top had been left down and the locals had turned it into a rubbish dump. For all that, the upholstery and hood were in good condition. It took me a day to clean it up, change the points and plugs, and run it back to the marina. I bought six cans of spray-on paint and turned the car into an eye-catcher that, wherever we parked, would bring offers to buy. Without the car I would have still enjoyed my stay in Cyprus, but it did make the world of difference.

The hot climate of Cyprus also brought an improvement in my breathing. The nose was still a major problem. Being unable to sniff or blow, it meant that every time I left *Solitaire* it was with one pocket filled with tissues. As they were used, they would be transferred to the empty pocket. There was a six-month waiting period in England for the removal of the polyp's growth or a payment of £600 for private treatment. When I visited a Greek Cypriot Ear Nose and Throat surgeon, I was told to report the following morning for the operation. I would have to stay for one night in a private room. The cost including any further visits was £100. Since then I've been reliving forgotten smells: the scent of a woman, fresh butter on early morning toast...

Solitaire came in for a good deal of attention. From Norway came new parts for the Saab engine, clutch and propeller; from Profurl in France, a new furling gear to replace the twin forestays I'd been using; from Hong Kong, a furling genoa; from Scotland, an anchor windlass and 200ft of chain; and a new GPS from America – at the push of a button I would know our position to within a few metres. To replace the plastic water containers I fitted stainless steel tanks. As a backup, should the furling gear break, I modified the top of the mast to take an emergency forestay. A new bow fitting was made to stow the anchor with two large rollers.

CHAPTER TWELVE
Breaking Out

Larnaca – Whangerai, New Zealand
May 1990 – December 1995

Our long and contented stay in Cyprus had only two black spots: the first annoying, the second devastating.

Most of the yachts in the marina would cruise the Turkish coast for three months during the summer. This had been on our itinerary and we left Larnaca during May 1990. Turkey had been described as a friendly welcoming country and a gentle introduction to the Middle East. The first sight of the mountains that started at the sea's edge and swept into the distance was breathtaking. Apart from that, the only thing to take my breath away was the blatant rip-offs.

As for a gentle introduction to the Middle East, I would have rather visited Saddam Hussein in Iraq. Only British nationals have to pay for their visas. This had to be paid with an English £5 note. I had only a £10 note, and this was refused. I finished up going to four banks before I got it changed. To get a transit log you end up walking to widely scattered buildings. The process takes for ever. When it was time to leave Turkey and turn in this log, I was told that one of the officials hadn't put his stamp on it. I had been in the country illegally for three months and would have to pay a fine of £50.

When I said, 'I don't have enough money', I was told not to

worry, they would put me in jail until I found it. 'While you are in jail, your boat will most likely be broken into.'

I paid the £50.

Later I was to hear from other visitors who had refused to pay these fines and had their yachts tied up for months, with costs running into hundreds of pounds.

The devastating news came by telegram that Sally, Irene and Tony's youngest daughter, had died giving birth to her first baby. The child only lasted a few hours, before following his mother. I tried to talk to them on the phone, but they were too broken up. All the flights to England were fully booked.

Solitaire was taken out of the water, her topsides painted and the hull antifouled. I borrowed charts to take us as far as Australia and had them photocopied. Stores, diesel and water were taken on board. The old Beetle that had given so much pleasure was sold on to a good home. The TV set was returned. The only thing I was worried about was my Flavel gas cooker. All the burners were in a bad way. In fact the only one working was on the top for boiling water. I'd tried to buy new burners, but the price quoted was nearly the same as for a new stove. It had become too late to place an order. At the last moment, I did find the same type of stove on the boatyard's rubbish tip and managed to salvage the oven burner. We could set sail on Friday, July 2nd, 1993.

The trip to Port Said of 230 miles was uneventful, until we started to enter the harbour. We had a Customs boat with large oily tyres banging into our side. They were shouting for cigarettes. I threw them two packets, but it seems they wanted complete cartons. After that I started doing a bit of screaming myself and was directed to the yacht club. The passage through the Suez Canal was more of the same: presents, cigarettes and money. I was just pleased to have got through without any serious damage.

Our next port of call would be Aden in South Yemen. I'd spent two years (1967–68) working there, just after they threw the British out. You could still see the bullet holes in the buildings and ride in taxis that had previously dragged bloodied servicemen through the streets by their feet. The question was always the same: 'When are they coming back?' I was there when the giant Russian transport arrived over the airport to unload crates of Mig fighters. I had watched as the prosperous duty free shops and restaurants closed.

The voyage down the Red Sea had been long and tiring. Mostly with light, following winds that blew exhaust gases into a scorching cockpit that I hardly dared to leave for 1,300 miles of crowded sea. At night, as ships constantly seemed to be heading for us, I'd shine a powerful torch on our sails. Then panic calls over the VHF: 'British yacht *Solitaire*, do you see us? Do you see us?!' For all that, as I walked through the derelict streets with their boarded shops, the question was still the same: 'When are the British coming back?' I took on water and diesel, some oil for the motor, a few vegetables. There was very little tinned food and, since I had enough to reach our next port, the Australian Cocos Islands, I didn't bother searching.

The voyage would cover approximately 3,600 miles. We would sail down the Gulf of Aden and into the Arabian Sea, pass through the Maldives Islands, and under India and Sri Lanka into the Indian Ocean. We would head for a position 300 miles north of the Cocos Islands to allow for the strong winds and currents in the area that would try to force *Solitaire* west of the Islands.

We set sail on July 26th, 1993. A week later, while still in the Gulf of Aden, we ran into a bad gale. *Solitaire* suffered a knockdown, which brought seas flooding into her cabin, ripped out both her spray dodgers, broke the battery out of the compartment and sent containers with 15 gallons of diesel flying over the side. The storm lasted for three days, but during that time we made good progress, despite only using a few metres of the genoa. We arrived at our position 300 miles north of the Cocos Islands. Soon after that, we ran into heavy squalls and confused seas. With headwinds and breaking waves, we finished 37 miles to the east of the islands. To waste any further time trying to beat into these conditions I thought was risky. All the water in the tank had gone. We had 10 gallons left in plastic containers. Food supplies were low. Perth, our main port of call in Australia, was 1,600 miles away. The following night, after giving up any idea of reaching the Cocos Islands, a U-bolt that was holding up the rigging and the mast broke at the lower shroud. I dropped all sail and waited for daylight, when I found an old eyebolt to replace it. The worrying thing was that if the mast went, with the prevailing winds and current, the nearest land wouldn't be Australia, but South Africa – over 3,000 miles away.

The rigging had broken on September 11th. On October 1st, Perth was still 550 miles away. It had taken 20 days of beating strong winds and current to make good only 1,050 miles. Our food was nearly finished, with 2 gallons of water left. The day before I'd topped up the engine oil with the oil I'd bought in Aden. The dipstick now showed a thick treacle mixture and the engine was proving hard to start.

Carnarvon on the north-west coast of Australia was 350 miles away. Being due east of our position, we wouldn't be battling into the strong north current and I expected to make better progress.

By the time we reached Carnarvon, things had gone from bad to worse. All the food I had left was a packet of spaghetti and half a bottle of tomato ketchup, and a few cups of water, which I couldn't boil since the stove had given up the ghost. My engine had died on me. I had no chart for the harbour. I'd spent a good deal of time trying to contact Australian Customs on the VHF, but had no reply. I could see the beach with a large satellite dish on it. There were a few houses but no marker buoys, only a few poles with green and red boards. I tried sailing down these, but the channel got narrow, made a sharp turn to port (which I couldn't follow), and finished up with *Solitaire* in some long grass, being dragged along on her side. I put an anchor down, but it didn't help.

I made the front page of the local paper the following day: 'The men at Customs House first knew Les Powles was in town when a strange message came over their radio on the afternoon of October 8th. Ignoring all standard protocol, his message was a simple one: "This is *Solitaire*, I have some difficulties and need help. I have no food or water on board and I'm having trouble controlling the boat. I'm over some sort of weed and my anchor won't hold. I urgently need assistance."' The paper devoted a full-page spread to my sailing background. What it didn't say was that I was in a complete panic and offered to pay anyone that would tow me into the harbour.

What they did send out to me was a 40ft cabin cruiser that belonged to the Australian Fisheries Department. There were four people on board, one of them a Customs Officer. I later found this was Hugh. At the time, my head turned into a cash register and I started to worry about the cost of all this attention.

Hugh came on board *Solitaire*, hauled up the anchor, took the tiller and soon had us tied along the pier in a small, enclosed fishing harbour. Immigration and quarantine procedures can be long and costly. Hugh quickly went through the lockers – checked that there was no water in the tank, threw the few cups over the side, took my packet of spaghetti, and invited me back to the Customs House to meet the rest of his mates. First I was shown their toilets and showers. After that, completely refreshed, I found a steak dinner and a cold beer waiting for me. I was then driven to the bank and supermarket, then back to the Customs House, to fill in all their forms. By this time, my cash register was showing at least $1,000. Worried, I asked if I could pay my Customs bill. I was amazed to be told there was nothing to pay. When I asked if they would phone the Australian Fisheries so that I could pay for the tow, I was told the same thing.

That night, I was invited to Carnarvon's Social Club for dinner. The following day, I'd just taken the cylinder head off the engine to discover that the gasket had gone, when a couple of Australian mechanics arrived. When they failed to find a replacement they made one, which they fitted and the engine started first go. When I tried to pay them, I was told that the guy they worked for had sent them. In fact he'd told them to take the engine out if it was necessary and to refuse any payment. These acts of kindness continued while in Carnarvon and in fact at every port I visited in Australia. At times I felt like a fish out of water. My mouth would open and close, but completely lost for words, nothing would come out. October 24th, 1993 arrived and brought with it my 68th birthday. I spent the afternoon flying over the town in a friend's plane. That night I had dinner with his family.

Within a week I was on my way down to Perth and the marina in Fremantle. There weren't many yachts that sailed up to Carnarvon from Fremantle. The problem was that with the strong north-flowing current and headwinds, it was difficult to make the trip back. Bill Burbridge had a 36ft light displacement racing yacht, and with a good crew he would be able to stay close inshore. It had been known for boats to be sent south by road rather than face the trip. Bill had given me all the charts and I'd decided to make one big tack out to sea of 200 miles and then cut back.

Fremantle Marina and the clubhouse are out of this world. Built for the America's Cup, the facilities and restaurants are first class. I was tied up to the visitors' pontoon the morning I arrived when I had my first visitor. Bruce Stone came along on his bike to tell me he was a dentist and always gave free treatment to any cruising yacht. I had dinner with him that night and met his wife Carol. By the next day I had my own berth, a colour TV on board, and was hooked up until Christmas, which I would spend with Bill and his wife Shirley. I watched the replica of Captain Cook's ship *Endeavour* being built and later its launch. I went out with Bill to see the Whitbread yachts arrive and again when they left.

I had intended spending Christmas in Hobart, Tasmania, but was delayed when a cooker I'd ordered from England to replace the old one arrived without its pan support. Later, when the part arrived, we found that all the markings on the knobs were out of place. When indicating that the gas was off, in fact it was fully on. The oven could not be adjusted and always burnt any food placed in it. I should have returned it to the makers, Plastimo, but there was no time.

As it was, we didn't set sail until February 16th, 1994. We arrived in Hobart, having logged over 1,850 miles, on March 18th.

One of the reasons for the slow voyage was that ten days after we had left Fremantle, the roller furling lower coupling broke.

At the time we were sailing through a strong gale, with only a few feet of genoa. The first I knew of it was a loud crash as the rig came back and smashed into the mast. With nothing holding the genoa reefed, it had unfurled to its full size and the screaming winds were trying to tear it to bits. There was nothing holding the mast forward and at anytime I was expecting it to break backwards and over the stern. With only an hour to darkness, I would have said that we were in a life or death situation. Later, when I was able to go below and change my soaking clothes, I couldn't believe that within that hour I'd pulled the gear forward and roped it in position, furled the genoa by hand, fitted the emergency stay and was once more under way with a working jib. Later, safely in Hobart, I would try to fit a new coupling and it took over two hours.

Hobart was a great place. Its small harbour for yachts was situated in the middle of town. They had to lift a road bridge for you to gain entrance. You could watch the early morning rush while sipping coffee in the cockpit. I'd heard the story of my non-stop voyage in 1980–81, and the parties, on my radio. The promise that one day I would return once more got *Solitaire*'s name in the papers and on national broadcasts. This brought loads of visitors. When asked if I would recommend they cruise around the world, my answer was always the same: 'Why bother, you've got everything here.'

For any yacht cruising around the world, Sydney is a must. I'd missed it on my first voyage, but, like Hobart, there was no way I would miss it this time round. I'd heard that the Cruising Yacht Club of Australia, which was about halfway up Sydney's main harbour, would allow cruising yachts to spend the first night free. With all the letter writing I had to catch up with, the first night stretched into 10 days. By that time, I owed about £75 in berthing fees. When I went to the Marina Office, the Club's secretary said that the Commodore had left instructions that all my berthing had been free. This once more turned me into a fish with its mouth open, unable to utter a word of thanks.

The next two days were spent doing the tourist bit, cruising around that great harbour past the famous Opera House and under Sydney's bridge. The month of May was coming to an end. My 12-month visa to stay in Australia would come to an end in October. The marinas in the main harbour were in great demand and expensive. There was a middle harbour, which you entered by passing through a swing bridge. This only operated at certain times of the day, which kept anchoring and berthing fees low. Cammeray Marina lay at the top of this bay and was owned by Fran and Bunny Babbits, who did everything possible to encourage overseas cruising yachts. The marina itself was in the middle of a bird sanctuary. It was like living in a wooded valley, with millionaires' homes dotted in the trees on one side, a golf course on the other. I could have happily spent the rest of my life there. *Solitaire* was contented to rest with swans and wild ducks swimming around her.

I'm sure that Fran wanted me to settle there. Once more I'd made the papers. Fran ran a programme on the local radio and we did a chat on that. She introduced me to the North League Club, with its free cinema, swimming pool and snooker tables. Twice a week you could buy a full lunch for 50 pence. I could never understand why there was crime there – so much was given away free. I tried to repay all this generosity with talks for charities. I gave one after lunch for the Cape Horner's Club and made more lifelong friends.

The main reason I thought Fran wanted me to settle there was all the elderly ladies she'd try to fix me up with. On one occasion I really thought she'd gone bananas. Invited to her house for dinner one night, I arrived to find thirty or forty of the old dears. It turned out that we were all there for a light meal, followed by a religious service in which we all prayed for world peace. After we were all seated around the room and holding hands, the lights were turned out and this weird Indian music started to play. Suddenly a lady cried out, 'Lord give us peace!'; the next woman, 'God save us!' I realised these cries were slowly working their way around the circle and I couldn't think of a thing I wanted to say. The lady on my right let go my hand and I felt an excruciating pain in my testicles. Looking down I saw I had a bloody great brick sitting on my crown jewels. It turned out that this was the holy stone: when it was passed to you, it was your turn to speak. Later, I still had tears streaming down my face and all the ladies were gathered round to congratulate me. They said they'd never heard 'JESUS CHRIST!' said with such feeling.

Despite all of Fran's efforts and my own strong desire to stay in this paradise for another year, my visa showed my twelve months in Australia was coming to an end and it was time to leave. The last story to be in the newspapers was very flattering. Apparently I was keeping alive the tradition of the British sea dog, a tradition which stretches from Sir Francis Drake to Francis Chichester, and then some; gales, squalls, dead calms were all the same to me. The story was way over the top. However, since we hadn't seen any sign of a strong wind since we'd been in Sydney, I thought it safe to do a bit of strutting.

Full of confidence, I started giving September 21st as the date we would set sail for the Bay of Islands in New Zealand. Three days before we were due to leave there was a change in the weather with a strong wind warning. Trees, even in our protected valley, started to rustle and come to life. The next day I phoned Customs House, which was about half the way up the main harbour, to book a departure time. I was told that due to the strong gales, shipping was being restricted and it would be impossible for me to tie up at their jetty. The worried look left my face. Saved by the bell.

Next morning there were still gale force winds and a warning going out to all small ships to remain in port. Sitting comfortably in my berth, feeling relief at my near escape, I was told I was wanted on the phone. The Customs Officers said that rather than delay me further, they would drive round to the marina and clear me there. When I got down to the swing bridge there were people waving and pointing for me to go back. The main harbour was being agitated by violent breaking waves. As *Solitaire* cleared the heads and made out into the open sea, we found the winds coming over our stern. With just a few turns of the genoa out, we started to make good progress and were soon out of sight of land.

The Tasman Sea is well known as being like the inside of a washing machine. Strong currents and swinging winds make for a disturbed, confused passage. The worst part of the voyage for a single-hander is after sailing across the top of the North Island, the slow drag down the east coast of Opua, the port of entry in the Bay of Islands. The Bay of Islands is a resting place for around 500 yachts every year. Its people are well known for their warmth and kindness. For me it will always be remembered as a lonely place, with days of sitting on *Solitaire* with nothing to do.

It started off well enough; the Customs were helpful and friendly. June, an English lady, invited me to lunch and offered to drive me around during my stay. Things started to go wrong the first night while still tied to the Customs pier. After having no sleep for two days, I woke in the morning to find that about 12ft of the wooden toe rail that runs around the top of *Solitaire*'s deck was missing. I was later told that a fishing boat had been seen to hit me. Dead to the world, I hadn't felt a thing.

I was hoping to round Cape Horn that year, but the damage to *Solitaire* was the final straw. I would have to put the voyage off for a further year and set out the next Christmas. The fact that I wasn't happy in the Bay of Islands was mainly because most of the cruising yachts had been together in the South Pacific. With only a small general store and post office in Opua it was difficult to be part of the adventures they shared. After a stay of four weeks, I put *Solitaire* alongside a boatyard jetty, cleaned her hull, and sailed overnight to Whangarei.

Whangarei lay at the top of a 15-mile-long harbour. It was important to arrive at its entrance at low water and make the passage on its fast ingoing tide. The marina was a part of the town basin. You could tie between piles, which meant using your dinghy to row ashore, or you could take one of the more expensive berths. When *Solitaire* arrived, work had just begun to make the area a tourist attraction, with landscaped gardens, museums, art galleries, restaurants, plus a new marina office to replace the old clubhouse with its washing machines, toilets and showers.

I still had my asthma problem. It was my intention to stay in Whangarei until the New Zealand winter months began in April, then sail north to New Caledonia, returning to take on provisions and antifoul for the voyage home. I had been given the addresses of people to contact, but these were over a hundred miles south in the Auckland area. Still short of money, I thought it best to tie to the piles and try to keep to myself as much as possible. The town had a modern shopping centre with a cinema and theatre. But really it was one big storehouse. Most of my days were spent walking around the supermarkets or visiting shipyards to check on prices. Christmas came and I spent it alone on *Solitaire*. The New Year arrived and we started getting heavy showers, which meant I was constantly bailing out the dinghy. It would have been difficult to carry out any woodwork or fibreglassing and I had thoughts of buying the materials and carrying out the jobs in New Caledonia.

During all the unhappy months, the only good times were spent talking to the marina manager, Lew Sabin. Lew was one of the kindest gentlemen I'd ever met. He could have well become a diplomat. He became a close friend I would have trusted with my life.

It was to Lew I turned when I walked into the clubhouse one morning to find a letter written by the Director of Maritime Safety, Russell Kilvington, stating that as from February 1st, 1995, all foreign yachts from around the globe, no matter what safety standards they had complied with before leaving their home ports, and no matter how experienced their crews, would be forced to submit to a safety inspection by the New Zealand Yachting Federation or they wouldn't be given Customs clearance to leave New Zealand. Section 21 of the Maritime Act listed 56 items to be checked, plus the requirement of an adequate crew. At the age of 70, suffering from asthma, I had no chance. The letter finished with the warning that failure to comply could lead to a fine of $10,000 and a period of up to a year in jail. I couldn't believe that a country of just over three and a half million people could fly in the face of Article 94 of the United Nations Convention on the Law of the Sea 1982. This clearly states that the country of registration is responsible for setting standards for vessels flying its flag.

I could only think that it was someone's idea of a very sick joke. When I asked Lew about it, he said that the letter had arrived in that morning's mail. A week later, an American was refused permission to leave. It seemed his lifejackets, which had passed the American Coast Guard specifications, were not the type used in NZ. The yachties started having meetings. When it was put to the vote as to whether we would have come to New Zealand if aware of the inspection, it was unanimous that no one would have come.

I really didn't want to get too involved since I was having serious problems of my own. Although you're given 12 months Customs clearance when you arrive, they could demand in my case 14,000 NZ dollars (then £7,000) if I stayed longer. I was already in trouble with Immigration. In this case they only gave me a visa for six months. I'd sent my passport to their office in Auckland. It finally took me three months to get it back. All letters, faxes, phone calls were ignored. It wasn't until I wrote to the British High Commissioner that it was returned. I just didn't want to make any more waves. New Caledonia and Australia would take you without Customs clearance and many yachts started leaving illegally. In my case, I couldn't do that since I'd never be allowed to return to pick up stores.

I did manage to make more waves when on one occasion I went on national radio. There were only two stations: the one played classical music, the other mostly talk shows. The talk show I tried not to miss was Kim Hill, an attractive English lady, with a biting tongue and a ready wit. When I was asked to talk to her over the phone at 9 o'clock one Monday morning, I wasn't too keen, but finally agreed. Unfortunately I got my days mixed up and reported to the marina office on the Tuesday, to learn that Russell Kilvington had been on the show and everyone was asking where I was. It seems the idea was that the broadcast was supposed to be a head to head argument between us, with Kim as referee.

Some of the yachties had made a tape. Kilvington had come across as a pompous toffee-nosed prat. He had called yachties who couldn't afford the inspection 'impoverished'. I phoned the station and agreed to give our side of the case. It might have been my working-class background, the fact I was in my 70th year, or maybe that I was on my third circumnavigation, but the lady showed me only kindness, the same kind of caring and kindness I'd been shown during all my voyages. There was no way I was impoverished. When I came out of the office it was to find a crowd that had been listening on a portable. It seems I had said all the right things. After that I was in the newspapers, with a full story in a *Yachting Magazine*. Like it or not, it seems my colours were nailed high on a post and *Solitaire* was committed to sail for home by the end of the year.

Soon I started to have visitors with offers of help. British, American, Canadian, French – they all came with flares, EPIRB, and liferafts that would be out of date when they left, but suitable for me to use. Warm-hearted New Zealand crews arrived with the idea that I could borrow all the equipment from them and hand it back when 12 miles off the coast. It wasn't possible for me to consider either of these answers. Although I've always sailed single-handed myself, I've always considered the practice to be foolish. To allow a yacht to sail through a black night with no one on watch is in my view dangerous. If I'd still been married with a family and had responsibilities, I would have had second thoughts. As it was, I would never carry equipment with which I could cry for help and put someone else's life at risk. I'd already said in the strongest terms that I would never agree to a safety inspection. To do so now would be letting down too many friends and adding another string to Kilvington's bow.

Lew allowed me to go alongside Peter and Val's 45ft steel yacht. With their four grown-up children I started to feel part of the family again. Moored to the quay, we were able to get electricity on board and start to make repairs and modifications for the coming voyage. I replaced the damaged wooden toe rail. The large 150% furling genoa, which had given trouble during the trip to Tasmania, was replaced with a smaller 10oz/105 headsail. To the heavy stainless band that I had fitted at the top of the mast to take the emergency headstay, I now attached one more to make twin stays. The foredeck was strengthened and a bracket fitted. We had become more or less cutter rigged. I had two extensions made so that if the furling gear gave trouble we could go back to our original rig of twin forestays and carry storm jib and working jib.

During our first circumnavigation through the Southern Ocean, I'd been forced to fibreglass the cockpit locker covers in position to prevent *Solitaire* sinking. Now frames fitted around these lockers, to which plywood covers could be screwed, to give a double seal. I bought a hand-held Garmin GPS from America as a backup to the fixed one.

On our move to a nearby boatyard to antifoul, remove the mast, and fit new rigging, the engine stopped. Fortunately, I had Peter with me and we managed to drift down on the outgoing tide. We contacted the boatyard by VHF to get them to send out a dinghy to tow us in. When it became time to return alongside Peter's boat, we went up on the ingoing current using Peter's dinghy. When I stripped the engine down I found the cylinder head gasket needed replacing. I had no trouble finding a new one. I was thankful it happened when it did and not later, when I might be trying to dodge Customs boats.

By this time it was October 24th, and my 70th birthday had arrived. As it happened, two close Canadian friends would be leaving the following day. I was told they were giving a party in the now new clubhouse. When I arrived with my six-pack of beer it was to find the door closed and I couldn't hear a sound. I'd started to walk away, thinking I'd made a mistake, when the door opened. Stepping inside, I found the place packed with yachties and children from the local school. There were tables laden with food, dozens of cards and presents. I'm not sure if these surprise birthday parties work, but it gave me a memory I'll treasure for the rest of my life.

Apart from the 45 gallons of water in our tanks, there would be 40 gallons in plastic containers, plus containers for sugar, rice and flour. In order that they could be secured, I fitted bolt rings into the cabin floor. Gas bottles were filled. Day after day I visited the local supermarkets and came back to load *Solitaire* up with stores. I couldn't afford to buy new charts and we would have to do with the old coffee stained, disintegrating charts of 1980–81. This would give added interest since we would be leaving the top of New Zealand at about the same time we were passing below last time. Our paths should meet somewhere in the Southern Ocean. With our new furling gear we should make far better progress and be well in front at this stage. The only new chart I bought was for the Falkland Islands. The harbour of Port Stanley would be our first destination.

With time running out, I went into a routine, which I'd used before setting out on any voyage. I drew a small chart and typed a full report giving details of my plans. The distance to the Falkland Islands was just over 5,000 miles. The pilot charts showed I should have strong following winds from the west, increasing to gale force as we dropped further south into the Roaring Forties and the Furious Fifties. I thought it was safe to say that one could expect to hear from me within sixty days. I mentioned that if for any reason I didn't stop, I would make contact with the Islands by VHF radio. I sent about sixty copies of this letter off. Had I known the worry and concern I would cause friends around the world, the letters would never have been mailed.

I had Christmas dinner with some Americans on their boat. Boxing Day, December 26th, 1995, started perfectly, with clear blue skies and a steady south-west wind blowing at Force 4, making an easy passage down Whangarei's long harbour and out to sea. High water was at noon, which gave me time to do last minute shopping for bread, fruit and veg. I phoned Irene and Tony in Birmingham and my aunt Jean. I said I would be leaving within the hour.

As I stepped from the land for the last time, I felt as though I was about to break out of prison. This was not the fault of the New Zealand Yachting Federation, whose inspectors were quitting rather than enforce an unjust law; not the Customs Service, who refused to run with the muddy ball; certainly not the New Zealand people. I'd sat in a crowded clubhouse watching this country win the America's Cup, cheering with the rest of the foreign yachties. Even the Americans were shouting the NZ black yacht on, despite the fact that it was racing against their own boat. We had come to love and admire the people of this country. Most of us were there because of the love of the sea and the freedom it gave. A few bureaucrats were trying to change all that. They said they were leading the world with their new regulations. That's how dictatorships start.

As I let go our lines I felt as though I was stepping out of an aircraft without a parachute, knowing that I would never be able to return. *Solitaire* slowly moved down the line of inmates she was leaving behind. Crews started to appear on decks. There were the normal foghorns, the waving of arms, the shouts of 'Good luck!' The laughter was missing – only sadness that another yacht was being forced to leave by the back door. I did remember one sick joke I'd heard as we cleared the Whangarei town basin. It was the story of a man standing by the window in a skyscraper, when someone falls past him saying, 'So far so good.' No Customs boat appeared – so far so good.

We enjoyed our pleasant little push start and for the first four days we had good sailing: winds from the south-west, Force 4 to 5, *Solitaire* making 100 miles a day without even trying. After resting for over a year, we were easing our way back into being at sea. On the fourth day, the winds went light – swinging, so we never knew which tack to be on. Long bad-tempered calms. To cheer things up, I tried baking bread, expecting to fill *Solitaire* with glorious smells. Instead all we got was black smoke, as the unadjustable burner tried to cremate the dough. From time to time I'd open the oven door to get rid of some of the heat. When this failed, I tried turning the loaf four times and finished up with a poor offering that was black on all corners and soggy in the middle. More frustrated swearing. At the end of the first week we had made good only 416 miles – 376 miles in the first four days only, 40 miles in the last three days. We were at latitude 39°S, only a cat's whisker away from the Roaring Forties, with their constant westerly gales. Things would improve.

CHAPTER THIRTEEN
No Regrets
Whangerai – Lymington
December 1995 – July 1996

Just before we left Whangarei I'd studied our falling-to-bits old chart, along with the 15-year-old ship's log of the last time we were in the Southern Oceans. The more I thought about it, the more I realised how I'd changed over the years. Looking back at the 55-year-old man who had made the previous voyage, he gave the impression of being so full of confidence and purpose, able to make immediate decisions, and carry them out with a natural instinct and ability. At the age of 70, the strong unwavering drive to finish anything I'd started was as strong as ever, but I was much slower, taking longer to sort out even simple problems. The year spent in New Zealand hadn't helped matters. It had been a time of worry, tension and apprehension. As I read the young man's log, I became jealous: he seemed closer to *Solitaire*; together they were making longer, smoother passages.

During that first week at sea we passed over the date line. On December 29th, 1995, our longitude went to 180°E. The figures changed to the west, reducing as we headed home. The young man didn't cross over the date line until January 5th, 1981. We were a full week in front of him. He did have the advantage of being further south by 540 miles. With our larger furling headsail and strong winds from the west, we would be well in front of him when our paths crossed.

The second week at sea was an even bigger disaster. Instead of winds roaring like a lion, we had a pussycat that spent most of its time cleaning and purring. When we did get a breeze, it was hardly enough to fill the sails. At the end of our second week, we had made only 264 miles. The young man covered 682 miles.

The third week was even worse, with days of complete calms followed by gale force winds from the south-east. While trying to beat into one of these storms, the mainsail was ripped. It took all day to repair it, a day when we were blown 4 miles back towards New Zealand. During the long calms, I went back to trying to bake bread, this time making the dough into round cobs. The results were the same: I kept opening the oven door and they became flat burnt offerings, which only made me pleased that for this voyage I had plenty of other food on board. We made good only 397 miles. The young man 640 miles. By the end of that week, I had to admit that he had passed me by at least 200 miles, according to our longitudes, and was still 120 miles south of us. The thing I found annoying was that he was complaining about his slow progress. I said, 'You should be in our bloody shoes!' and slammed his stupid log down.

The fourth week was one of the worst I could remember at sea. The winds kept swinging around the compass. Storms from the south-east would tear into us at gale force and we would have to reduce sail to prevent them being torn to shreds. Then they would back to the west, where we wanted them, dying in strength as they went. Finally, when in the perfect position, they'd die to a complete calm. Once more we would stow all sails to prevent them being damaged by the monstrous seas. That week we logged only 192 miles. I finished my report with the prayers: 'Please God, send us the westerlies!'

Solitaire crossed the path of the young man at the end of our fifth week at sea, on January 29th, 1996. The trouble was that he had arrived at that position on the 19th, a full ten days before us. He could have been much further ahead, but he had eased his way further north – not out of any concern for me, but simply to stay above the extreme limit of the icebergs.

Week six ended with more of the same frustrating conditions. Sick of the slow progress, sick of always complaining, my only remarks were that we had reached the 2,000 mile mark to Cape Horn and that during the calms, with nothing better to do, I'd taken sights with my sextant. It didn't help any; I got only the same depressing news that the GPS gave.

During week seven we were halfway to Cape Horn and for a while I thought the end of our voyage was near, and possibly the end of our lives. To add to the misery of the days of calms, we seemed to be in a world of fog and drizzle. Even without the wind the seas were heaving as though some monster was about to break the surface. Our latitude was now 49°40'S. We were just about to enter the Furious Fifties. It was a glorious day with a blue sea and sky. We had very light following winds and a high swell that kept backing the genoa. In the end I just had the main out as far as possible, with a preventer on a broad reach. The wind increased towards dark and I stowed the main and went to a full genoa. By the morning of the 9th, we were in a full gale and reduced to only a few metres of the headsail. I couldn't make any sense of the conditions and screwed all the cockpit plywood covers in place. Still uneasy and apprehensive, I strapped the plastic water and food containers to the ringbolts in the cabin floor. During my last voyage through the Southern Oceans, I'd always kept some sail on, if only a storm jib. To go to bare poles, I'd always considered, was to put *Solitaire* at the mercy of the seas.

Just after midday, *Solitaire* started to shake like a rat that some dog had by the scruff of the neck. The wind in the rigging went to a high-pitched scream that vibrated down the length of the mast. For seven weeks I'd been crying out for more wind. It now seemed that during all that time the winds had just been building up for this, for this one supreme, killing blow. When I went on deck, *Solitaire* was being buried by mountains that were attacking from every direction. If I didn't do something the mast would go. I furled in the last few feet of genoa and removed the wind vane from the self-steering. Terrified that I had made my final mistake and condemned *Solitaire* to her death, I went below.

I was sitting on the starboard bunk, and was just about to go back on deck to check the rigging, when the lockers on the port side seemed to lift above my head. I finished up lying on my back with the sensation that we were flying. Our landing would have done credit to Concorde. There was one heck of a crash. All the lockers burst open. Books and stores shot across the cabin, punching me with heavyweight blows. The plastic containers had been retained by their lashing, but they were now lying at all angles. Struggling out of the mess, I started to straighten the boat out. When I finished, I once more sat on the lee side. It was then I realised that *Solitaire* had completed a 180-degree turn as she came upright. I'd hardly caught my breath when the same thing happened again. Frightened and in a daze, as I was clearing up after the third knockdown, everything went blank.

When I regained consciousness, it was dark. So I guessed I'd been out for at least five or six hours. For weeks, I'd been wearing heavy weather gear with a towel wrapped around my neck. When I put my hand on the towel it seemed to be covered with wet tacky jam. Tracing its source, it appeared to come from a hole somewhere in the front of my head. My legs and part of my body were trapped under the water containers. When I tried to move my legs, I felt like someone had kicked me in the back. Paralysing pains shot through me, finishing at my fingers and turning them into clenched fists of agony. I thought my ribs were broken and the rough bones were trying to grind their way into my kidneys.

To add to my discomfort, I heard one of the big rollers crash into *Solitaire*'s side. Half the cold Southern Ocean flooded through the hatch, straight into my upturned face. I could see that the hatch was closed, which meant that the first line of defence, the canvas hatch cover, had gone.

I would like to be able to say that it was only British determination that forced me to grit my teeth and crawl up the companionway steps. The truth was, it was the normal strong desire to see if there was anything I could do to remain on this planet for a few more hours, minutes, seconds.

When I managed to pull my eyes to deck level, I could see that the canvas cover was in fact ripped in half. Worse still, the new rigging, fitted in New Zealand, had stretched and the mast was swaying from side to side – dancing to a Latin rhythm only I could hear. There was nothing I could do to adjust the rigging screws in the dark. The job would have to wait for dawn. I just hoped we would still be here to see it. By this time, I'd found that if I stayed on my hands and knees I could just about crawl.

As I went back to wrap my safety harness around the mast support, I stopped long enough to grab a bag of medical supplies and a bottle of whisky. Secured to the support, the first thing I took out of the bag was a bottle of iodine. Since I couldn't locate the hole in my head, I poured the full bottle over the top. This turned it into a raging furnace. Leslie, I thought, that wasn't the most brilliant idea you've come up with. At least you've found out where the hole is and it's taken some of the attention from the pain in the back. I started taking painkillers and antibiotics, but gave the whisky a miss since I can't stand the taste of the stuff. There was a loud double crack, as though someone had fired a rifle off the starboard side. At first I thought the stainless steel rigging shrouds were breaking away. Then, thinking of the double crack, I decided that the heavy teak beam that holds the rigging U-bolts had broken. When the sound was repeated louder than ever, I forgot my dislike of whisky and took a long hard pull from the bottle.

Dawn arrived on Saturday, February 10th, to find me still tied to the mast: freezing cold, huddled, trying to stop my teeth from chattering – partly due to the cold, but more because of fear. Water was still streaming through the hatch as the waves continued to pound into *Solitaire*'s side. Seawater was running from the electrics into the radio. They would be gone for sure. Most of the terror came from watching the cabin floor. By this time, the bilges would be nearly full. At any moment, I expected to find icy waters oozing around my legs. I was still taking painkillers and swigs from the whisky bottle. It didn't seem to be having any effect. The day before I could crawl; now I couldn't even move from the mast support. I had decided that I would save half the whisky to take with the rest of the painkillers once my legs were covered with water. If I hadn't fitted the plywood hatch covers that would have already happened. I kept mumbling, 'Thank God, thank God.'

Sunday, February 11th, I was still attached to the mast support. The storm force winds seemed to be as strong as ever. The only difference was that the seas were more uniform and coming from the one direction.

For nearly two days I'd become a part of the mast support, unable to move, to find food. To pass water, I was using a bottle. Even moving that through my wet weather gear and my trousers was painful and there had been accidents. Due to the fact I wasn't eating, the whisky and painkillers had started to take effect. I felt light-headed and at times floating. I kept hearing someone grumbling and was surprised that when I tried to sing, the complaining would stop. I don't have a singing voice, so just remembering the words and saying them seemed to help: 'It's been a hard day's night and I've been working like a dog!'

By this time the bilges were full with about 60–70 gallons of water. The carpets had always been soaking; now it was oozing through them. The pains in my back were as bad as ever, but I did seem able to move my legs without too much trouble. I vaguely remember crawling into the cockpit and pumping out the bilges, but I don't remember much else that happened that day. It was much later, when I read the ship's log, that I realised that in my drunken state I'd carried out a good deal of work. The entry in the log for Sunday, February 11th, read: 'Still in storm conditions, lying a-hull and taking a hammering. Need to work on rigging, but it's impossible. GPS position latitude 49°19'S, longitude 125°17'W; Cape Horn 2,085 miles, bearing 95°.'

Monday, February 12th, came at the end of our seventh week at sea. It was the day that I did manage to get *Solitaire* moving again. Yet apart from the date and a scrawl that said 'Severe gales', nothing else was reported.

I knew that at some time I would have to readjust the six rigging screws. There were three either side of the boat and two in the stern. To adjust each screw, you had to straighten and withdraw two small split pins. Having adjusted the screw, the pins had to be replaced. It was more or less like trying to thread a needle. In the comfort of your own home it was easy. On a rolling, pitching boat with seas breaking over it, it was another kettle of fish. When I took a long swig of whisky and a couple of painkillers, and stuffed screwdrivers and pliers in my pocket, I knew the job was impossible. All I intended to do was check on the self-steering gear and pump out bilges. As I went through the hatch, I was singing one of the drunks' all time favourites: 'Show me the way to go home!' By the time I'd done the pumping, I was ready to crawl back and hug my friendly mast. One wave had already clobbered me, pushing back the hood on my jacket, soaking all my inner clothes. The salt water had mixed with the iodine in my hair and was making its way into my eyes. My reading glasses were covered with spray. Half blind, the sensible thing would have been to try again the next day, but there again, by then I might be sober!

As each wave hit *Solitaire*, the water would be thrown into the air, falling to flood over her decks. Spray would follow, until the next wave arrived. With each roll, *Solitaire*'s lee side deck was completely under water. At times, the rigging screws would disappear. When I crawled along to the first screw, I knew I couldn't do the job. When I pulled the first pins out, I knew I couldn't do it. When trying to make adjustments and my hands, screwdrivers and rigging screws went under water, I sat waiting for them to come back – I knew I would fail. And when the pins were back and it was time to go onto the next one, I knew I couldn't do it. Slowly, I found the rhythm that *Solitaire* was moving to. I started to keep time with her. With each roll we would both hesitate for a few moments, then move at a slow steady pace. When it was time to move over to the windward side, with the breaking waves, I thought it would be more difficult. In fact, once I picked up the new beat, it wasn't so bad. I would hear the waves roaring in, hold onto the rigging and duck my head. Once they had gone through it seemed the decks would dry faster and last longer.

The whisky had started to wear off as I went back to the cockpit. I was about to risk a few feet of the genoa when I thought of the two rigging screws for the backstays. At least I would be working from the cockpit this time. After these final adjustments, I eased out enough genoa to allow *Solitaire* to make steerage way on a broad reach. I put back the self-steering wind vane and once more we were in control.

Apart from the stretched rigging, I thought another reason for the vibration was that as the new furling sail was reduced in size, the effect was to move it further up the stay, turning the rigging wire into a bowstring. On my non-stop second voyage, I'd had twin forestays with a storm and working jib hanked on. In use I kept them as low as possible, just clearing the pulpit. In future I would be forced to use smaller sails earlier and put up with slower speeds. By this time, the young man we had been racing against was miles ahead. I no longer felt jealous about his achievements and better times. All that mattered now was surviving, and rounding Cape Horn.

Pleased with the day's work, I was about to go below when I saw the ripped canvas hatch cover. I removed it and took it with me. I still didn't feel like eating, but I needed to replace all the blood I'd lost. During blood donor sessions in the past I'd been given hot, sweet cups of tea. By now it was late afternoon. I put the whisky bottle away and the kettle on. That night, my back started to hurt and I took a double dose of painkillers. I was still strapping myself to the mast support, but I was using a long lead and sitting in the corner of the bunk. It was difficult to sleep. Every now and again there would be the loud double report from the rifle.

Tuesday, February 13th. After drinking a few cups of tea, and taking my painkillers and antibiotics, I started to sew the hatch cover together. My safety harness was removed from the mast support and attached to one of the ringbolts in the cabin floor. By the afternoon the pains in my back were very bad.

The cracking sound from the beam was making me very edgy. Unable to concentrate, I gave up on the job for the day and started to look at the electric panel. The GPS had its own switch and that was still working. All the pilot lights for the rest of the equipment were very dim, some showing no signs of life. When I switched the transmitter on, the radio made a few squeaks and died. I removed all the front panelling and, to get my own back, I started spraying the lot with a lubricant that drives out moisture. I had thoughts of taking off my wet weather gear and changing my clothes, but there would have been little advantage: everything on the boat was soaking wet.

By that time, I could walk about bent over double. This seemed to be the normal position for lying on my bunk. A last cup of tea and two more painkillers and I lay down, pulling a sleeping bag over my head.

During that 24 hours with the furling sail reduced to storm jib size, we made one of the best runs for a long time of 116 miles. The total distance for the week was 643 miles. Considering we should have been lying in Davy Jones' locker, I thought we'd done pretty well. The hatchway cover had been sewn and fitted. I didn't think it would last very long and when in any violent storm I knew I would have to stow it. At least in the present gales and high seas it was keeping most of the water out. I was back in the old habit of pumping the bilges out first thing in the morning and last thing at night. But they were never more than a third full.

Towards the end of that eighth week at sea I did change my dirty, cold, soaking wet clothes for clean, cold, soaking wet clothes. Stripped off, it was the first time I'd seen my body since our troubles. I was a mass of black and blue bruises. My back was still painful, but I no longer thought I had broken ribs. Providing I didn't make any sudden moves, I could stand upright.

At the end of week nine, we had covered another 642 miles, only one mile short of the previous week's run. My back was still painful and I was still taking the painkillers and antibiotics. The main worry was the rifle cracks that seemed to be increasing in volume. The heavy beam that the rigging U-bolts came through had stainless steel backing plates. I believed that it was behind this plate that the beam was broken. There was one way I could stop the noise. That was to simply place my hand on the plate to feel the vibration. I could stand there for minutes and nothing would happen, move away and crack, crack...

Having found out how I could stop the noise, I then found out how it could be increased: by swearing at the bloody thing, it would soon be laughing, crackling away fit to bust. During the week I did find some drops of moisture in the fixed GPS. It was still working fine, but just to play it safe, I decided to try the hand-held standby GPS. I'd tested it before leaving New Zealand and it seemed OK. Now I couldn't get it to lock on to the satellites.

When I checked on the young man I found he was having his own problems, mostly due to a lack of food and a weight loss. Despite the fact we'd been stationary for three days, he hadn't gained that much distance. Our weekly runs were about the same. The same gale force winds, the high breaking seas, even the same calms. Our main complaints were about the freezing seas and the cold damp cabin. He was being held up by the fact he had only small sails that he could use: a working jib and a storm jib. Whereas I had a much larger furling genoa, but I couldn't use it in case I pulled the mast down.

Solitaire started her tenth week at sea on Monday, February 26th. Cape Horn was 800 miles away. By the end of the week we had sailed a further 600 miles. It had been a week of severe gales. Once more, we had sailed well below Cape Horn's latitude, to make sure we weren't driven on a lee shore. Our own latitude was now down to 57°24′S, 76 miles below the Cape. *Solitaire* had tried to edge her way north, but merciless seas had kept howling from that direction, driving her further away. She'd had two more knockdowns, which left a bit of straightening up, but nothing more serious.

We sailed below Cape Horn at 4.30pm on Wednesday, March 6th. Our latitude was 57°15′S, approximately 76 miles below. For the first time in weeks we had a blue sky and a calm sea. I tried to dry a few towels.

The Falkland Islands and Port Stanley were around 489 miles away to the NNE. The pilot charts showed that prevailing winds should be blowing from the south-west, Force 5 to 6. With luck, I thought, we should be in Port Stanley by the end of the week.

The young Leslie had sailed past Cape Horn on Monday, February 23rd, 1981. His latitude had been 57°00'S, approximately 61 miles below. He had enjoyed the same weather conditions. Instead of towels, he had tried to dry carpets. He was now 12 days in front. He had gained a further two days. I felt sorry. He was starving. If I had met him 15 years ago, I would have gladly given him some of my food.

Our week after rounding came to its end on Wednesday, March 13th, 1996. We were still 124 miles from Port Stanley. Instead of the winds blowing from the south-west, *Solitaire* had been punching her way into strong winds from the north. At times these winds had reached gale force. During the week of frustration, the one great pleasure had been listening to the radio broadcasts from Stanley. Apart from the great music, I'd felt I knew the people. There was always a report on the flights between the islands and the names of the passengers were given. I knew the name of the local pub and that volunteers were needed for some varnishing. I couldn't wait to be sitting in its warm friendly bar.

The following day I gave up all thoughts of sitting in that pub. The weather report had forecast gale force winds from the west. With the breaking seas, we were slowly being forced away from the island. On Friday, March 15th, I scribbled a few remarks in the ship's log:

Latitude 51°29'S, longitude 56°39'W. Port Stanley was only 38 miles away, but we had been driven past the Island. Things going very badly. A few knockdowns while trying to lie a-hull. Hatch cover once more in bits. Spent all morning trying to sort things out. GPS is still working, but now has condensation inside. Just found that I've lost two lighters, the one remaining doesn't work. I have a few matches left by Tony and Irene during our holiday. It could be a serious problem. To be honest, I don't think we can finish this voyage. We will just keep trying to head north. Everything is so cold and wet – NO REGRETS.

I took all the sail off *Solitaire* due to the pounding she was taking and the loud cracking complaints from the beam. Without the sails, she started to do the same 180-degree turns after each knockdown. With the hatch cover gone, once more seawater started flooding into the cabin. Before things got completely out of hand I unfurled a few metres of the genoa and went onto a reach, pulling away from land. I deeply regretted that my VHF radio was U/S and I hadn't been able to make contact. Food would now be a problem and I could see that soon I would be in the same condition as the young man, with his agonising sores and bleeding gums. He had already gained an extra day on me, sailing past the Islands on March 2nd, 1981, a full 13 days in front of us.

By the end of our 12th week at sea we had managed only 398 miles. The Falkland Islands were 215 miles astern. I'd once more repaired the hatch cover. The crack, crack from the rifle continued. With each sound, my nerves and temper got worse. Worrying about my friends didn't help.

Week 13 was a funny old week, with many ups and downs. The biggest down was that we only made 264 miles.

Tuesday, March 19th. The winds were light from the north. With a full genoa and mainsail, we managed to make 93 miles, staying hard on the wind. In the past I'd always tried to run the engine every two or three weeks. When I tried this time, I found seawater in the oil. I managed to filter it out and start it. I tried to get a fix with the standby GPS, without any luck.

Wednesday, March 20th. More gale force winds from the north-east. I removed the weak hatch cover. The seas seemed to be warmer, so I removed my boots – no progress.

Friday, March 22nd. I fed the latitude and longitude for Horta in the Azores into the main GPS. It gave a reading of 5,248 nautical miles, on a bearing of 022° Magnetic. Lymington would be about 6,750 miles. That day, in gale force winds, we only took 32 miles off the distance.

Saturday, March 23rd. Becalmed all night, I tried to start the engine, only to find the starter motor U/S. When I tried to use the main GPS, I found it had given up and thrown in the towel. Having taken my sextant out, I decided to give the hand-held GPS a last try. I read in the instructions that when first used from new it would take up to twenty minutes to lock onto its first satellites. I now believed that the reason it wouldn't work was that it was trying to lock onto the satellites over New Zealand. I thought that if I removed the batteries while it was still switched on, it might cancel these and start searching. Fifteen minutes later I got my position and heaved a sigh of relief. We had taken 58 miles off the distance home.

Sunday, March 24th. Distance covered 34 miles, winds gusting from the north-east. The good news was that I had found one of my new lighters. I cut a 5-gallon plastic container in half and fitted a hosepipe tube into its cape, ready for when we had rain.

Monday 25th brought drizzle from a grey sky. We managed to catch 2 gallons of water in a very slow trickle. 23 miles covered through confused seas.

Week 14 wasn't much better: gale force winds from the north-east that had me once more removing the hatch cover to prevent damage.

On Wednesday 27th we were in another bad gale and mountainous seas. It was a clear bright day when I saw our first ship for a month, a supertanker passing down our starboard side about half a mile away. I wrote in the ship's log that I thought they'd seen us. I regretted I didn't have a radio I could make contact with. I would have given anything to have been able to put *Solitaire* on board her. This had been a bad voyage and I'd been afraid too long. I just wanted to leave those seas and never return. I was sorry to let Irene and Tony and all of my friends down.

At the end of week 14 the good news was that our position was latitude 39°45′S, longitude 46°27′W. We had made good only 300 miles. But great news: we were out of the Roaring Forties.

Whenever we had a day without strong winds I would try to bake bread. The only way I could do it was to wrap dough in tin foil. The cobs that I made came out black and flat, but I was already rationing my food so anything would help. I'd started to think that I might be forced to call into Rio in Brazil.

By the end of week 15 I was sure that food and water would be a problem and that we would be forced to stop in Brazil. There were more gales from the north-east, then long calms that at least allowed me to repair my wet weather gear and the starter motor. Distance covered was a disappointing 270 miles. By this time we were well out of the Roaring Forties at latitude 35°S. The pilot chart showed only six per cent gales in this area, against twenty-six per cent at Cape Horn. We were having gales nearly every day. It was frustrating. With the cracking rifle, nerves were at breaking point.

Week 16, Monday, April 15th. Distance covered 305 miles. There were more gales from the north and north-east, and rough seas, but they were no longer life threatening. When the cracking from the beam got too bad, I could drop all sail without the knock-downs and the whipping 180-degree turns. I tried driving wedges between the bulkhead and the beam. This seemed to deaden the sound slightly. I wrote in the ship's log that 'the Azores are approxi-mately 4,448 miles, Rio 720 miles, ENGLAND 6,000 miles'.

I checked the food and found that on the present rations, we had enough to last 56 days. I removed the oil from the motor and put more fresh oil back, fitted the starter motor, and ran the engine. I made a note that the fuel lift pump had a bad leak. The last entry was that still in the Variables, with 600 miles to go to reach the south-east trade winds. Now down to low rations of half a tin of food and half a cup of rice. I didn't really want to go into Brazil. I would even consider St Helena, 2,000 miles to the north-east.

Week 17, Monday, April 22nd. Distance covered 480 miles. We had started with a strong gale, but the rest of the week it was strong squalls, with gusting winds from every direction and confused seas. As things became warmer my weather gear had been stored away, sea boots removed and toes wriggled. After the Southern Oceans, even in the worst conditions, it seemed like *Solitaire* was sailing over blue velvet.

Over the years I had constantly listened to the BBC overseas broadcasts. These started to give disturbing information about Brazil: 13,000 convicts were being released from their crowded jails, high inflation, drugs out of control. Worried I might have problems due to my passport showing no Customs clearance from New Zealand and not having a visa, I decided to cut down once more on my food and water and try to make the Port of Horta in the Azores. Now, for the first time, our measuring changed from cups to tablespoons. Our ration became five tablespoons of rice, half a tin of corned beef, beans, sardines or tuna.

As week 17 came to an end, we were slipping by Rio, 460 miles to the west off our port side, heading for home. Perhaps that was the magic word driving us: 'Home!' Being British was in my blood. My father, his father, and for as far back as there were records, my family had been born in Herefordshire, in the heart of England. After being away for eight years, I needed to walk in its green and pleasant lands, and stand in an English pub and talk to the weird and wonderful characters the country seems to produce.

The young man had sailed past Rio on Tuesday, March 31st, 1981. His log showed that he was 600 miles off the coast, 140 miles further out to sea. He had gained an extra 10 days since we had rounded Cape Horn and was now 22 days in front.

Week 18 started with light winds, the temperature going up into the 80s. I removed my shirt and changed into shorts. There was about 10 gallons of water in the tanks and 4 more in a plastic container. We were getting squalls with a light drizzle and fresh gusting winds. There was hardly any water off the end of the boom. What there was was too salty to drink. The fuel lift pump was still leaking. I kept wrapping tape around it, then covering it with sealant. The thing slowly turned into a rubber ball, but it still leaked.

The week ended with a distance of 490 miles completed. I was now constantly hungry. But with hours spent in the cockpit, temperatures in the mid 80s, I felt more content. I started putting notes in the ship's log to remind me how much bread and rice I was eating. The week's run had been 490 miles. With a latitude of 16°57′S and longitude of 32°40′W, we should be in the south-east trade winds and making better progress. I'd given up believing in pilot charts years before. I was just pleased to still have a mast and be going home.

At noon on Monday, May 6th, I made the entry in the ship's log:

Spent 19 weeks at sea! Covered only 242 miles. Becalmed for three days. Let's hope these light southerly winds mean we are now coming into SE trade winds. Work carried out during the flat calms. Changed the Hydrovane's self-steering rudder for a smaller spare. More work on lift pump, managed to stop the fuel leak and start the engine.

Week 20 was a good week, despite the fact that I lost my last remaining bucket, and a very powerful spotlight that Chris Parry had given me blew its bulb. The light had been used coming down the Red Sea to warn shipping that they were too close. This had been the first ship that came close enough at night to give me concern since I left New Zealand. My tri-navigation lights at the top of the mast had stopped working after our knockdowns and I'd been hoping to use the spotlight while going up the English Channel. The temperature had increased to 95°F. We logged 657 miles in the south-east trade winds.

If week 20 was a good week, week 21 was even better. On Tuesday, May 14th, we crossed over the Equator at 8.08pm. When I used the GPS it gave a reading of latitude 00°08′N, longitude 028°52′W. To celebrate, I used the last few granules of coffee to make my last cup.

When I checked on the young man, he had crossed over the Equator on Wednesday, April 15th, 1981, and toasted the crossing with a wee glass of sherry. He was now 29 days ahead of me. Food-wise he was much better off than me. That week I had cut my daily ration of rice down from five to four tablespoons.

Despite the fact that the young man was still pulling away from me and I'd been forced to cut down yet again on my rations, I would look back on that week and the days May 17–19th with greater pleasure than I had experienced on any previous voyage. On those three days we had monsoon rains with just enough wind to hold a good course with a full main. For the past two weeks I'd been getting a sucking sound from the water tanks that had make me think twice before making a cup of tea. There had been a threat of rain with heavy black clouds. Then we had the first heavy drops hitting *Solitaire* and bouncing off her decks. For a few minutes I watched the rivers of water run down the sail to rush along the boom and gush forth like a torrent from Niagara Falls. Never seen anything like it in all my 70 years. Never known such pleasure. Stark naked I stood in the cockpit and washed the salt from my tired body.

Having given time for the salt to be washed from the sail, I fitted my Mk1 water-catching funnel to the end of the boom. Water shot out of the end of the hosepipe as though it was connected to some high-pressure tap. Back in the cabin I dried myself. Then, selecting one of my plastic containers, I held it on the companionway steps with my stomach. When I fed the hose in, the vibrations started to say, 'Cups of tea, cups of tea!' By golly, I thought, this isn't as good as holding a woman, but it runs a bloody close second. I collected 40 gallons that day and then spent some time on deck, transferring the water into the tanks. The following day I filled the containers again. Our water problems were over. I now had enough to see us all the way back to England, enough even to clean my teeth and shave. At the end of our 21st week at sea we had only made 450 miles, but the water really lifted our hearts.

By the end of week 22, we had logged a further 540 miles. The winds had been mostly from the north-east and since our course for Horta was due north, we were sailing as close as possible into wind. The cracking from the beam was becoming even more worrying. Every time I put an inch too much sail up, I thought the mast was coming down. The winds were forcing *Solitaire*'s track to curve to the west, away from the Islands. With our weak condition, I didn't want to waste too much time tacking back and forth. At the end of the week, Horta was still 1,500 miles away.

At the end of week 23, we logged 650 miles, but lost over 100 miles as we were pushed to the west of the Islands. Instead of Horta being 850 miles away, the port was in fact 960 miles. More and more time was spent with my hands on the beam, trying to find where the break was. By now they didn't seem to help. If only the winds would swing away from the north and we could come onto a reach, things would improve, I thought. Nerves were really starting to show the strain. On Thursday, May 30th, I baked my last bread. All I had left was four small burnt cobs.

By the end of week 24, things were no better. We had sailed 400 miles. Horta was 660 miles away. The Island of Santo Cruz, with its Port of Flores, the most westerly of the Azores Islands, was closer at 640 miles. On Wednesday, I'd just cut my ration down to three spoonfuls of rice a day, when a 65ft red yacht came tearing across our stern. All the crew were on deck shouting. I was doing my own shouting (and waving): 'Food! Give me food!' But in the blink of an eye, they were gone.

The following day, Thursday, June 6th, after winds gusting from Force 2 to Force 7 from the NNE, I wrote in the log: 'If these winds continue, I will pass well clear of the Azores to their west and try to reach England non-stop.' Food was a real problem. Even a small tin of sardines was having to last for two days. I found a small tin of chestnut puree, which tasted terrible, but with three spoons of rice that was my ration for another two days.

During week 25, the tins of corned beef went down to a ration of a quarter tin. I found a few dried beans. Soaked overnight, they would swell to twice their size. As we came into the high-pressure area that lies over the Azores, the winds became fickle with long calm periods. I started to run the motor with the autopilot steering. Short of diesel, I could only do this during flat calms. Week 25 ended on Monday, June 17th. We had logged 445 miles. Horta was now 310 miles away, Flores 235 miles.

Week 26 was a great week. I cut down on the rice to two

spoons a day, but found that the dried beans ration could be increased to three spoons. A tin of chilli lasted five days. For the first time since leaving New Zealand, the winds started to read the pilot charts and blow from the right direction. On Wednesday, June 19th, 1996, we sailed past Flores – 55 miles to our East. All that was ahead of us now was home and England.

In the ship's log I wrote that day:

Still it continues: grey skies, some drizzle, but constant winds from the west at Force 5. Due to the conditions over the past few days we will now try to make it all the way back to Lymington. The last few days we might be without food, but it will be well worth it, just so I can think I told New Zealand's Safety Officer Russell Kilvington to get stuffed.

By the end of the week, we were running short of dried beans, so I opened up a tin of pineapple and had half a tin of that with half a tin of tuna and two spoons of rice. At the end of the week we had made 670 miles, all in the right direction. Falmouth, the first possible port in England, was now only 860 miles away. The noise from the broken beam was increasing, but now we were in the Gulf Stream with friendly winds. Even if we lost the mast *Solitaire* could find her own way.

By the end of week 27, Falmouth was only 285 miles away. We had logged 570 miles for the week, all in the right direction. I'd been back to wearing heavy sweaters since passing the Azores, with heavy weather gear. A great comfort was the lovely music I'd started to receive from an Irish station. The good old BBC was now coming in loud and clear too. The weather report was for strong winds and rain for the next three days, not the best conditions for sailing up the English Channel. I had managed to get the ship's steaming and deck lights to work, but the all important navigation lights at the top of the mast were still not working. It would mean that, apart from dashing below for a quick cuppa, I'd be spending all my time on watch in the cockpit.

Week 28 was to be our last week at sea. All that I had left now for food were two tins of mixed fruit and a few dried beans.

Tuesday, July 2nd. Winds died during the night, hardly making steerage way. Wind Force 2 to 3 from south-east. Full genoa and mainsail. BBC forecast strong winds later. Good radio reception from Islands BBC and Devon. Fishing boats came close during the night. One came over this morning. Ration for the day: half a tin of mixed fruit with two spoons of dried beans. Falmouth 215 miles. Distance logged 70 miles.

Wednesday, July 3rd. Winds from the south-west, Force 4 to 5. Broad reach with genoa. Very bad visibility, drizzle and rain. Seas very green. Good progress in the past 24 hours. Using the GPS more to keep track of our position. Falmouth 115 miles, Lymington 270 miles. Distance logged in 24 hours: 100 miles.

Thursday, July 4th. English Channel. Strong winds from the West, still good sailing, two-thirds genoa. With luck we should be close to Lymington by tomorrow night. Then, lovely food. Lymington 170 miles. Distance logged 100 miles.

Friday, July 5th. Noon, winds from the west, gusting Force 2 to 7. Should be able to enter Lymington Yacht Haven tomorrow morning.

I was sure I had caused my many friends unnecessary worry, but was just hoping that they would appreciate how sorry I was and that it had not been done intentionally. With the perfect winds blowing us up the Channel, our first sight of England was Portland Bill.

Next came the Isle of Wight and then we were sailing by the Needles into the Solent. Old Crack-Crack made his final weak complaint. This time there were no popping eyeballs, only a smirky smile as I thought, 'You're dead, mate.' Safe in harbour, I would sort him out for good.

I started to get fenders and mooring lines ready. I stowed all sails and hoisted the yellow quarantine flag. My intentions were to stay in the Yacht Haven for two nights. Then, after contacting friends, I'd go down and tie alongside Lymington Town Quay.

As *Solitaire* made her way up the river to the Yacht Haven, a yacht passed, going out. Her skipper shouted across, 'Are you Leslie?'

I said, 'Yes.'

The guy said, 'We'd been worried about you!'

I shouted, 'I was worried about me, too!'

The guy told me I was dead and it was then I learnt that I'd been in the national press, and on radio and TV, reported as missing at sea. My first thoughts were that I was in worse trouble than I'd realised and I wasn't even being given the chance to apologise.

The man I'd met going out was Peter Smales. He followed me back to the visitors' berth, where he told me he was the Haven's PR man and Dirk Kalis had left instructions that when I turned up I was to be given a year's free berthing. Richard and Audrey Chase took my lines. Audrey asked if there was anything else I wanted. I asked for a piece of bread. Later Dirk Kalis came down to tell me that a mistake had been made about my year's free berthing: it wasn't for a year, but for life!

The young man had arrived back in the Lymington Yacht Haven on Wednesday, June 3rd, 1981. We returned to the Yacht Haven on Saturday, July 6th, 1996. Our race from New Zealand had finished with him beating me by 33 days. The 15 years difference in our ages was no longer important, nor even who won the race. All that was important was we had both completed our voyages and were safely back home.

That night I was wearing pyjamas when I went to sleep on *Solitaire*, sure that it was all a dream and I would wake up to find I was once more in the Southern Oceans, tied to *Solitaire*'s mast support, a bottle of painkillers in one hand and a bottle of whisky in the other.

Next day, the newspapers and broadcasters started a mini media frenzy, reporting how 'the starving Ancient Mariner sailed home'. *The Times* reported on my 'full English breakfast, followed by strawberries' as I did my best to restore the 5st I had lost. The *Daily Mail*'s David Munk wrote: 'He is so thin you could play a sea shanty on his ribs.' My weight had been reduced to 8st.

Even though I had returned from the dead I didn't expect the media attention to last for more than two or three days. In fact, it went on for quite some time. The BBC asked me to go to London to do some filming for a TV show. I was told I would be paid my expenses. On arrival at the studio I was asked for my railway ticket – a cheap one-day return, costing £19. I watched in amazement as 19 one-pound coins were counted into my hand. No taxi fare. Not even a couple of bob for a cup of tea!

In the months after I returned home I was given two awards. Not so much for seamanship, I felt, but more because I'm an amateur who will not take sponsorship. One of these accolades was from *The Oldie* magazine, which gave me the Ancient Mariner Award, presented at a posh lunch at the Savoy Hotel, London. There were about 150 very famous people there. In fact the only one I didn't recognise was me! After being called dead, I thought being called Ancient was a step in the right direction. I was also awarded The Ocean Cruising Club's Award of Merit. I was over the moon with this one, since it was given by people for whom I have great admiration.

In the beginning, all the fuss, all the hugs, handshakes and questions were enjoyable. Then as I started to put on weight, people stopped recognising me in the street and life returned to something approaching normal. After the long days alone at sea it had been marvellous to be shown all that warmth and kindness – something I would remember for all my remaining years but I was pleased it was over.

Soon after I arrived back in England I bought an old 1983 Mini Metro car, which I used to drive around the country giving talks. Driving back to Lymington at 2 o'clock in the morning with maniacs in 30-ton trucks screaming past at 80 miles an hour did nothing to help the old blood pressure. I chickened out of this pastime after several months.

Meanwhile, *Solitaire* was still in the poor condition she was in when we arrived home from New Zealand. It really didn't seem fair. She had done all the work and here I was fully recovered, apart from the ever-present asthma problem. My first job was to replace the wooden toe rail that runs around *Solitaire*'s deck.

EPILOGUE

away again

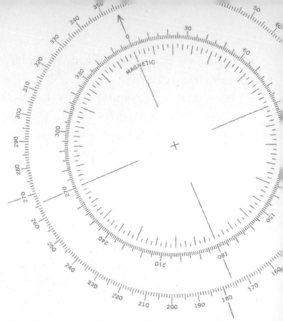

During the storms in the Southern Ocean, the starboard tang that secures the lower standing rigging to the mast (shrouds) had broken, leaving a 5-inch tear. It was the opening and closing of this gap that was responsible for the cracking sound and not the wooden beam. The masthead navigation light was missing, along with a large part of the forward toe rail. Despite these injuries *Solitaire* had rounded Cape Horn and sailed over 10,000 miles to make her way home. I ordered a new mast with the same specifications as the old, apart from changing to cutter rig with a furling staysail and running backstays.

By 2000, *Solitaire* was spending her second cold English winter out of the water, but at least all the major re-fitting work had been carried out and she was now ready for her fourth circumnavigation.

Having nursed *Solitaire* back to good health, I was able to go into hospital myself for a prostate operation in August. They call it keyhole surgery but at the time it seemed like they used a camera crew and a digger (and afterwards you spend five days passing water – and double-decker buses – through a tube). For me, that was the easy part. The hard part came when it was time to leave hospital and I was told that, because I had to climb a 12ft high ladder to get aboard the yacht, I wouldn't be able to return to *Solitaire* for six weeks.

Instead, it was arranged for me to go into a memorial hospital and rest home at Barton-on-Sea. The nurses and staff were all angels and couldn't have been kinder, but to watch the elderly patients was like seeing my own future. The dining room was full of old people taking pills. Some just watched daytime TV. Others were desperately lonely and waiting for family to turn up and visit them. To see the expressions on their faces was dreadful. It was far more terrifying than the worst storm at sea.

The biopsy for cancer proved to be negative. However, I still had breathing difficulties with asthma and my lungs needed kick starting from time to time with inhalers. Summers were fine. I could sit in the cockpit with spectacular views overlooking the Solent. The winters were another story – *Solitaire* became an 8ft-squared box without running water or a toilet. There were showers and toilets in the main building but they were a 200-yard dash away.

Over the four years since my non-stop voyage back from New Zealand, I'd been considering what to do when I reached this time of life. At the age of 74, the sensible thing to do would be to leave *Solitaire*, but that was unthinkable.

If I hadn't had difficulties publishing a new edition of my book, *Hands Open*, I would have had funds for a flat ashore in winter. I could even have returned to Cyprus with its warm climate. But then, of course, there's no British National Health Service on the island.

To once more gain the interest of publishers I would need to have fresh up-to-date material. There seemed to be two options. The first was to sail for Boston on the east coast of America, and then follow the route Joshua Slocum took between April 1895 and June 1898, passing through the Straits of Magellan. For this voyage I needed a reliable engine so I had my Saab diesel reconditioned by the agents.

Three times after the start of the new millennium I attempted to leave Lymington to start a new long-distance voyage. The first time my diesel tank split and by the time I got to the French coast, off Ushant, the carpets were soaked in fuel and with my asthma the fumes made me feel pretty bad. I sailed back to Lymington in southwesterly gales.

It took me a couple of years to sort out *Solitaire* before I was ready to try again. By the time of the second attempt, in 2006, I had bought a new Volvo Penta 18hp engine. I got as far as Old Harry, off Studland Bay, Dorset, when the engine stopped. I was becalmed as there was no wind. Since it was a brand new engine that had been fitted, I contacted Lymington Yacht Haven. They wanted me to call the Coastguard. But I said, 'No, you've got to fetch me!' So they sent out a towing vessel. It turned out the gearbox was faulty and by the time it had all been fixed under warranty it was too late in the season to cross the Bay of Biscay.

For my third attempt, in order to increase speed under power I changed from a two-bladed propeller to a three. The drag from this mistake only came to light when I tried to sail for Cape Town on October 13th, 2005, hoping to continue to Australia during the Southern Ocean's more kindly months. With my asthma and breathing problems it was really far too late to sail through the Bay of Biscay. The alternative, however, was to spend another cold damp winter in England surviving on steroid tablets and inhalers.

With following winds the trip down the English Channel was easy. It was only when we turned into the Bay for the 380-mile crossing to Cape Finisterre that things became unpleasant. By the third day we were battling into gale force winds from the south-west. On past voyages under these conditions, I would remove all sails, allowing *Solitaire* to fall onto a reach, then unfurl just enough headsail for steerage way. Little progress would be made, but she would be fairly stable and hold her position. Now when I tried, high seas and fast flowing rollers were pushing her sideways at a terrific speed and I ended up using the engine just to break through.

I had never known the boat so wet; charts became soaked and fell apart. With the vibration and shaking it became difficult to boil water for a hot drink. On October 24th it was my 80th birthday and I managed to celebrate with a cup of tea.

Exhaustion made me decide that, once past Cape Finisterre, I would make for the harbour of Porto, in Portugal, to rest and carry out repairs. When I checked with our GPS position the distance was 20 miles, but when I next looked, the distance had increased to 40 miles.

I'm not sure what happened during that 24 hours. I noticed there was blood on some of the lockers and seats. There was a large lump on the back of my head and more blood. I was very cold and had trouble breathing. After using my inhalers and taking a few steroid pills, I decided to return to Lymington and try again in the spring. Fortunately, the strong southerly winds continued to blow and we surfed back through Biscay on a broad reach with a small amount of headsail.

It was only when we were well clear of the French coast that I had a panic attack and stopped breathing.

The ship's compass showed we were on course to take us up the English Channel to Lymington, but when I checked our position with the GPS it showed we were tracking north towards the Scilly Isles at 2–3 knots. I managed to get my lungs working with kick-start from my inhaler and tried to make contact with the Coast-guard. Seawater had put my main VHF radio out, but I still had my hand-held set. When I called on Channel 16 I was answered by an Australian helicopter pilot who said he was in my area and had been asked to confirm my position. Soon afterwards he flew over and called to say I was still 40 miles south of the Scillies. I said I'd been injured and was very tired and would they listen out for me.

Soon after he left, the tide turned and we started to make good progress on course. I tried again to contact my Australian mate, but now my hand-held was not working. We had passed Dartmouth and were outside Lyme Bay with all our lights on when the ship hit us. I was standing in the main hatch and turned to look over the bow, only to find the area filled with a great black mass. There was a tremendous bang and I went flying. By the time I had recovered, the ship had long gone.

Solitaire's bow was damaged and her pulpit pushed over to the port side. Her engine was still running and we were still on course, but then the engine stopped. When we had our collision, the sheets from the headsails had been thrown over the side. Now they were wrapped around the propeller. We had no engine, no sails and no means of contacting the Coastguard. Dawn was breaking when I saw in the distance a thin white shape, which I took to be the Needles on the Isle of Wight. I cut both the sheets as far down as possible, leaving a few feet still around the prop. When I started the engine we could just about head in the right direction.

When leaving England on October 13th, the last call I had made on my mobile phone had been to Lymington Yacht Haven. Now, when I switched it on, they answered and I told them I could see the Needles, but when I gave them my GPS position they said I was 20 miles away and was looking at the cliffs at Anvil Point. They called the Coastguard, who arrived sometime afterwards and towed *Solitaire* into Poole Marina, where they had an ambulance waiting to rush me into Poole hospital. Tests proved that in addition to cuts on my head, I had suffered a mild concussion.

They allowed me to return to *Solitaire* the following day and, after a diver had removed the sheets from the propeller, we returned to our old berth in the Lymington Yacht Haven.

Since then, I haven't, at the time of writing (2011), done any long passages. I've helped on some deliveries and taken friends out for a sail. One Christmas, Dylan Kalis (the son of Dirk), who took over running Lymington Yacht Haven when his father 'retired', presented me with a laptop computer. I told them there was no point. I'd never be able to use it. But he sent a technical wizard down to my boat next day to teach me the basics. Having a computer has changed my life. It's better than a mobile phone because you've got time to think and focus.

At 8 o'clock most mornings I fire up the laptop, log on, and check my emails. I can contact friends in Australia, New Zealand and America, as well as the UK and all over Europe, at virtually no cost. When Dylan's father gave me a free marina berth for life, I was also given free electricity – and then came free wireless internet.

In 2001, following the death of my father's sister Jean, the last of my family, I received a small inheritance. This gave me some extra security so I don't have to rely on charity. I don't drink or smoke and I live frugally. After my convalescence in that old folks' home, I vowed never to let that happen to me. I've had a good run, two good wives and a whole host of adventures.

Who knows what's next? Just recently, a friend, Clive Rockford, helped me get my engine running again. He took the cylinder head off and found water inside as well as corroded valves. He's reconditioned it. It took a lot of persuading to get it started but now I run it every week. I've also got a folding prop. In the summer I painted the decks.

I celebrated my 86th birthday on October 24th, 2011. But I'm still very pig-headed. If I make up my mind to do something, then you would have to cut my legs off to stop me. I'm an Englishman, for God's sake. You know what the English are like – if you say they can't do something, they will bloody well go and do it!